To Kelly + whom interested in reading it.

FATHER ARSENY

Dear Kely, I hope you enjoy and get something out of this book. A new insight concerning humanity and how we are all united in the end.

Please don't rush through this book just to finish reading and forget all about it. But slowly, take your sweet time with it, savor it.

Try to place your feet in some of the shoes of the people in this book. And imagine how you would react if you were forced to experience such heart shattering difficulties.

Would you have survived or would you of lost hope and submit into despair. I myself can't even imagine going through what these people went through. It's hard to believe half of what your reading even took place. How could humans be capable of such atrocities and evil wickedness, I pity the poor souls who didn't survive to see their families again

FATHER ARSENY

1893-1973

Priest, Prisoner, Spiritual Father

———

*Being the narratives compiled by the
servant of God Alexander concerning
his spiritual father*

Translated from the Russian by
VERA BOUTENEFF

HUMAN KINDNESS FOUNDATION
PO Box 61619, Durham, North Carolina 27715
2001

Library of Congress Cataloging-in-Publication Data

Otets Arsenii. English

    Father Arseny, 1893-1973: priest, prisoner, spiritual father: being the narratives compiled by the servant of God Alexander concerning his spiritual father/translated from the Russian by Vera Bouteneff.

    p.   cm.

    ISBN 0-88141-180-9

    1. Arsenii, otets.   2. Russkaia pravoslavnaia tserkov'—Clergy—Biography. 3. Orthodox Eastern Church—Soviet Union—Clergy—Biography.   4. Persecution—Soviet Union.   I. Alexander, servant of God.   II. Bouteneff, Vera.   III. Title

BX597.A7407413   1998

281.9'092—dc21

[B]   98—4429

    CIP

Translation Copyright © 1998 by Vera Bouteneff

This edition prepared for publication by
St Vladimir's Seminary Press for the
HUMAN KINDNESS FOUNDATION

Originally published in Russian as *Otets Arsenii*
by St Tikhon's Orthodox Theological Institute Press,
Brotherhood of the All-Merciful Saviour
Second Expanded Edition, Moscow, 1994
(Originally published, 1993)

First printing 1998
Reprinted 1999, 2000, 2001

ISBN 0-88141-180-9

PRINTED IN THE UNITED STATES OF AMERICA

CONTENTS

Translator's Foreword

As You Embark on reading this book, you will most likely find that its historical setting, the period of Stalin's dictatorship in the Soviet Union, presents situations which are hard to understand or even believe.

My own father and a number of other family members in Russia were victims of Stalinist repression. Their accounts enrich my understanding of this period, which forms the backdrop for the extraordinary people and events described here. I therefore feel it important to set out a few details about that era which may help to explain some of the situations in the book, and to provide the context in which its characters find themselves.

The Stalin years (1924-1953) were particularly dark ones in the history of the Soviet Union, and at the time very little information about what was going on filtered out to the outside world. The term "Iron Curtain" described a system which effectively prevented the West from learning about the extent of the repression of thought and the extinction of human life. While most of us knew, for example, that labor camps existed, few could imagine how horribly cruel they were, nor how huge were the numbers incarcerated in them. It was Alexander Solzhenitsyn's *One Day in the Life of Ivan Denisovich* that gave us one of our first glimpses into the conditions in a Soviet labor camp.

Religious Persecution

The Iron Curtain also kept most of us ignorant about the antireligious atmosphere which pervaded the Soviet Union. Recognizing the important influence of religion, the authorities moved to counteract it, labeling it as "obscurantism" and "the opiate of the people," claiming that it prevented human progress and enlightenment. The "fanatics" who persisted in openly expressing belief in God and sharing it with others were at risk of being labeled mentally ill, consigned to the inhumane conditions of mental hospitals, or sent to labor camps.

Since the fall of the Soviet regime, it has been revealed that six hundred bishops, forty thousand priests, and one hundred twenty thousand monks and nuns were killed during this period. Many of these died in the harsh conditions of prison or labor camp; others were shot or buried alive. By the end of Stalin's dictatorship, only some two hundred priests remained active in the Soviet Union. The scale of this martyrdom is unprecedented in the history of the Christian Church.

Those who attended church services were watched carefully; they often lost their jobs and other opportunities—their children could be refused entry to universities. People had to be secretive about their faith, even at home. Icons on display were dangerously visible proof of one's faith. People who felt it important to have icons in their homes were forced to hide them, or keep them locked up or covered by curtains or secular works of art. Schoolchildren were encouraged to report to their teachers if someone was praying at home: they were told that by betraying their families, they were helping their country.

In addition, religious education of any kind at home, in church, or at school was strictly forbidden, as was all religious literature. The ban on private prayer also meant that priests were not allowed to serve outside the few churches left open by the authorities, nor were they allowed to receive in their homes anyone who wanted to come for confession or simply to talk or pray. After the death of Stalin, this sort of persecution continued, though to a lesser extent, up until the fall of Communism in 1991.

Perhaps the strength of religious faith in Russia can be measured by the ferocity of the battle which the communist regime thought it worthwhile and necessary to put up against it.

Political Persecution

Political persecution was especially fierce during Stalin's time. Anyone who thought differently from the party line was considered an enemy of the people, and could be arrested and interned. People lived under the constant threat of "the knock at the door."[1] The knock heralded the abrupt appearance of the secret police, who usually came in the middle of the night to ensure that they would find the residents at home, befuddled with sleep. The search would begin. It would be painstakingly thorough and cruel, and spiked with humiliating personal insults. Having turned the apartment upside down, the police would arrest one or more members of the family living there. The others, quietly and in haste, would gather warm clothing and food for the one being taken away, bless him or her with the sign of the cross, and say goodbye. Then would begin a wrenching new life of constant worry for the prisoner—husband, wife, son or daughter—whom they might never see again. (These are details I have gleaned from a number of relatives in Russia who went through this experience first-hand.)

To build a case against someone who was considered a political enemy, the authorities often employed false witnesses, or denouncers. Because you could be betrayed by anyone, this ploy created an insidious suspicion of just

1 This knock was so integral a part of Soviet life that Shostakovich features it in his String Quartet no. 8.

about everyone you knew. Your own child could denounce you for praying at home. A friend could denounce you to protect himself or his family from arrest. Furthermore, the party line changed so often that even Communists who had conformed to a certain ideology could suddenly find themselves exiled to prison or to the same camp where they had consigned others.

Soviet labor camps had mixed populations: religious and political prisoners were interned together with criminals. This made for unbearably difficult circumstances for the "politicals" (i.e., both religious and political prisoners), who were in constant physical danger from the criminal element.

"Special" labor camps, such as the one where we first meet Father Arseny, followed a stricter regime; these were for the worst criminals as well as for "incorrigible" politicals. In the horror and desolation of those places there were yet people who provided light, sanctity, and limitless love to all those around them. Father Arseny was one such person.

The Text

Piotr Andreyevitch[2] Streltzoff was an art historian who, on becoming a priest-monk, was given the name of Father Arseny. It appears from the text that he was born in the first decade of the twentieth century, was first arrested in 1933 and then again in 1939 for his activities as a priest, and survived in prison camps where he stayed until 1958. He died in 1973.

This book first appeared during communist rule in samizdat form.[3] Even then the book circulated widely and nourished the spiritual lives of many. After the fall of communism when it could be published officially, it was reprinted twice (200,000 copies each time), the last time in 1994. Its success in Russia has been enormous.

The man who calls himself "the servant of God Alexander" compiled the book from accounts written by people who knew Father Arseny himself. One such man is a journalist, whose experience in documentation accounts for the clarity of detail in Part I. Yet this book is not a biography; it is a spiritual encounter. It introduces us to a man whom we can love and respect, whose example can lead us throughout our life.

Vera Bouteneff
Synaxis of the Mother of God, 1997

2 As with many other names in this book, this name was changed.

3 Samizdat means "self-published," referring to manuscripts typed in carbon copy and distributed without the permission of the government or the Writer's Union.

Introduction

IN PAST YEARS many memoirs have been published which describe the life of political prisoners in Russia in the days of Stalin. These were written by scientists, military people, writers, former Bolsheviks, educated people of all professions, kolkhoz workers, etc. But I think that nobody until now has written about the millions of the faithful, Orthodox believers, who died in prison camps or prisons, or suffered indescribably during interrogations. They suffered and died for their faith, for the fact that they did not renounce their God. In dying they sang His praises, and He did not abandon them.

To "put a seal on one's lips" and keep silent about this would mean leaving to oblivion the sufferings, the cross-bearing, and the death of many millions of martyrs who suffered for God and for us who live on this earth.

Our duty before God and His people is to tell about these martyrs.

The finest people of the Russian Orthodox Church died during this difficult time: priests, bishops, elders, monks, and simply deeply believing people in whom the flame of faith could not be extinguished. This faith was equal to if not stronger than that of the early Christian martyrs. In this book we shall meet one, only one of these many as yet uncanonized saints. And how many there were who died for us!

For twenty centuries humanity grew in knowledge; Christianity brought people light and life, yet in the twentieth century there were people who out of this rich heritage chose only evil and, multiplying it through the achievements of science, sent millions to drawn-out suffering and painful death.

God led me into spending only a little time in the camp with Father Arseny. But even this was enough for me to be brought to the faith, become his spiritual child, walk his path, understand and observe his deep love for God and for people, and see what a real Christian is.

The past should not be lost; it is the foundation for the present and the future. This is why I felt it my duty to gather all I could about Father Arseny's journey through life. In order to gather these precious facts about him I spoke to his spiritual children, read letters which he had written to them and to his friends, and read the memoirs of people who had known him.

The spiritual children of Father Arseny were many. Wherever God sent him, new ones appeared. They were in the city where earlier he had been an art historian and was then ordained a priest and formed a community of believers;

they were in the village to which he had been exiled; they were in the little town, lost in the endless northern forest where he lived a number of years; they were in the fearsome "special regime" labor camp. They were factory workers, peasants, members of the intelligentsia, criminals, political prisoners, former Communists, and camp administrators of all ranks. Coming into contact with Father Arseny they became his spiritual children, his friends, believers, and they followed him.

Yes! Many were those who, having met him, followed him! And those I met each told me what he or she had seen and what each knew of him.

Meeting with Father Arseny, I tried to learn the details about his life, but in spite of the fact that we talked a great deal, he told me very little about himself. I was able to get a little of my writing done while he was still alive. I gave him my notes to read over, and asked, "Was it really like this?" He would always answer, "Yes, it was," but he would always add, "God led us all on many paths, and each person, if you bother to look deeply at his life, has something worth being written about. My own life, as that of all other people, was always intertwined with and ran alongside that of other people. There was much of everything. But everything was always sent by God."

Often he would correct some details in what I had written. Then of course I had to change the names of places and almost all the people I refer to. Some of them are still alive, and times can always change.

The search was difficult, but as a result of it much information is gathered here. It is not perfect in the way it is written, but it does recreate before us the image and the life of Father Arseny.

When I started my work I did not know how much material I would be able to gather or of what nature it would be. Now I see that there will be three parts: "The Camp" is the first part; the second part, written but not yet fully edited, is entitled "The Path." It will include letters, memoirs and stories told by people who knew Father Arseny. As for the third part, there is much material but it still needs a great deal of work. I pray God to help me.

It would be vain to say, "*I* gathered, *I* wrote." So many people wrote, gathered, shared with me their memories. Many dozens of the people who knew and loved Father Arseny are the ones who should really be thanked for this work. I only tried, like everybody else whom Father Arseny raised and set on the path of faith, to give back a minute part of what I owe him who saved me and gave me a new life.

Having read this book, pray for the health of the servant of God Alexander. That will be my great recompense.

I

❧ THE CAMP ❧

The Prison Camp

THE DARKNESS OF the night and the cruel cold paralyzed everything. Everything, that is, except the wind. The wind carried clouds of icy snow that broke to form a shard-like precipitation. Encountering an obstacle, the wind would throw clumps of snow, pick up new ones from the ground, and move on, ahead...to nowhere.

Sometimes, there would be a quiet minute, then, through the darkness, an enormous patch of light would appear. In these rays of light one could see barracks upon barracks, spread out like a town. Towers with searchlights and guards could be seen on the horizon. Stretches of barbed wire created protective rows between which the icy glow of the menacing lights could be seen. Between the first and last rows of barbed wire police dogs roamed lazily. The searchlight beams swept down from the towers onto the ground and slid slowly across the snow, then back to the barbed wire.

Soldiers with automatic rifles standing on the towers were constantly watching the space between the rows of barbed wire. Yet it was never quiet. The wind would pick up again, blocking out the beams with snow, further darkening the misery of the barracks.

The camp was in a deep slumber.

Suddenly, there was the sound of metal clanging against metal, first at the entrance of the camp, and then again and again in different places. The searchlights quickened their sweeping pace, the gates of the camp opened, and trucks full of supervisors and guards rolled in.

The vehicles spread out quickly all over the camp. Four men ran out of the trucks at each barracks, checking all aspects of the structure to verify that no escapes had been attempted. Having ascertained that nothing had been disturbed in any way, the supervisors unlocked the doors of the barracks. For the guards in the towers, this was the most sensitive part of the procedure. Lights came alive and rifles left the shoulders of their owners. Guard dogs began to growl and became restless. The gulag had begun its workday.

The cloak of darkness lifted slightly as the northern winter day began, but the wind seemed to take no notice of the change, and continued its merciless, groaning storm of snow. A short distance from the inner circle of the camp's security zone, the flames of bonfires licked the air. These served to melt the ice that blanketed the earth so that mass graves could be dug. This was the work of the men in the barracks.

The Barracks

THE CAMP CAME alive as prisoners filed out of their barracks for roll call. The cold, freezing wind and the darkness were an agony to the people outside. Lining up by barracks, the prisoners received their meals and went directly to work.

The barracks had been emptied of its inhabitants, but the smell of damp clothing, human sweat, excrement, and disinfectant filled it. It seemed as though the shouts of the supervisors, the sound of soul-shattering swearing, the suffering of people, and the cruelty of the criminals remained inside as well. This depressing feeling, among the naked benches and the rows of bunk beds, was counteracted by the warmth of the place, making it feel somehow lived-in, softening the feeling of emptiness.

At -27° F, the gusty winds today alarmed not just the prisoners who had gone to work, but even those dressed in their warm clothing who watched them.

The prisoners trudged off to their work in fear. They knew that their work was designed to be cruel to them, and that the requirements set forth by the camp's chief officers were nearly impossible to fulfill. Everything was done to lead these people slowly to their death. Both political prisoners and common criminals whose crimes were punishable by death were sent to this camp. Few came out alive.

Father Arseny, whose name had been Piotr Andreyevich Streltzov before his priesthood, had been assigned the title of "zek"(prisoner) No. 18376. He had been sent to this camp six months ago and understood that there was no hope for him to ever leave it.

The night was transforming into a dark dawn, and then into a short half-dark day. Searchlights were still lighting the camp. Father Arseny was always on duty; he had to split logs near the barracks and then carry them into the barracks to feed the stove.

"Lord, Jesus Christ, Son of God, have mercy on me, a sinner!" he repeated constantly while doing his work. The logs were damp and half frozen and were difficult to split. As axes were not allowed in camp, he had to split the logs by hammering a wooden wedge into them with another log. The heavy, frozen log slipped and jumped from the weak hands of Father Arseny, and he could not hit the wedge properly. The work was slow. Exhaustion and the lack of food made it impossible to work properly. Everything was heavy and difficult. Yet the barracks had to be heated for the arrival of the workers. It had to be clean, tidy and swept. If it was not ready on time, the supervisor would send Father Arseny to the punishment cell and the other prisoners would beat him.

The political prisoners were beaten often: the supervisors beat them as punishment, the criminals just liked to do what they were used to doing, and all their hatred and cruelty came out this way. Someone was beaten every day, and beaten with pleasure—for the criminals, it was a real distraction.

"Have mercy on me, a sinner. Help me. I place my trust in Thee, O Lord, and in you, O Mother of God.[1] Do not abandon me, give me strength," prayed Father Arseny, almost falling from exhaustion as he carried bundle after bundle of logs to the stoves.

It was now time to light the fires. The stoves were cold and no longer gave off any warmth. It was not easy to light the fire for the logs were damp, and there was no dry kindling. The day before, Father Arseny had found some dry branches and put them in a corner near one of the stoves thinking, "Tomorrow, I will be able to light the stoves very fast!" When he went to get the dry kindling, though, he found that some of the criminals had poured water on it. He knew that if he was late in lighting the fires, the barracks would not be warm for the return of the workers. Father Arseny ran to try to find some dry bark or anything dry behind the barracks. And all the time he was praying, "Lord Jesus Christ, Son of God! Have mercy on me, a sinner," but then he added, "Thy will be done!"

He looked everywhere, and could find nothing dry. He did not know how he would light the fire.

While Father Arseny was looking for the dry branches, an old man working in the next barracks walked by. He was a criminal of immense cruelty and power. People said that even under the Tsar his name had been infamous all over Russia. He had committed so many crimes that he himself could not remember them all. Not much was known about the details of his crimes, so numerous were his exploits. Yet when he was brought to trial, the judge had knowledge of enough of his crimes to condemn him to be shot. His sentence was later commuted to internment in this prison camp, which for some criminals was much worse: if you are shot, you suffer a short time; in this camp, death is slow and painful. Those who were released from the camp

---

1 "Mother of God" is the title most often used by Orthodox Christians for Mary, who is the mother of God incarnate, Jesus Christ.

came out as invalids. Knowing this, many criminals became cruel, and their cruelty was expressed by beating the political prisoners and sometimes even other criminals, beating them to death.

This criminal was the boss of his whole barracks. Even the camp officers were afraid of him. It would take only a wink from him to have an "accident" occur. His fellow inmates called him "Graybeard." He was in his sixties, and his appearance was gentle. He would often begin by talking to people nicely, sometimes joking. Then, suddenly, he would start swearing horribly and punching with his fists.

Seeing that Father Arseny was looking for something he shouted, "What are you looking for, you silly priest?"

"I had prepared some dry branches to start the fire today, and somebody poured water onto them, so I am looking for something dry. The logs are damp. I don't know what to do."

"That's right, silly priest, without kindling you are lost," answered Graybeard.

"People will come from work, they will be cold, and they will beat me," mumbled Father Arseny.

"Come, Pop, I will give you some kindling,"[2] Graybeard said, leading Father Arseny to a whole pile of beautiful dry kindling. Father Arseny had a thought that perhaps this was a joke; he knew Graybeard only too well, and could not expect any help from him.

"Take, Father Arseny, take what you need," the criminal said.

Father Arseny began to quickly gather some dry branches, all the time thinking, "I will take some kindling and he will shout that I am a thief." Then he realized that the man had called him Father Arseny. He prayed silently, crossed himself in his mind, and began to gather the kindling.

"Take more, Father Arseny! More!" Graybeard barked. Then he bent and started helping Father Arseny, carrying the kindling into the barracks and putting it next to the stove. Father Arseny bowed before him and said, "May God bless you!"

Graybeard did not answer, and left.

Father Arseny put the wood in the stoves and lit the fire. The logs began to burn. He had time only to throw more pieces of wood on the flame before he had to rush to clean the barracks, wiping off tables, sweeping, and getting more logs.

2 In Russia a colloquial (and usually disrespectful) name for a priest is "pop."

It was almost three o'clock. The stoves were red-hot and it was getting warm in the barracks. The smells became stronger, but because of the warmth, the barracks regained a familiar and almost cozy feeling. The supervisor came in several times as Father Arseny went about his work. As always, his words were angry and menacing. During one of his visits, he struck Father Arseny on the head with a piece of wood.

Carrying the logs and throwing them into the stoves tired Father Arseny to the extreme. His head hurt because he was so tired and weak, his heart beat irregularly, and his breathing was bad. His legs felt so weak that they could hardly support his tired body. "Do not abandon me, O God," he whispered, bending under the weight of the logs.

The Patients

In The Barracks, Father Arseny was not alone; three other prisoners had stayed in that day. Two were seriously ill, while the third, a loafer named Fedka, had cut himself with an ax on purpose. Lying on his bunk bed, he would fall asleep, and suddenly awakening, would shout, "Keep the barracks warm! I am cold! If you don't do your work I'll slap you!" and then would immediately fall asleep.

The two ill prisoners were in very serious condition. They had not been sent to the prison camp hospital only because it was full. At about noon a medic stopped by, and looking at the patients from a distance, shouted to Father Arseny, "They will soon be dead, a lot of them are croaking these days. It's cold!" He spoke not caring at all that the patients could hear him. And why should he care? Prisoners were supposed to die in this camp. Then he approached the third prisoner, the one who had hurt his hand, and who was moaning now to show off his pain. "Don't you fool around," he ordered. "Tomorrow you will go to work! If you don't, you will be sent to solitary confinement where you will really 'rest'!"

Every so often, Father Arseny would interrupt his work to go to the two very sick patients, help them however he could, talk to them, and pray for them. "Lord Jesus Christ! Help them; heal them, show them your mercy. Let them live until they can go free!" he whispered again and again, arranging their hard mattresses or covering them. Sometimes he gave them water to drink, or the medication that the medic had thrown onto their beds. In camp, the primary medication was aspirin, which was supposed to cure all diseases.

To the one who was most sick Father Arseny gave a piece of bread, a quarter of his own daily ration. Having softened the bread with water, Father Arseny fed the patient, who opened his eyes, and, looking at Father Arseny, pushed his hand away. Father Arseny quietly said, "Eat, eat with the help of God." The sick man swallowed the bread and said, "What do you want from me with your God! What do you hope to get from me? You hope I will die so you can take my belongings. I have nothing, so don't even try!" Father Arseny did not answer, carefully covered him, and approached the other patient to help him turn over before starting to clean the barracks again.

10

He decided not to hide the kindling given him by Graybeard and piled it right next to the stove. He thought, "Yesterday I tried to hide it, and see what happened: people poured water over it. Today God has helped me."

The stoves were red-hot and Father Arseny was pleased that the workers would come home and would be able to rest a little in the warmth of the barracks. While he was thinking this, a supervisor walked in. He must have been in his early thirties, and as he always appeared cheerful and smiling, his name was Pupkov, but he was called "the Optimist" by all the prisoners.

"What do you think you're doing, *Priest?* You're heating the barracks as if it was a sauna! You're using state logs for the enemies of the people. I'll show you!" He hit Father Arseny in the face, and left, still smiling. Wiping blood from his face, Father Arseny prayed, "Do not abandon me, do not leave me, a sinner. Have mercy on me."

Fedka the loafer sat up and said, "The dirty pig, he hit you hard on the snout, and all for fun! He doesn't even know what he did it for!" In an hour's time the Optimist came back and shouted, "Inspection time, all of you get up!" Fedka jumped down from his bunk bed, and Father Arseny stood at attention with a broom in his hands.

"Who else is here?" shouted the supervisor, in spite of the fact that he already had asked this question the same morning and knew perfectly well who was there. "Two very sick ones and one who will go to work tomorrow!" he continued, walking along the corridor between the beds. He saw the two patients and understood that they could not get up, but just for show, he started shouting. He did not dare come near though: who knows, perhaps they were contagious?

"You'd better watch out, *Priest,* and see that everything's in order! They'll call you for questioning. You'll have to answer for everything." And, mumbling obscenities, he left.

The day was coming to an end. Darkness came fast, and the prisoners were soon to return. They always came frozen, tired, angry, and weakened, and when they reached their bunks, they nearly fainted onto them. With the return of the workers, the barracks filled with cold, dampness, and a generally restless and unpleasant atmosphere.

Half an hour after their return, they were taken to eat. Mealtime was for many prisoners a time of suffering: the criminals would grab away political prisoners' food and beat those who tried to stop them. Those who were weak and could not defend themselves were deprived of food.

There were more political prisoners than common criminals, but the thieves and murderers had much power over the weaker zeks. Every day many zeks were deprived of their meager food ration. This brought indescribable suffering. Tired, hungry and constantly shivering of cold, the prisoners thought of nothing but of food, dreaming of full meals to make themselves happy.

The meals they did get were pitiful. The portions were minute, nearly rancid, and, for some unknown reason, smelled of kerosene. All of this was designed to kill them slowly.

Father Arseny was often deprived of meals, but he never complained. If his meal was taken, he would just return to the barracks, lie down on his bunk, and pray. At first his head would spin, he would shiver from cold and hunger, his thoughts cloudy. Still, he would recite the matins service and the Akathist[3] to the Mother of God, to Saint Nicholas and to Saint Arseny, and he would commemorate his spiritual children and all the departed he had kept in his memory. After praying in this way all night, he felt new strength in the morning, as if he had eaten and slept.

Father Arseny had many spiritual children outside and inside the camp, and his soul suffered for each of them. When he had been in regular camps, he was able to get letters from them, but since he was in the death camp, this was not possible. His spiritual children thought that Father Arseny had died. They inquired about him and always got the same answer, "If he was sent to the 'special camp' he is not on record anywhere."

Now it was dark. The columns of prisoners entered the camp zone, one after the other, and poured into the different barracks. In Father Arseny's barracks, people walked in angry and tired, but as they entered into the warmth they were comforted. Today nobody beat up Father Arseny and nobody took his bread.

The two sick men received only half their ration and Father Arseny hid a little piece of fish for them in his clothing. Later Father Arseny started feeding the two patients. He heated up some water with pine needles, mixed it with aspirin and gave some to both men. He divided the bread and the fish between them.

Five days later, the two sick prisoners started feeling a little better. They would probably live, but they could not yet get up. Father Arseny cared for them at night and, when he had time, during the day. He also gave them part of his own ration.

3 The Akathist is a church service in praise and honor of a saint. The word comes from the Greek "Akathistos," meaning "not sitting," for during this service the faithful stand.

Father Arseny did not know who the patients were. They had come to his barracks from another camp and had been very sick when they arrived. They accepted the care of Father Arseny with no enthusiasm, but they could not survive without him. They said nothing about themselves, and Father Arseny asked nothing. He had seen many people like these two patients and he had cared for them all. When they left, he seldom heard of them again.

One of the sick men told him that his name was Sazikov, Ivan Alexandrovich. Father Arseny prayed quietly while he was helping him. Sazikov noticed it and mumbled, "You're praying, eh, Priest?! You pray to get forgiveness of your sins and this is why you help us! You're afraid of God! Why's that? Have you ever seen Him?"

Father Arseny looked at Sazikov with surprise. "How could I not have seen him? He is here among us and unites you and me!"

"What are you saying, Pop? God is in this barracks?" he laughed.

Father Arseny looked at him and said quietly, "Yes, I see his presence. I see that your soul is black with sin, but there is room in it for light. Light will come to you, Sazikov, light and your Saint. Saint Seraphim of Sarov will not abandon you."

Sazikov's face distorted, he trembled and whispered with hatred, "I'll kill you, silly priest, I'll kill you — I don't know how you know things. I hate the way you think."

Father Arseny turned around and walked away repeating, "Have mercy on me, a sinner!" While he was doing his work he prayed the akathist, his rule of prayer, vespers, matins, and all the other prayers a priest must pray.

The second patient was one who was in the camp for a simple reason: he had to be removed from his position of authority so that someone else could take his place. His story was the same as that of so many. He had been part of the October Revolution in 1917, he had known Lenin, he had commanded a brigade in 1920, he had had an important position in the secret police, he had worked for the NKVD[4] and now he had been sent to die in a "special" death camp.

Some men were killed for things they had said, others for their faith, and then there were those like the second sick man: a Communist-idealist who had happened to get in someone's way, and was therefore put away. All of them were sooner or later to die in this camp.

4 NKVD was the Soviet Secret Police.

One of those removed from power was Alexander Pavlovich Avsenkov. As soon as he had heard this name Father Arseny remembered him. Avsenkov had often appeared in the newspapers, and he was the one who had signed Father Arseny's sentence. This was when Father Arseny had been sentenced to be shot for antirevolutionary activity. Later his punishment had been commuted to fifteen years in camp. Father Arseny remembered the name well.

Avsenkov was middle-aged. He looked forty or fifty, but life in camp had left a heavy imprint on him. Hunger, exhausting work, beatings, all these paled next to the awareness that only months ago he had sent others here, believing each time that he was ridding the state of the "enemy of the people." His stay in the camp had made him realize the enormity of his mistake. He realized that he had sent tens, hundreds of thousands of innocent people to their death. From his high position he had lost touch with the truth. He believed interrogation reports and the flattery of his subordinates; listening to absurd government orders he had lost contact with living human beings and life itself.

He suffered constantly, but could change nothing about what he had done. His feeling of spiritual emptiness and loss tore him apart. He was quiet, kind, and shared all he owned; he was afraid neither of the administration nor of the criminals. He was frightened when he was angry, but did not lose his head; he tried to protect the innocent and for this he often had to spend time in the punishment cell.

Avsenkov was attached to Father Arseny: he loved him for his generosity of heart and his warmth. He often told him, "You have a soul, Father Arseny." (Within the barracks most people did call him Father Arseny.) "You have a soul, I can see that, but I am a true Communist, while you serve your God; you are a priest. We have different points of view. In theory, I should be fighting ideologically with you."

Father Arseny just smiled and answered, "Hey, dear friend. Why would you want to fight? You fought as much as you could and where did your ideology get you? It took you to this camp, which swallowed you! As far as I am concerned I had my faith in Christ out there in freedom and I have it here within myself. God is the same everywhere and helps everyone! I trust and believe that He will help you too!"

And once Father Arseny said, "We have known each other for a long time. God brought us together a long time ago, and planned our meeting in this camp."

"What are you saying? How could I have known you?"

"Oh yes, you know me, Alexander Pavlovich. In 1933 when Communism was trying to eradicate religion, hundreds of thousands of believers were exiled, hundreds of churches were closed and this is when, for the first time, I was sent away to camp on your instructions. In 1939, I was in your jurisdiction again. I wrote an article. As soon as it was published, you arrested me again and convicted me to be shot. But, thank you – you commuted the sentence to exile in camp. Since then I have been living in various camps and all along I've been expecting to see you. So finally we meet!

"Please don't think that I am trying to accuse you. All this is the will of God, and my own life is just a drop in the ocean. Of course you cannot remember me. Among the tens of thousands you saw, how could you remember me? God alone knows everyone and everything. The fate of people is in His hands."

The Silly Priest

LIFE AND WORK in the camp were awful and inhumane; each day only brought one closer to death. Knowing this, many of the prisoners did not want to die spiritually, and strove to lead an internal battle for their lives and their spirits. These prisoners talked about science, life, or religion, sometimes held lectures on art or scientific research, or discussed books they had read before their arrest, read poetry, or talked about their lives before camp.

Against the backdrop of cruelty, coarseness, violence and the awareness of impending, unavoidable death, the hunger, extreme exhaustion, and the constant presence of the criminals, this was truly remarkable. The prisoners often tried to find in each other the support that would make their life bearable.

Depending on the nature of the most recent wave of arrests, different people would arrive at this camp—engineers, soldiers, clerics, scientists, artists, farmers, writers, agronomists, doctors—and then subgroupings of prisoners with similar interests would form naturally. Everyone was downtrodden and exhausted, but you could see that no one wanted to forget his past, his profession. Debate between groups was very heated—people would become impassioned, see only their own side on an issue, and argue as if their lives depended on it.

Father Arseny took part in none of these discussions. He aligned himself with no group, nor did he attempt to defend a viewpoint. Whenever a discussion began, Father Arseny would simply go to rest and pray on his bunk. The intellectuals in the barracks looked down their nose at Father Arseny. "Just a silly priest, uneducated. He's good-hearted, helpful, but uncultured. That's why he believes in God; he has nothing else to live by."

This was the opinion of the majority of the prisoners.

✣

Often, after roll call was taken and the barracks were locked for the night, a group of ten or twelve writers, art historians, and artists would gather. The discussion was always heated. This time the topic was ancient Russian art and architecture. One of the prisoners, a tall man who had kept his elegance and poise even in camp, spoke with great assurance on this topic. People around him listened with great interest. This tall and impressive man was surprisingly knowledgeable and very sure of himself; he spoke very convincingly. As he was talking, Father Arseny happened to pass by.

The speaker, who was in fact a professor of art history, spoke to Father Arseny condescendingly. "Tell us, *dear Father,* you are very pious and of the clergy; perhaps you could tell us how you understand the influence of Orthodoxy on ancient Russian art and architecture. Do you think there is such an influence?" He spoke and smiled. The people around him laughed. Avsenkov, who was seated nearby, also smiled.

Such a question addressed to Father Arseny seemed absurd. Some felt sorry for him, others wanted to have a laugh. Everybody understood that a simple priest like Father Arseny could not answer such a philosophical question. Since he didn't know anything, the question was intended to demean him—Father Arseny was just passing by. But he stopped, listened to the question, noticed the grinning faces and answered, "I will answer as soon as I finish my work," and kept going.

"He's no fool, he avoided being put on the spot!" someone murmured.

"Yes, the Russian clergy was always uncultured," echoed another. Ten minutes later, Father Arseny returned to the group that was talking and, interrupting the speaker, said, "I finished my work. Can you please repeat your question?"

The professor looked at Father Arseny the way he would look at a stupid student, and slowly said, "The question, Father, is a simple one, but interesting: how do you, a member of the Russian clergy, understand the influence of Orthodoxy on ancient Russian fine art and architecture? You may have heard about the art treasures in Suzdal, Rostov, Pereslavl, and the Ferapontovo Monastery. You may have seen reproductions of the Icon of the Mother of God of Vladimir, and the Trinity by Rublev. So please explain to us, what connection do you see?"

The question was that of a professor; every one understood this and thought that he should not have asked it of the simple but good little priest. It was clear, they thought, that he could not answer; you could see it just by looking at his face.

Father Arseny stood straighter, his appearance changed somehow, he looked at the professor and said, "There are many different theories about the connection between Orthodoxy and fine art. Many people have written about this including you, professor. You have spoken and written much about it. However, I feel that a great many of your theories and statements are convoluted, incorrect, and contrived simply to satisfy your readers, or the censors. What you were saying just now is much closer to the truth than what you said in your books.

"You believe that Russian fine art grew out of a secular base – you deny almost completely the influence of Orthodoxy. You write that it is only economic and social factors, not the spiritual basis of the Russian people and the beneficial influence of Christianity, which influence art and architecture. My opinion is the opposite of yours. I consider that Orthodoxy was the decisive influence on Russian culture from the tenth to the eighteenth century. In the tenth century, the Russian clergy found and accepted the culture of Byzantium and brought it home to influence all of Russia. They brought books, icons, models of Greek churches, and hagiography to the Russian people. This was the influence that built Russian culture.

"You mentioned the Icon of the Mother of God of Vladimir. Didn't this icon, like many other early icons, come to us from Orthodox Byzantium? And weren't these icons the foundation on which later Russian iconography and art flourished?

"Every Russian icon is inextricably connected to the soul of the Christian iconographer, of the believer who comes to the icon as a spiritual, symbolic representation of Christ, His Mother, or His Saints. The Russian people do not approach icons as idols, but as the spiritual image of the one to whom his soul addresses itself in sorrowful or joyous prayer. The Russian iconographer creates his icons with prayer and fasting, and it is understandable that it is said that the hand of the iconographer is held by an angel of God.

"The Russian iconographer never signs his work because he considers that it is not his hand but his soul that had created the icon, with the blessing of God—while you seem to see only socioeconomic factors.

"Look at a western Madonna and at an ancient Russian icon; you will see the difference. In our icons you can feel the spirit of faith, the imprint of Orthodoxy; on western paintings you see a Lady, a woman: spiritual yes, but full of earthly beauty. You do not feel the power of God's grace; it is only a woman. Just look at the Mother of God of Vladimir. Look at her eyes and you will read such strength of spirit, such faith in God's mercy, and such hope for salvation."

Father Arseny spoke clearly and expressively. Even his physical demeanor had changed. He spoke about well-known icons and explained each of them, thus revealing the soul of ancient Russian iconography. He then began speaking about architecture, giving examples such as those in Suzdal, Vladimir, and Moscow and showed its connection with Orthodoxy.

Father Arseny finished his answer this way: "In building churches, Russians made the stones sing the glory of God: they made the stones teach about God, and glorify God."

Father Arseny spoke for about an hour and a half and the people around him listened in dead silence. The professor had lost his half-mocking smile, and looked as if he had shrunk.

"Excuse me," he asked, "How do you know all this? You know fine arts, architecture, and even my own books? Where did you study? I thought you were a priest."

"One has to love and know his fatherland. It is essential that even the 'silly priests,' as you call them, understand the soul of Russian art and, being shepherds of souls, they must show their flock the truth as it is in reality. Because people like yourself, professor, cover in mind-twisting theories and lies that which is most holy and precious in man. This distortion is created for one's personal benefit and to cater to current political leanings and directives."

The professor changed his tack altogether and asked, "Who are you? What is your last name?"

"In the world I was Piotr Andreyevich Streltzov, now I am Father Arseny, a prisoner like yourself in this 'special camp.'"

Startled, the Professor spoke with difficulty. "Piotr Andreyevich, I apologize. Forgive me. I could never imagine that I was speaking to a famous art historian, author of many books and articles, teacher of many, a famous professor, now a priest, and asking him such a stupid question. For a number of years no one had heard from you. Nobody knew where you were; only your books and your articles continued expressing your thoughts. How is it that you, such a famous expert, became a priest?"

"I became the priest Arseny because I see and feel the presence of God in everything. Having become Father Arseny I understood as never before that a simple priest must know a great deal. And while we are on the subject of 'simple priests,' you of all people know that they were the power that made Russia what it was in the fourteenth and fifteenth centuries, and helped the Russian people overthrow the Tartars. It is unfortunately true that in the sixteenth and seventeenth centuries morality was at a low among the Russian priesthood, and only a few rare 'lights' lit up the horizon of the Russian church. Until then, the priesthood had been the dynamic force of our country."

With that, Father Arseny left, and all those who had heard him, among them Avsenkov, stood silently in awe and amazement. "Well, there we have it, my friends," someone said. "That was our simpleton priest." Each went to his bunk in silence.

Avsenkov noticed that from this time on, the intellectuals in the barracks looked at Father Arseny differently. It seemed that for many the concepts of God, science, and "intelligentsia" were becoming more closely related. Avsenkov had been a convinced Communist who had believed almost fanatically in Marxist ideology. During his first year in the camp he had lived as a loner; then he started to talk to some of the other prisoners and realized that most of his old friends, also Communists, now hoped only for a return to the old days when their life was comfortable. They did not care to do battle with the unjust rule of Stalin. Avsenkov disliked these attitudes and stopped talking to them. He looked back at his own life and understood that he had in fact lost all his idealism a long time before; these ideas had been replaced by parroting formulaic "truths" and obeying orders. He had lost contact with humanity; lectures and newspaper articles had replaced living human beings.

In his contact with other prisoners, Avsenkov saw authentic, unartificial life. He was attracted to Father Arseny with his rare attitude towards others and his constant readiness to help everyone with true kindness. Father Arseny's intellectual qualities won him over completely. His limitless faith in God and his unceasing prayer had at first alienated Avsenkov, but at the same time had strangely attracted him. He always felt good when he was with Father Arseny. All the difficulties, the sadness, the oppressive atmosphere of the camp became bearable in his presence. Why? He could not understand.

Ivan Alexandrovich Sazikov, one of the ill prisoners whom Father Arseny had cared for, had been, as they learned, an infamous criminal. He loved power, he was a hard man, he knew the community of camp criminals well and had soon subjugated them all to himself. They all obeyed him. His word was law; the prisoners were all afraid of him—but he did not like to mingle in the affairs of the barracks, preferring to stay apart.

For a few months after Father Arseny had nursed him to health, Sazikov did not want to be near him and made believe that he did not even know him. But it so happened that Sazikov hurt his leg and had to lie in his bunk for four or five days; the wound became infected, gangrene set in and he was afraid his leg would have to be amputated. The medics did not force him to go to work, but he was not getting any better. Father Arseny once again patiently nursed him, fed him, and with his support, Sazikov finally got better.

Sazikov tried to give Father Arseny some money for this, but Father Arseny answered with a smile, saying, "I am not helping you for money, I am doing it for you, the person—for yourself."

Sazikov's feelings toward Father Arseny became warmer; he told Father Arseny about his life, and once he said, "I don't trust people, in general. I believe priests even less. But you, Piotr Andreyevich, I trust. I know you won't turn your back on me. You live in your God, you do good not for your own benefit, but for the sake of others. My mother was like that." He said this, and left.

⤳

This story was recounted by Avsenkov and Sazikov. It was confirmed by a number of other prisoners who were interned in the same barracks at that time.

"Stop This!"

THE WEATHER OUTSIDE was ferocious. Many prisoners froze to death and many new prisoners arrived to work in their stead. It was a difficult time for everybody, but the "political" prisoners had it worst of all. For two days in a row their rations were stolen by the prisoners who were criminals. That night, after roll call and the locking of the barracks, a large fight erupted between the two factions over these rations.

Avsenkov took the leadership of the "politicals." The criminals were headed by "Ivan the Brown." He was a hardened criminal, a good-for-nothing, and a murderer many times over. In camp he had also killed more than once; he liked card games in which the one who lost paid with his life.

The battle that evening was over the rations which the criminals had taken laughingly—they said that they were used to taking what did not belong to them. The camp administrators, for reasons of personal safety, were always on the side of the criminals.

The fight started with fists, and then logs, then knives appeared in the hands of the criminals. Knives were, of course, forbidden. The guards searched for them but never seemed to find them. One of the prisoners, a soldier, was cut up; several "politicals" had their heads cracked. The criminals knew how to work together; most of the "politicals" could only shout and were afraid to help their own.

The criminals were cruel. They were winning over the "politicals"; blood was flowing.

Father Arseny ran to Sazikov and begged him, "Help! Please help, Ivan Alexandrovich! They are cutting people up. There is blood everywhere. I ask you in the name of God to stop this! The criminals will listen to you!" Sazikov only laughed and said, "Sure, they will listen to me, but why don't you help with your God? Ivan the Brown has already killed two of your friends, and now he is going to kill Avsenkov. Your God seems not to notice this!"

Father Arseny looked all around him. He saw blood on people, he heard screams, swearing, and moans, and his soul was full of pain for their suffering.

He lifted his arms, went into the very midst of the heated fight and said in a clear and loud voice, "In the name of God, I order you! Stop this!" He blessed them with sign of the cross and said in a whisper, "Now, help the wounded," and he headed for his bunk. There he stood, as if in a different world, as if surrounded by light. He stood there, having receded into himself, praying. He did not hear the dead being carried to the door, nor did he see the wounded being helped. He stood, his attention focused on prayer.

All was quiet in the barracks now. You could only hear people getting into their bunks, and the moaning of a seriously wounded man. Sazikov came near Father Arseny and said, "Forgive me, Father Arseny. I doubted your God. I see now that He exists. It even scares me. A great power is given to one who believes in Him. Even I am frightened. Forgive me for making fun of you."

In two days, Avsenkov came to Father Arseny after work and said, "Thank you. You saved my life! You believe in God unconditionally and, looking at you, I'm also beginning to understand that He exists."

✠

Life plodded along. Prisoners came, worked, then were buried in the frozen ground. Others came to replace them and the cycle started over.

There was no more stealing of rations. If some criminals forgot this new way of life and did steal, the others taught them a hard lesson. Father Arseny worked as usual, beyond his own strength, but he was never discouraged.

In the barracks in which Father Arseny lived, many people from different backgrounds were thrown together to die. This situation caused much friction between different groups and Father Arseny served as a buffer for the pain and suffering of all the factions involved. With a warm and kind word he knew how to comfort their souls. A person could be a believer, a Communist, a criminal, or any other kind of prisoner – Father Arseny always found the right words for each individual. These words went deep into one's soul and helped him live, gave him hope for the future and often helped him become a better person.

In some strange way Sazikov and Avsenkov became closer. What could a criminal and a Communist idealist have in common? They were somehow invisibly united by Father Arseny.

⁀

This story was recounted by Avsenkov, Sazikov and three other prisoners.

A Summons to the Major

THE SUPERVISOR HAD begun frequently to stop in and make a fuss about every little detail as Father Arseny cleaned the empty barracks and tended to the stoves. One day he was especially fierce: he hit Father Arseny in the face, swore filthily, and tried to scare him. That evening Father Arseny received a summons to appear before the Major.

Everyone knows that to be summoned at night is a bad sign. There was word that a new major had been named as chief of the special camp. This caused fear in all the prisoners. A call to the "special sector" was not a good thing. It usually meant that the camp officers would try to make you admit to something, or they would try to make you a "secret coworker" (a sort of internal spy). If you said no, they would beat you savagely. Beatings occurred during interrogations too. The only time they did not beat you was when they called you to announce the decision to extend your sentence. The prisoners feared the special sector. Some 25 people worked there. Many of these workers in the special sector drank heavily. They knew how to interrogate; they knew how to beat. "You will admit to everything," they would say.

Father Arseny was met by a young lieutenant. It all started as usual: name, patronymic, last name, what are you accused of, as well as screams of "We know everything." Threats followed, and then one would always hear, "Now admit you were spreading propaganda in this camp."

Father Arseny answered all the usual questions and was silent. He started to pray. The lieutenant swore, beat the table with his fist, threatened, and then rose, saying, "We'll take you to the major – you will talk," and cursing, he left. In about ten minutes he came back and led Father Arseny to the major, the chief of the special sector. Father Arseny, knowing the rules of the camp, understood that this was bad.

"Leave us," said the major taking Father Arseny's file. The lieutenant left. The major got up, closed the door tightly, returned to his desk, sat down, and started reading the file.

Father Arseny stood and prayed, "Lord have mercy on me, a sinner."

The major finished going through the file, and said in a plain, pleasant voice, "Sit down, Piotr Andreyevich. I am the one who called you in here." Father Arseny sat down, silently repeating, "Lord have mercy on me! I put my trust in you." And he thought, "It will start now."

24

The major looked again in Father Arseny's file, checked the photograph, unbuttoned his jacket pocket and took out a small piece of paper. He gave it to Father Arseny saying, "This is for you from Vera Danilovna. She is alive and in good health. Read it!"

"Dear Father Arseny," it read. "God's mercy is endless, He kept you alive. Be afraid of nothing! Trust. Keep preying (sic) for us sinners. God has preserved many of us. Pray for us. Vera."

This letter startled him. Vera was a nun and his closest spiritual child. It was Vera's handwriting. There could be no doubt that she was the one who had written all this. He knew it because the two of them had agreed together that if they were able to write they had to make a spelling mistake in the word "praying."

"Lord, I thank Thee for Thy gift of letting me know how my children are, I thank Thee for Thy mercy!" The major then took the letter from Father Arseny's hands and burned it. They were both silent. Father Arseny was stunned and extremely moved. He could not understand what was happening. The major was silent because he understood the state of shock which Father Arseny was in. He looked at the person in front of him: an old man with a thin beard, a shaved head, wearing an old, heavily patched cotton jacket and torn quilted trousers.

Having studied Father Arseny's file, the major knew that his was a "serious" case. The prisoner's family included a famous scientist; he himself had graduated from Moscow University and had become known in the Soviet Union and abroad as a brilliant art historian. He was the author of renowned studies on ancient Russian art and architecture, and was now a hieromonk. He was the leader of a large and strong religious community that had not dispersed as the authorities had hoped even after Father Arseny had been arrested. This same old man who stood before him, way back when he had lived in the free world, had known how to combine deep faith and a serious scientific mind. In his books he spoke about the beauty of his homeland and asked his readers to love it. Now the major saw that all this had died in the man sitting before him. He had been trampled on and was broken. Death was upon him. Only the begging of his wife, whom the major loved unconditionally and whom he always heeded, and the request of Vera Danilovna, who had been of great help to his wife and daughter in the past, had led the major to this dangerous act of passing on a letter to a prisoner.

Vera Danilovna was a doctor, and it so happened that the lives of several of the people closest to the major had been saved by her care and devotion. In a camp where all watched each other in the hope they could inform on someone to the administration, it was extremely dangerous for the major to do what he had done. But there was yet another reason why he wanted to make contact with Father Arseny in this camp.

Father Arseny was praying with such intensity that he seemed separated from the world around him but, suddenly, he looked up at the major and calmly said, "I thank you for bringing me this letter. I thank you in the name of the Lord."

The major looked into the eyes of Father Arseny, and he understood that he had in front of him not an old and decrepit man, but an extraordinary person whom the years spent in this camp had not broken. On the contrary, they had strengthened the power of his spirit. For the eyes of Father Arseny shone with a light and a power the major had never seen before. And in this strength and this light you could see infinite kindness and a deep knowledge of the human soul.

The major sensed that Father Arseny had only to look at someone or say something, and it would be done. Father Arseny's eyes could see the innermost reaches of a person's soul and read his thoughts. His faith had a power over others and it seemed to radiate visibly from him. The major understood that this man was not going to ask him why he, the newly assigned chief of this special camp, had dared to pass him the note.

Father Arseny was looking at something above and just past the major. He stood up, made the sign of the cross several times, and bowed to someone. Seeing him the major stood up too, for before him at that moment stood not an old man in a patched up vest and torn pants, but a fully vested priest, who was performing the sacrament of prayer to God.

The major shrugged at this unexpected and incomprehensible event, and he recalled something he had long forgotten. He remembered the time when his mother used to take him, as a little boy to the small wooden country church to pray on the great feast days. A feeling that was at once gentle and kind seized his soul.

Father Arseny sat down and again the major saw in front of him an exhausted old man, but one whose eyes still radiated light.

The major spoke: "Piotr Andreyevich! They sent me to work here. I found out you were here. I was in Moscow and told Vera Danilovna, and undertook to bring this message to you. I also wanted to ask you to help a man who lives in your barracks I..." and the major stopped short.

"I understand, I understand! Of course I will help Alexander Pavlovich Avsenkov. I will pass on to him what you asked me to. I understand it is difficult for you here, Sergei Petrovich; you are not used to this new work of yours. It is extremely difficult to get used to this life. So many awful things happen here! But be as merciful as you can be, and that in itself will be a help to the prisoners."

"Yes! It is difficult. It is difficult everywhere now, this is why I ended up here. My heart bleeds when I see what is happening around me. People are followed, they denounce each other, secret instructions are given that contradict one another. I do what I can, but it's almost worthless. I am ashamed to admit it, but I am afraid for myself.

"The supervisor Pupkov keeps sending reports about you; he obviously does not like you. We will replace him with somebody more decent. It's hard for you, Piotr Andreyevich I cannot help you much, as I said, but I plan to try. I will be sending for you through Markov, the one who just interrogated you. He is a difficult man, always suspicious. That is why I will ask him to keep a special watch on you, and after your interrogations, to bring you to me. Do not worry, this special surveillance will not be written into your file.

"Do tell Alexander Pavlovich that General Abrosimov has been demoted to the rank of major. Many people in high places still remember Alexander Pavlovich Avsenkov, but it is extremely difficult to help him. Several went to Stalin to request his release, but he only says 'Let him stay in camp for a while.' Meanwhile the man who got Avsenkov's post is trying to get rid of him for good, in order to keep the position for himself. Alexander Pavlovich knows a great deal, he is a true idealist, and he is straightforward. This kind of person is disliked in the ranks. They want him shot, but Stalin has not given the final order. So Stalin's subordinates are trying to get rid of him unofficially, through the camp criminals. It is rumored that "Ivan the Brown" has been asked to get rid of him somehow.

"Please give Alexander Pavlovich this note from his wife. This will give him moral support. Help him. Tell him to beware of Savushkin; he is trying to invent accusations against him. He also lives in your barracks.

"Well now, you have to sign the record of our interview. I am going to write it in at our next meeting."

Father Arseny signed a blank piece of paper and said, "Write in what you must."

The major stood up, walked to Father Arseny and, taking him by the shoulders, said, "Please remember me."

Filled with impressions and emotions and unceasingly praising God, Father Arseny went back to his barracks and lay down on his bunk, tired from all he had just experienced.

All the prisoners in the barracks breathed a sigh of relief. It had seemed likely that Father Arseny would never return. Lying down he prayed prayers and psalms thanking God and repeating, "Lord, I praise Thy deeds. I thank Thee for having shown me Thy mercy. Have mercy on me, Lord."

There is an unwritten rule in camp: after somebody has been interrogated you do not approach him. You ask nothing. The person will tell if he wants. If you do ask, your fellow inmates might get suspicious of you. They might think you're worried that your name came up in the interrogation. Father Arseny did not sleep that night; he was rejoicing in the mercy of God. Father Arseny glorified Him and prayed to the Mother of God. In the morning he got up and started his daily work with a light heart.

That morning, Pupkov dropped in on the barracks, looked around and said, "So, Pop, they didn't finish you off yesterday? They will!" And laughing, he left.

In the evening, when the prisoners came home, Father Arseny said to Avsenkov, "I cannot split these logs alone, they won't be done in time. Please help me."

There was about an hour left before the roll call. The searchlights were already running back and forth along the ground. The sky was turning black and Father Arseny told Avsenkov, "I will pass the logs on to you; meanwhile take this note, read it, and swallow it. I will tell you everything later."

Stunned Avsenkov asked "What note?"

Father Arseny slipped him the note that the major had given him. Avsenkov snatched it and started splitting logs with the wooden wedge. Then, as if he was checking a log under the light, he started reading the note. He read it once, twice, and tears started running down his face. Father Arseny whispered, "Now swallow the note and try to control yourself."

As they worked, Father Arseny was able to tell him what Abrosimov had said: that he had been demoted from general to major, that Avsenkov's friends wanted to help, but were finding it extremely difficult, and that there were orders to get rid of him.

"Piotr Andreyevich, Father Arseny! I do not believe in God, but now I am beginning to believe. I just have to believe. I got a letter from my Katia, my wife, and in it there is word from a dear friend of mine, a very important person. He wants to help even though he knows that if somebody finds this note it will be the end of him. There are still honest, sincere people even outside the camps; not all of them are drowned in dirt. Katia says that she prays to God for me. She probably prays well, because here you are helping me. You keep my heart warm, you do not leave me alone with my thoughts. And not only me. You help so many people. Look what happened to Sazikov, such a cruel man and so fearsome and now he is gentler, he listens to you and trusts you in everything. You probably do not even see this, but I do. I do now believe; your God does it all through your hands. I do not know if I will ever become a true believer, but I know now, I see that God does exist!"

They carried the logs in; when Sazikov saw them he jumped down from his bunk and started helping. Later, Father Arseny told Sazikov about his conversation with the major and the fact that Moscow wanted to get rid of Avsenkov at the hands of the criminals.

Father Arseny called Sazikov not Ivan but Seraphim, which was his true name. He was not worried that Sazikov would report this conversation since he had changed a great deal.

"It's an unusual situation," said Sazikov. "Yes, we will help. We will protect Alexander Pavlovich. He is a good man, a worthy man. We will protect him, don't worry. We have ways among us, I will tell my people about it. We will protect him."

This story was told by Avsenkov, Abrosimov, Sazikov, and was partially taken from the scant notes left by Father Arseny.

Life Goes On

WINTER CAME TO an end and spring arrived. More and more prisoners were getting sick and dying. The camp hospital was so packed that sick men were forced to stay in their barracks. Father Arseny was very weak, but performed all his duties as before. The weather got warmer, but it was humid—the barracks had to be heated as often as during the winter so that the walls and the clothing would not become moldy.

Exhausted, almost unable to walk, Father Arseny still helped everyone he could. His help was always surprisingly warm and reached people deeply. He did not wait to be asked for help. He always seemed to know where his help was needed, and after giving it he would leave silently, never expecting to be thanked.

The Major did replace the supervisor Pupkov as promised. The new one was not talkative; he was stern, but fair. The prisoners started calling him "The Fair One." He was strict about his rules being observed—he especially required cleanliness—but he did not hit people and almost never swore.

The brief summer finished its tortuous sweep with clouds of mosquitoes spreading discomfort and disease throughout the camp. The barracks no longer had to be heated, but Father Arseny, in view of his age, was not sent out to dig. His work was cleaning the barracks and their surroundings and emptying the latrine pits.

Father Arseny was called into the special sector twice. The first time, he was interrogated by Markov and not sent to the Major. After the second interrogation he did see the Major, who looked concerned and nervous and said, "It is a hard period. The rules are even stricter; everybody watches everybody. I am an important figure, everyone is afraid of me, but I am unable to help. I don't have trustworthy people under me. I don't know when I will be able to see you again. I am afraid, but neither you nor Alexander Pavlovich ever leave my mind. Give him this note, and do tell him that he is remembered in Moscow. Now sign the records of our interview. I wrote it up before you came."

Father Arseny passed the note on to Avsenkov, and this again raised his spirits.

"Where Two or Three Are Gathered in My Name"

DURING ONE OF the winters, a young man was assigned to Father Arseny's barracks. Aged 23, he was a student and had been sentenced to twenty years in the camp. He had no experience of camp life because he had been sent to this special camp directly from the strict Butirki Prison in Moscow. Still young, he did not fully understand what lay ahead for him. As soon as he entered the death camp, he encountered the criminals.

His clothing was still good for he had only been in prison a few months. The criminals, led by Ivan the Brown, decided to get hold of the young man's apparel. They proposed a card game with clothing at stake. Everybody knew that this lad would soon be naked, but no one could do anything about it; even Sazikov dared not intervene. The camp rule was that whoever interfered would be killed. Those who had been in camp for a while knew only too well that if the criminals decided to play for your rags, to resist would be the end of you.

Ivan the Brown won all the young man's clothes. Ivan approached him and said, "Take everything off, my friend."

At that point things started to go sour. The young man, whose name was Alexei, thought that the game had been for fun and refused to hand over his clothing. Ivan the Brown decided to make an exhibition of it. He began with mocking kindness; then he started beating him. Alexei tried to resist, to fight back, but by now the whole barracks knew that he would be beaten until he could no longer move, or even to death. Everyone sat still and watched as Ivan bashed Alexei. He bled from the mouth and face and was swaying. Some criminals mockingly urged him to fight.

Father Arseny had not seen the beginnings of the fight; he had been piling up logs near a stove at the other end of the barracks. He suddenly saw what was happening. Ivan was going to kill Alexei. By now Alexei could only cover his face with his hands; Ivan was slamming him and smashing him repeatedly. Father Arseny silently put the logs down near the stove, calmly walked over to the fight and, before the amazed eyes of the whole barracks, grabbed the arm of Ivan the Brown. Ivan looked surprised, shocked! The priest had interfered in a fight. This meant he must die. Ivan hated Father Arseny. He had never dared touch him for fear of the rest of the barracks, but now he had a true reason to kill him.

Ivan stopped beating Alexei and pronounced, "O.K. Pop, it's the end for both of you. First the student, then you." A knife appeared in his hands and he lunged toward Alexei.

What happened? Nobody could understand, but suddenly the gentle and weak Father Arseny straightened himself up and slammed Ivan on the arm so hard that the knife fell from his hand. Then he pushed Ivan away from Alexei. Ivan stumbled, fell, and hit the corner of a bunk with his face. Father Arseny went to Alexei and said to him, "Go, Alyosha, wash your face, no one will hit you anymore." Then, as if nothing had happened, he went back to his work.

Everyone was taken aback. Ivan the Brown stood up. The criminals did not say a word. They understood that Ivan had lost face in front of the whole barracks. Somebody discreetly wiped the blood from the floor with his foot. Alyosha's face was completely smashed up, his ear was torn, one eye was closed, and the other one was dark red. Everyone was completely silent. They knew that it was all over now for both Father Arseny and Alexei. The criminals would kill them both.

But in fact things turned out differently; the criminals looked upon Father Arseny's actions as bold and brave. Even though everyone feared Ivan, Father Arseny had not faltered when Ivan the Brown had held a knife, and they respected a man who showed no fear. They already knew Father Arseny for his kindness and his unusual ways; now they respected him for his courage. Ivan retreated to his bunk and whispered with his friends, but he realized that they did not really support him—they had not come immediately to his aid.

The night passed. In the morning everyone went to work; Father Arseny was busy tending the stoves, cleaning up and scraping dirt off the floor. In the evening the prisoners returned from their labor and suddenly, just before the barracks was locked for the night, the supervisor ran in with several guards.

"Attention!" he shouted. All the men jumped down from their bunks. They stood motionless while the supervisor walked along the line of men. When he came to Father Arseny he began to beat him. Meanwhile Alexei was dragged from his place in line by the guards.

"P18376 and P281 to punishment cell No. 1, for 48 hours, without food or water, for breaking camp rules, for fighting," shouted the officer.

Ivan had reported them to the authorities. To do so was considered by the criminals to be the lowest and most despicable act possible.

✠

Punishment cell No. 1 was a tiny house that stood by the entrance of the camp. In this house were several rooms for solitary confinement; there was also one for two people which held a narrow board instead of a bed. This board was less than 20 inches wide. The floor and walls were covered with sheets of metal. The whole room was not wider than three quarters of a yard and two yards long. Outside it was -22° F and windy, so that it was hard to breathe. You had only to step outside to become immediately numb. The occupants of the barracks understood what this meant: certain death. Father Arseny and Alexei would be frozen within two hours. No one had ever been sent to that cell in such cold. Occasionally, someone was sent to it when the temperature reached -21° or -22° F, but this only for 24 hours. The only ones who stayed alive were those who could jump up and down the whole 24 hours to keep their blood from freezing. If you stopped jumping, you froze. And here it was -22° F, Father Arseny was an old man, Alexei had just been beaten up, and both men were exhausted.

The supervisors seized them both and started dragging them out of the barracks. Avsenkov and Sazikov dared to come out of the line and said to the officer, "Comrade Officer, they will freeze to death in this weather. You can't send them to that cell!" The supervisor slammed them both so hard that they flew dazed against the barracks wall.

Ivan the Brown lowered his head. Fear gripped him as he realized that his own people in the barracks would kill him for this.

Father Arseny and Alexei were dragged to the punishment cell and shoved inside. They both fell, cracking their heads against the wall. It was pitch black inside. Father Arseny stood up and said, "So, here we are. God has brought us together. It is cold, Alyosha, and there is metal all around."

They heard the outer door close, the locks click, the voices and the steps of the guards fade away. The cold seized them and constricted their chests. Through the small window with iron bars the moon shone its milky light into the cell.

"We are going to freeze, Father Arseny," moaned Alexei. "It is because of me that we are going to freeze. We are both going to die. We need to keep moving, to jump up and down, but it is impossible to keep that up for 48 hours. I already feel so weak, so battered. My feet are already frozen. There is no room here, we cannot even move. Father Arseny, we are going to die. They are inhuman, it would be better to be shot!" Father Arseny was silent. Alexei tried to jump, but it did not warm him up. It was hopeless to try to resist such cold.

"Why don't you say anything, Father Arseny?" Alexei shouted.

As if from somewhere very far away Father Arseny's voice answered, "I am praying to God, Alexei!"

"What's there to pray about when we are going to freeze?" Alexei muttered.

"We are here all alone, Alexei; for two days no one will come. We will pray. For the first time God has allowed us to pray aloud in this camp, with our full voice. We will pray and the rest is God's will!" The cold was gradually conquering Alexei and he was sure that Father Arseny was losing his mind. Making the sign of the cross and quietly pronouncing some words, Father Arseny stood in the ray of moonlight. Alexei's hands and feet were numbed by the cold; he had no strength in his limbs. He was freezing and no longer cared.

Father Arseny was silent now, and suddenly Alexei heard Father Arseny's words clearly, and understood that this was a prayer. Alexei had been in church only once, out of curiosity. Although his grandmother had baptized him when he was a child, his family did not believe in God. They simply had no interest in religious matters. They did not know what faith really was. Alexei himself was a student, a member of the Komsomol. How could he believe?

Through the numbness and the pain from the blows he had received, Alexei could clearly hear the words that Father Arseny was saying: "O Lord God, have mercy on us sinners! Ever-merciful God! Lord Jesus Christ who because of Thy love became man to save us all. Through Thine unspeakable mercy save us, have mercy on us and lead us away from this cruel death, because we do believe in Thee, Thou our God and our Creator." And so the words of prayer poured forth, and in each of these words lay the deepest love and trust in God's mercy, and unconditional faith in Him.

Alexei started listening to the words of the prayer. At first he was perplexed, but gradually he began to comprehend. The prayer calmed his soul, took away the fear of death, and united him with the old man standing beside him.

"O, Lord our God, Jesus Christ! Thou didst say with Thy purest lips that if two or three agree to ask for the same thing, then Thy Heavenly Father will grant their prayer because, as Thou didst say, 'When two or three are gathered in my name, I am among them.'" Alexei was repeating these words after Father Arseny.

The cold had taken over Alexei completely; his entire body was numb. He no longer knew whether he was standing, sitting, or lying down. But suddenly the cell, the cold, the numbness of his whole body, his pain from the blows he had received and his fear all disappeared. Father Arseny's voice filled the cell, but was it a cell? Alexei turned to Father Arseny and was stunned. Everything around had been transformed. An awful thought came: "I am losing my mind, this is the end, I am dying."

The cell had grown wider, the ray of moonlight had disappeared. There was a bright light and Father Arseny, dressed in brilliant white vestments, his hands lifted up, was praying aloud. The clothing on Father Arseny was the same as on the priest Alexei had once seen in church.

The words Father Arseny spoke were now easy to understand, they had become familiar—they entered directly into Alexei's soul. He felt no more anxiety, no more suffering, no more fear, only the desire to become one with these words, to understand them, to remember them for the rest of his life. There was no more cell: now they were in a church. How had they gotten here? And why was there someone else here with them? Alexei saw with surprise that there were two men assisting Father Arseny. Both were dressed in the same bright vestments and both shone with an undefinable white light. Alexei did not see their faces, but sensed that they were beautiful.

Prayer filled Alexei's being. He stood up and started praying together with Father Arseny. It was warm and easy to breathe, and happiness filled his soul. Alexei repeated everything Father Arseny was saying, yet he was not simply repeating, but praying together with him. It seemed that Father Arseny had become one with the words of his prayer, but Alexei understood that Father Arseny had not forgotten him and was helping him all the while, helping him to pray. The certainty that God existed, that He was with them, came to Alexei. He saw God with his soul. At times Alexei thought that perhaps they were both already dead, but the firm voice of Father Arseny and his presence kept bringing him back to reality.

How much time had passed he did not know, but Father Arseny turned to him and said, "Go, Alyosha! Lie down, you are tired. I will keep praying, you will hear me." Alexei lay down on the metal-covered floor, closed his eyes, and kept on praying. The words of prayer filled his whole being: "...will agree to ask anything, it will be given to them by my Heavenly Father..." In thousands of ways his heart responded to these words: "gathered in my name..." "Yes, yes! We are not alone," thought Alexei from time to time as he continued to pray.

All was peaceful and warm. Suddenly out of nowhere his mother appeared. She covered him with something warm. Her hands took his head, and she pressed him to her heart. He wanted to speak to her, "Mama, can you hear, can you hear how Father Arseny is praying? I've learned that God exists. I believe in Him."

As if she had heard him speak, she answered him, "Alyoshenka! When they took you, I also found God. This is what has given me the strength to live."

Everything that was awful had disappeared, his mother and Father Arseny were near him. Words of prayer which had been unknown to him now rekindled and warmed his soul. It was important not to forget these words, to remember them all his life. "I never want to be far from Father Arseny, I want always to be with him," thought Alexei.

Lying on the floor at Father Arseny's feet, Alexei listened, half-asleep to the beautiful words of the prayer. Father Arseny prayed, and the two others in bright garments prayed with him and served him. They seemed amazed at how Father Arseny could pray. Father Arseny no longer asked for anything, he only glorified God and thanked Him. How long all this lasted no one could say.

The only things that remained in Alexei's memory were the words of the prayer, a warming and joyful light, Father Arseny praying, the two others in clothes of light, and an enormous, incomparable feeling of inner renewing warmth.

Somebody struck the door, the frozen lock squealed, and voices could be heard from the outside of the cell. Alexei opened his eyes. Father Arseny was still praying. The two in garments of light blessed him and Alexei and slowly left. The blinding light was fading and the cell at last became dark and, as before, cold and gloomy.

"Get up, Alexei! They have come for us," said Father Arseny.

Alexei rose. The head of the camp, the doctor, the main head of the special sector, and the Major were coming in. Somebody behind the door was saying, "This is inexcusable—someone could report this to Moscow. Who knows how they will look at this. Frozen cadavers— this is not the modern way."

In the cell stood an old man in a patched up vest and a young one in torn clothes with a bruised face. Their faces were calm and their clothing was covered with a thick layer of frost.

"They're alive?" the Major asked in amazement. "How did they survive here for two days?"

"We are alive, sir," said Father Arseny. All looked at each other in amazement.

"Search them."

"Come out!" shouted one of the supervisors. Father Arseny and Alexei walked out of the cell. The supervisors removed their gloves and started frisking them. The doctor also removed a glove, put it under Father Arseny's and then Alexei's clothing and, to nobody in particular, said, "Amazing! How could they have survived? It's true, though; they're warm." The doctor walked into the cell, looked around it and asked, "What kept you warm?"

"Our faith in God, and prayer," Father Arseny answered.

"They are simply fanatics. Send them back to the barracks right away," said one of the supervisors in an irritated voice. As he was walking away, Alexei heard somebody say, "It's amazing. In this cold they should have lived no more than four or five hours. It's unbelievable, considering that it's -22° F out. You supervisors sure got lucky. There could have been some unpleasantness in store for you."

The barracks met them as if they had risen from the dead.

Everyone asked, "What saved you?"

They both answered, "God saved us."

Ivan the Brown was transferred to another barracks within days. A week later he was killed by a falling rock. He died in terrible pain. It was rumored that his own friends had helped the rock fall.

Alexei became a new man, as if reborn. He followed Father Arseny whenever he was able to and asked everyone he could about God and about Orthodox services.

⌒)

This story was told by Alexei and confirmed by several witnesses who lived in the barracks at that time.

"The Fair One"

THE PREVIOUS SUPERVISOR had been replaced. In his place a new one was sent who, because of his strict demands that camp rules be followed, and because of his fair approach to the prisoners, was nicknamed "The Fair One." The new supervisor was indifferent to Father Arseny; if he found something not quite to his liking, he would say mockingly, "Father, it is important to perform the services right." Then he would leave and come back in a hour to see if Father Arseny had done the work to his satisfaction.

In the course of the summer something most unusual happened to the Fair One. One day he went to check the barracks and the whole territory around them; meanwhile Father Arseny was sweeping the paths between the barracks. He saw that when the supervisor finished his tour of the barracks he stopped, took something out of his pocket, opened his wallet, looked at the something, put it back, and kept on walking.

While sweeping the paths, Father Arseny came to the place where the supervisor had stopped and saw on the ground a little red book. He picked it up and saw that it was the Fair One's Communist Party card. Father Arseny picked up the card, put it in his pocket and, after he had finished sweeping the paths went to sweep the barracks. While he was doing this, he looked every so often through the window to see if the Supervisor was coming. In about two hours, he saw the Fair One running in a panic. Father Arseny walked out of the barracks, and went to meet him.

Losing your Party Card, especially in the camp at that time, meant death, and the Fair One knew it perfectly well. He ran along the barracks paths, his face dark with terror. He looked right and left, but people had already been walking along there. Father Arseny came to him and said, "Comrade! Please allow me to talk to you." The face of the supervisor clouded with anger and he shouted, "Out of my way, you silly priest," and wanted to hit him. Father Arseny silently gave him the Party Card and turned back to the barracks.

The supervisor snatched the Card and shouted, "Stop!" and drawing near he asked, "Who saw you?"

"Nobody saw me, Comrade Supervisor. I found this on the path some two hours ago."

The Fair One turned around and walked away. Nothing seemed any different, but the Supervisor became more and more demanding of Father

Arseny. People thought that perhaps he had decided to rid himself of Father Arseny as a dangerous witness. In camps such things happened; a supervisor would kill a prisoner and then say: "He attacked me!" and he would even be praised by the administration.

There were many ways to get rid of a prisoner, all of them without punishment.

Time passed.

≈

This story was recounted by Andrei Ivanovich, a former supervisor in the barracks where Father Arseny had spent so many years. Certain incidents described and written by Father Arseny were also used.

"O Mother of God! Do Not Abandon Them!"

THIS STORY IS based on one Father Arseny himself retold to his closest spiritual children; I was one of them.

The reports I heard when I met Avsenkov, Sazikov, and Alexei (the student, who was by then already out of camp) helped me to describe what follows. These people were present when Father Arseny physically died in the barracks, and they witnessed how he came back to life.

When I finished writing all this, I felt I had to show the manuscript to Father Arseny. He read it, was silent for a long while and when he heard my question "Was it not really so?" he answered:

"I was granted great mercy by the Lord and by the Mother of God, who showed me the most sacred and magnificent treasure—that of the human soul, filled with faith, love and kindness. They showed me that faith will never die on earth. Many people carry it within them—some with ardor, others with a trembling respect, others again just carry a spark—and it is essential for them that a good priest help them as a pastor to turn this spark into an unquenchable flame of faith. The Lord showed me that the people who carry the faith, and especially the shepherds of human souls, must help fight for each person to the end of their own strength, until their last breath. The basis of the fight for a soul is love, kindness and helping your neighbor, help given not for one's own sake, but for the sake of one's brother. People judge faith, and judge even Jesus Christ Himself, based on the behavior of others. It is also written: 'By your words you will be saved, and by your words you will be condemned' (Matthew 12:37) and, 'Bear one another's burdens, and so fulfill the law of Christ' (Galatians 6:2).

"What happened to me was for me an enormous lesson and an admonition. It put me back in my place. Having lived in camps for so long, and having been saved so many times by the mercy of God, I began to believe that I was strong in faith. When I died the Lord and the Mother of God showed me that I am not worthy even to touch the clothes of many of those who are also in camps. I have much to learn from them.

"The Lord humbled me, put me in my place, the place where I should have been all along. He showed me my great unworthiness and granted me time to improve myself, to correct my mistakes and errors. But have I? O Lord, help me!"

Having said this Father Arseny took my manuscript and returned it to me in a few days. Rereading it, I saw that he had changed a few words and added others. The manuscript he gave back to me is what is before you now.

Returning the manuscript to me, Father Arseny said, "Please, while I am alive, do not show this to anybody. When I die—let people read it."

☩

The exhausting hot summer with its clouds of mosquitoes had been replaced by a rainy, humid, and cold autumn. The ground was sometimes frozen and sometimes streaming with rivers of melted mud. It was damp and cold in the barracks, which made life particularly difficult. The clothing of the prisoners never could dry out, their feet were constantly wet and covered with blisters. A flu epidemic began. Every day three to five people died. It was now Father Arseny's turn. He could not rise from his bunk. His temperature was 104°, he had chills, he was coughing, he was congested, his heart refused to function.

In the special camp, during such epidemics of flu, patients were not even put in the hospital. Only if your skull was cracked, or if your leg or arm was cut off or broken were you taken to the hospital. Flu had to be dealt with within the barracks. The rule of the camp was—if you can stand, you work; if you can't stand, then prove you are not faking an illness. If you prove it, they will take care of you, if the authorities approve.

In the camp there is a plan as to how much work must be done by each prisoner. If he is made to do more more work than expected, the authorities are remunerated. Of course the prisoner himself did not even know it, but his work brought money to somebody. The authorities exist to keep to their plan, so there is no time for softheartedness.

When a prisoner is sick or has a high fever, he has to ask permission to go to the infirmary. There they will take his temperature. If it is below 103°, he is sent back to work; should he argue, they will send him to the punishment cell, and on top of it the supervisor will hit him in the face to remind him of his responsibilities. If the fever is higher than 103°, he may stay in the barracks in bed, but he must appear every day in the infirmary. If he becomes unconscious in the barracks, the medic will come to check his temperature and throw some medicine onto his bunk. Then he can stay in bed; but take care he doesn't remain there after his temperature drops below 102°.

So this was the general rule: if you can walk, walk to work; don't use the camp doctors. They are usually hired by the government, and know their job. It doesn't take much for them to shout, "You're faking—off to work! If you don't I'll send you to the punishment cell!" It is true that many of the prisoners had been doctors before they were arrested, but those were never allowed to practice in camp. They had to do physical work like anybody else, and particularly hard work at that.

On the third day after Father Arseny became ill, one of the doctors among the prisoners looked him over and called a lung specialist to discuss the case. They called Avsenkov over and told him, "The patient has pneumonia, complete exhaustion, a serious vitamin deficiency, and his heart is worn out. It looks very bad. We do not think he can last more than two days. We would need medication, oxygen, care. But under these circumstances, there is nothing we can do."

Father Arseny was almost an old man. He had lived in this camp for a number of years and over that time many people in the barracks had died and been replaced by new ones. Only perhaps twelve people were such "veterans" as he was. Everybody looked at these old-timers with surprise—how and why were these patriarchs still alive?

A medic was called in. He looked at Father Arseny from a distance of two meters, tossed some aspirin onto his bunk, gave Avsenkov a thermometer to check his temperature, saw that it was over 104°, and saying, "He has the flu," he left.

Father Arseny grew steadily worse. His friends could see that it was the end, that his time had come. They sent a man to the hospital to try and get help; his friends from among the criminals tried to soften up the supervisors; they managed to obtain some mustard powder for a plaster, and some raspberry jam; they brought anything they could. A messenger managed to get into the hospital with great difficulty, and with the help of some true friends he begged for help, for medicine, and explained what was going on with Father Arseny.

The doctor listened and asked the messenger, "How old is the zek, and how long has he been in this camp?" The messenger answered that the patient was 49 years old and had been in the camp for three years now.

The doctor answered, "Do you think that a special camp is a sanatorium, and the zeks in it should live until they are 100 years old? Your patient has beaten the odds, and it is time for him to go. He has lived long enough. There is no medicine for him, it is needed for the army."

The fever rose higher and higher, Father Arseny lost consciousness more and more often. Avsenkov tried to give him aspirin with raspberry jam to drink. Sazikov put a rag with mustard powder on his chest and back. The doctors among the prisoners helped as much as only they could the minute they returned from their labor; but Father Arseny grew worse and worse; at times he was nearly motionless. He was dying.

Death is a common occurrence in camp, everyone is used to it. But in this case everyone felt it in a special way. (From one end of the barracks to the other you could hear, "Father Arseny is dying! Piotr Andreyevich is dying!" For each one of them he had done something good, something kind. A most unusual man was dying; this was something the politicals as well as the criminals understood)—[This last sentence, in parentheses, I added to his memoirs already after Father Arseny's death; it was contributed by Sazikov and by Alexei—the student.]

Father Arseny prayed on and on, and felt the support and help of his friends. Gradually he grew silent.

"He is going," said someone. Father Arseny felt also that he was dying; the barracks, Sazikov, Avsenkov, Alexei, the doctor Boris Petrovich – he could see them no longer, everything had disappeared, had faded away...

After some time Father Arseny felt an unusual lightness grip him and heard an absolute silence surrounding him. He grew calm. His difficulty in breathing, the mucus that had blocked his throat, the fever that had been burning his body, his weakness and helplessness all disappeared. He felt healthy and energetic.

Now Father Arseny stood by his own bunk, and on it he saw a thin, exhausted, unshaven, almost white haired man with pinched lips and half open eyes. Near the man he could see Avsenkov, Sazikov, Alexei and a few more of the prisoners whom he, Father Arseny, especially knew and loved. Father Arseny looked attentively at the man on the bunk and suddenly realized with amazement that the man on the bunk was himself.

His friends who were gathered near his bunk, the enormous barracks with its numerous population, the whole vast camp—Father Arseny was suddenly seeing it all with absolute clarity. He understood that just now he could see not only their physical appearance, but their souls.

Through the silence that was in him, he saw the movements of the prisoners, and although he could not hear them, he could somehow understand clearly what they were saying and thinking. With awe, he realized that he could see the state of each of their souls, but he knew that he was no longer with them in this world.

An invisible line separated him from this world, and he was unable to cross it.

Now Sazikov brought a cup to "his" lips, and tried to pour something into his mouth, but could not. The water spilled over his face. Avsenkov and Alexei were talking about something with a few of the others. Father Arseny stood at the foot of his own body looking at himself and at the other people as though he were an outsider. And suddenly he understood that his soul had left his body, and he, the Priest Arseny, was physically dead.

Father Arseny turned around in wonder; the barracks was disappearing into darkness, but somewhere in the distance there was a blinding light.

Recollecting himself, Father Arseny started to pray and immediately was at peace; he understood that there was somewhere he had to go. He started walking towards the blinding light, but having made a few steps, he turned back into the barracks, and went up to his bunk. Looking at Alexei, Alexander Pavlovich, Ivanov, Sazikov, Avsenkov and the many, many others with whom he had shared the thorny path of suffering, he understood that he could not leave these people. He could not leave them.

He kneeled, and began to pray, begging God not to leave Alexei, Avsenkov, Alexander, Theodore, Sazikov and all of the others with whom he had lived in this camp.

"O Lord, O my Lord! Do not leave them. Help them and save them!" he prayed. And especially he asked for the intercession of the Mother of God, begging her in her mercy not to abandon the prisoners of the special camp.

As he prayed, he cried, begging God, the Mother of God, and all the Saints to have mercy on them all. But his prayer was wordless. And now the barracks and the entire camp appeared before his spiritual eyes in a very different way. He saw the whole camp with all its prisoners and its prison guards as if from inside. Each person carried within himself a soul which was now distinctly visible to Father Arseny. The souls of some were afire with faith which kindled the people around them; the souls of others, like Sazikov and Avsenkov, burned with a smaller but ever growing flame; others had only small sparks of faith and only needed the arrival of a shepherd to fan these sparks into a real flame. There were also people whose souls were dark and sad, without even the least a spark of Light. Now, looking into the souls of the people which God had allowed him to see, Father Arseny was extremely moved. "O, Lord! I lived among these people and did not even notice them. How much beauty they carry within them. So many are true ascetics in the faith. Although they are surrounded by such spiritual darkness and unbearable human suffering, they not only save themselves, but give their life and their love to the people around them, helping others by word and by deed.

"Lord! Where was I? I was blinded by pride and mistook my own small deeds for something grand."

Father Arseny saw that the Light of faith burned not only in the prisoners, but also in some of the guards and administrators, who, within the limits of what they could do, performed good deeds. For them this was extremely difficult, because it was very dangerous.

"What is all this for?" flew through the mind of Father Arseny. "What is it all for?"

He stood and observed the spiritual world of the people, the same people with whom he had lived, talked, or had only just seen. How surprisingly varied and spiritually beautiful this world appeared before him. People who in the crowd of others had seemed to Father Arseny to be spiritually empty and depersonalized, he now saw anew. He saw that they carried so much faith, so much inexhaustible love for others, did so much good and bore their cross without complaint. And he, Father Arseny, living among them, he, the Priest and Hieromonk Arseny, had not seen them, had not noticed them, had not connected with them.

"O Lord! Where was I? Pardon me and have mercy on me. I only saw myself. I was deluded, I did not have enough faith in people."

Bowing down, Father Arseny prayed for a long time. When he stood up he saw that he still was in the camp, but he no longer had his new perception of it; the bunks and the barracks had disappeared. Father Arseny stood at the gate of the camp. The sharp beams of the search lights were sweeping the region and by the gate stood a sentry. It was night. The camp was asleep.

Father Arseny turned towards the camp, blessed it and prayed for all those still living in it.

"Lord! How can I leave them? How will I be without them? Do not leave all those who live here without your mercy. Help them!" And kneeling in the snow, he prayed.

It was cold, the wind threw clumps of snow but Father Arseny felt none of it. He prayed for a long time, then stood up and left the camp. He passed the sentries and walked along the road. Somewhere far away he saw a bright, inviting light and walked towards it. He walked easily and calmly. He passed the forest and the village and suddenly found himself in his own town, the one with his church, his very church, the church where he first served as a new priest, where he with the help of his many spiritual children had worked hard to restore its ancient beauty. "How can this be, my Lord? Why am I here?" he murmured, and entered into the church.

The first thing he saw was the familiar icon of the Mother of God, the ancient miracle-working one whose sorrowful face looked deeply and attentively at each who approached her. Everything in this church was as he had left it, but now it was full of people, even overflowing with people. The faces of the people praying were joyous and they looked at the icon of the Mother of God.

As Father Arseny walked towards the altar, the people squeezed right and left to leave a passage for him. He walked towards the altar with a light and happy step. Having entered the altar, he wanted to vest himself and began to remove his camp jacket for the service, but someone who was standing nearby said firmly to him, "Don't take it off! These clothes are also vestments for service."

Father Arseny looked at his padded cotton prison jacket. It was shining and blindingly white. He put on his priest's stole to begin serving and he was amazed. The altar was flooded with a bright light, the whole church gave out light, and the icons looked quite extraordinary on the walls; they seemed almost alive. There were many praying people; they were praying deeply and joyously.

Serving the liturgy, Father Arseny saw that together with him served the Hieromonk Herman, the priest Amvrosy, the Deacon Piotr and several more priests. And he, Father Arseny, knew all those who served with him now. At the side of the altar quietly stood Bishops Jonah, Anthony, Boris, his spiritual father and friend Bishop Theophil, and they all looked at him with joy.

"Lord," thought Father Arseny. "They all died a long time ago, and now they are here. It is so good to be here together!"

Father Arseny served and his soul was full of joy; prayer filled all his being and uplifted him.

Blessing the people praying with him he understood that he knows them all as well. They are his spiritual children, his parishioners, and others he had met in different places, in different camps: he had shared his life with these people. And all these people were praying for someone, they were asking for something. And looking more carefully at them, he realized that just like the priests serving with him and the bishops standing in the altar, all these people had died, some a long time ago and some more recently.

"O, Mother of God, how can this be?" thought Father Arseny. He did not wait for an answer, but he entered deeply into the service, into prayer. As he served the liturgy he felt that he was burning with joy and inner warmth. He received Communion, finished the liturgy, and knelt before the icon of the Mother of God of Vladimir asking her to forgive all his sins.

"O, Mother of God, the Heavenly Father has called me to judgment, because I have died. Do not leave me; be my intercessor before your Son. Do not leave me. I put my trust in You: I am an unworthy sinner." As he prayed for the forgiveness of his own sins, he also begged the Mother of God not to leave all those who were still alive. He prayed for his spiritual children, for the prisoners with whom he had lived and who were still in camps. He prayed for Alexei (the student), for Avsenkov, for Sazikov, for Abrosimov, for Alchevsky and for many, many others. He lost the concept of time and prayed so hard that he felt that all those praying in this church prayed with him; repeating again and again, "O, Birthgiver of God! Do not forget them, the long-suffering!" He cried, he sobbed and tears flowed all over his face.

Father Arseny's heart ached and was tight in his chest—how would they survive, all those who were there? Again he asked the Mother of God not to forget them, whose suffering is beyond what man can bear... And suddenly, he heard a voice, a clear extremely gentle, but firm clear voice, saying, "The time of your death has not yet come, Arseny. You must serve people some time longer. God is sending you back to help His people! Go and serve. I will not leave you."

Father Arseny lifted his head, looked at the icon and saw that the Mother of God seemed to have come down from the icon and stood in its place. He fell on his knees at her feet and could only repeat, "Mother of God, do not leave them. And have mercy on me a sinner!" And again he heard her voice: "Lift up your face, Arseny, look at me and tell me what you want to tell me, tell me your thoughts!"

Father Arseny lifted his face, looked at the Mother of God and, overcome by her kindness and her unearthly greatness, bowed low, and said:

"Mother of God, your will be done, yours and the Lord's, but I am old and ill. Will I be able to serve these people as you, the sovereign one, want me to?"

"You are not alone, Arseny, there are many people serving me. You will serve alongside them. And, together with them you will help many. God has just shown you that He has many people helping Him. He has shown you the souls of the people who live in the camps. Faith does live in many of them, faith and love. You are not alone in the kindness you bestow. Go, serve me. I will help you!" And Father Arseny felt the hand of the Mother of God touch his head.

Father Arseny arose, took off his priest's stole, bowed to all those gathered, the priests and the people, and saw once again that he knew them all, and that he had accompanied most them to their eternal rest; his life was in some way tied to each of them. He approached the Royal Doors, knelt, arose, and asked the congregation gathered there not to forget him in their prayers, and walked to the door of the church. As he was walking by them, the people blessed him. He came out of the church with his soul overflowing with joy. It was easy to walk. He was walking towards the camp, towards his barracks. The forest, the road, the houses, all raced by him. He passed the sentries, entered his barracks, walked to his bunk, saw his body on it, with the people gathered around it. He lay down on his bunk and heard someone say, "It's all over! He is getting cold. Our Father Arseny has died. It's almost five o'clock, and will soon be time for reveille; we will have to inform the supervisors."

Someone added, "We all have been orphaned: he helped so many of us. I fought against God my whole life, but he showed Him to me. He revealed Him by his own actions."

Father Arseny sighed deeply—it surprised them all and it frightened many—he calmly said, "I was in my church, and now you see the Mother of God has sent me back to you!" And nobody felt that these words were strange, although they were still amazed at his return. Some two weeks later Father Arseny was able to get up. Everything seemed strange to him: life in general and people, all looked different. Each person wanted to help, each brought him a little bit of his own ration. Even the Fair One brought some butter and gave it to Sazikov for Father Arseny.

Father Arseny got up, came to life. The terrible illness left him. The Lord and the Mother of God had sent him to serve people, had sent him back into the world.

Mihail

ALL THE PRISONERS were accounted for, and had been pushed back into the barracks; the doors were locked. Before sleeping you could talk a little, share impressions of life in the camp, play dominoes or simply lie on your bunk and remember your past. Even two hours after the doors were locked, you could still hear some chatting; then the voices would get quieter, and silence would overtake the barracks.

After the barracks had been locked Father Arseny stood for a long time near his bunk to pray, then he lay down and continued to pray, and finally he fell asleep. His sleep was never very deep. Around one o'clock he felt someone pushing at him. He jumped up and saw an unknown man whispering to him:

"Come! My neighbor is dying! He is calling for you!"

The dying man, on the other side of the barracks, was lying on his back and breathed raggedly, with difficulty. His eyes were unnaturally wide open. "Please forgive me! But I need you. I am dying," he said to Father Arseny and suddenly said—almost ordered: "Sit down!"

Father Arseny sat on the side of the bunk. The light that was coming from the passageway between the bunks weakly lit the dying man's face, which was covered with beads of sweat. His hair was wet, his lips were closed tightly. He was worn out, he was dying, but his eyes looked at Father Arseny like two burning torches. In these eyes lived, burned, and rushed the whole life this man had lived. He was leaving this life, he had suffered, he was tired, but he wanted to bring an account of his life to God.

"Please, hear my confession. Forgive me my sins. I am a monk, a secret monk." Those whose bunks were near Mihail's got up and found another place to sleep. They could all see that death was upon him, and even in barracks one had to be merciful and indulgent towards a dying man. Father Arseny bent over the monk, straightened the torn blanket which covered him, put his hand on his head, whispered the prayers before confession and, gathering his own spirit, prepared to hear his confession.

"My heart is giving out," said the man. Saying that his name as a monk was Mihail, he began his confession.

Bent over, his face near the face of the dying man, Father Arseny listened to his barely audible whisper and looked into the eyes of Mihail. Sometimes the whispering would stop and you could hear wheezing when Mihail had difficulty breathing; he was gasping for air. At times he would become silent, and one might think he had died, but his eyes remained alive, and Father Arseny, looking into them, could read all that the sick man was trying to say in his difficult whisper.

Father Arseny had heard the confession of many people on their death beds, and always these confessions shook him deeply; but now, listening to the confession of Mihail, Father Arseny clearly understood that he had before him a man with an unusually great spiritual life. A man of prayer, a righteous man was dying, a man who had given his life to God and to his fellow men. A righteous man was dying, and Father Arseny understood that the Priest Arseny was unworthy to kiss the hem of the garment of the Monk Mihail, and that he was nothing in comparison.

The whispers came in shorter and shorter bits, but the eyes were burning, radiating light, they were alive. And again Father Arseny was able to read in these eyes everything the dying man wanted to say.

In his confession Mihail was severe with himself, he accused himself without pity. At times there was the feeling that Mihail had already separated himself from the man who was on the bunk and was talking about him from the outside. Father Arseny saw that Mihail's worldly life, like a ship loaded with his pains, worries, and griefs past and present, had already sailed away from him to the distant world of forgetfulness and now only the essentials remained, for him to bring before God for scrutiny. Having discarded everything which was not essential, all that was essential had to be entrusted to the hands of the Priest Arseny, and he, through the authority vested in him by God, was to forgive and absolve it all.

In the few minutes that he had left to live, the Monk Mihail had to bring everything to God, acknowledge all his sins, and clear his conscience before appearing before the judgment of God.

A man was dying the same that way so many had died before him in the hands of Father Arseny. But this death made Father Arseny tremble, and he understood that God had done him a great kindness in allowing him to hear the confession of this righteous man.

The Lord was showing him His greatest treasure, which He had lovingly cultivated. He was showing him to what height of perfection a man can rise, a man who loved God, who took up the "yoke and burden" of being a Christian and carried it to the end. All of this Father Arseny saw and understood.

The confession of the dying Mihail brought Father Arseny to see how even under the unbelievably complicated circumstances of modern life, with its political upheavals, its complex human relations, the officially supported atheism, the trampling of the faith, the fall of moral values, the constant suspicions and false reports, and the lack of any spiritual guidance, a man of deep faith could overcome everything which came between him and God.

The Monk Mihail had not traveled towards God from inside a monastery or a skete, but out in the harsh conditions of life, during the harshest of times, in a bitter battle against the forces of evil, against aggressive atheism. He had had almost no support or guidance; he had met two or three priests and had had the joy of a year in contact with Bishop Theodore, who had tonsured him; later Mihail had received two or three brief letters from him. But mainly he had been moved by his indestructible, burning desire to move nearer and nearer to God.

"Did I walk the right path, did I walk as I should have? Or did I take a wrong path? I do not know," said Mihail.

But Father Arseny saw that Mihail had not only not strayed from the path shown him by Bishop Theodore, but that he had walked this path far, very far, further than his spiritual guides ever had themselves. The life Mihail had led was like a battle for spiritual and moral perfection, and this amidst the everyday life of this century. Father Arseny understood that Mihail had won this battle, a battle engaged one on one with the evil all around him. Out among people he was doing good in the name of God and carried in his soul the words of the apostle like a burning flame: "Bear one another's burdens, and so fulfill the law of Christ" (Galatians 6:2).

Father Arseny understood the perfection and greatness of Mihail and acknowledged his own nothingness. He prayed fervently, almost aggressively, that God grant him, Father Arseny, the strength to ease the final minutes of the dying man. At times, Father Arseny felt utterly helpless but at the same time he felt great joy in feeling so close to Mihail, whose confession was opening for him the mysterious ways of God, teaching him about and setting him on the path to deepest faith.

And then the time came when Mihail had given all he had in his soul to Father Arseny and through him to God. He looked at Father Arseny with a question in his eyes. Taking the burden of Mihail's sins and holding it in his hands, Father Arseny took it all upon his own priestly soul, and trembled. He trembled again as he realized his human nothingness and helplessness.

Having said the prayer of absolution over Mihail, he at first sobbed internally and then wept uncontrollably in full view of the dying man.

Mihail raised his eyes and, looking deeply at Father Arseny, he said, "I thank you! Be calm again! The hour of God's will has come. Pray for me while you are on this earth. Your life's journey is still long. I beg you to take my hat; a note addressed to two people is sewn into it. They are people of great faith. Very great faith. Their addresses are there. When you are out of this camp, when you are free—give the note to them. They need you, and you need them. Sew your own zek number into my hat. Pray to God for the Monk Mihail."

During the whole confession they had been alone in the barracks. The barracks itself, the people living in it, the whole atmosphere had been somewhere far away, had disappeared into some kind of non-being. A state of closeness to God, prayerful contemplation and silent inner unity seized them both and placed them before God. All that was painful, stormy, or human had gone away. There was only the Lord God, to whom the one was now going, while the other was being permitted to contemplate something so great and mysterious—death, the departure from this life.

The dying man squeezed the hand of Father Arseny, and prayed, prayed so deeply that he had left everything of this world; and Father Arseny, his soul so near to Mihail's in prayerful union, released all that was around him, and with reverence, humbly followed in the prayer of the Monk Mihail.

But now came the time of death. The eyes of the dying man lit up with a silent light of joy and he whispered, "Do not forsake me, O my Lord!" Mihail sat up, stretched out his hands, almost made a step forward and said loudly, twice, "Lord! Lord!"

Then, he fell backward. The hand that had been holding Father Arseny's opened; Mihail's features grew peaceful, but his eyes were bright and gazed upwards with joy; it seemed to Father Arseny that he saw with his own eyes how the soul of Mihail was leaving his body.

Shaken, Father Arseny fell to his knees and began to pray, but not for the soul and salvation of the departed. He was thanking God, who in His mercy had made him worthy to see the Unseen, the Unknowable, and the most mysterious of mysteries—the death of a righteous man.

Father Arseny arose from his knees and bent over the body of Mihail, whose eyes were still open and bright, but whose light was slowly fading. A barely perceptible mist covered them as the eyelids slowly closed: a shadow ran over his face, and because of this it became majestic, joyous and peaceful.

Bent over Mihail's body, Father Arseny prayed, and although he had just witnessed Mihail's death, he did not feel grief—only peacefulness and an inner joy. He had seen a righteous man, and had touched God's mercy and His glory.

Father Arseny lovingly arranged Mihail's clothing and bowed to his body; the thought came to him again and again like a lightning bolt that God, the Lord himself, had been here and had received Mihail's soul.

Day was breaking; soon everybody would be awake, Father Arseny took Mihail's fur hat, exchanged his own number for Mihail's and went to the man responsible among the prisoners to report the death of Mihail. The man, the oldest among the criminals, asked for the zek number of the deceased and expressed sympathy. The barracks were opened, and the prisoners filed out for the morning roll call. In front of the barracks stood the supervisors; the one responsible approached them, saying, "We have a corpse, No. 382."

One of the supervisors went into the barracks, looked at the dead man, kicked him with his boot and left. Two hours later a sleigh came to pick up the corpse. A medic entered, glanced carelessly at the body of Mihail, lifted an eyelid with his gloved hand and said in disgust, "Get him out fast."

There were already several corpses in the sleigh, so they took Mihail and put him on top of the other dead prisoners. The driver settled himself comfortably by resting his feet on the frozen bodies. It was freezing and quiet; a light snow fell onto the faces of the dead men, it melted slowly, so that they seemed to be crying. Next to the barracks stood the supervisors, the medic and Father Arseny, who was praying silently, with his hands on his chest.

The sleigh moved off, Father Arseny bowed and blessed the dead with the sign of the cross. He went back inside the barracks.

The driver, swearing filthily, pulled on the reins, shouted at the horses and the sleigh moved slowly to disappear behind the barracks.

This was written from the words of Father Arseny in 1960. In 1966 the scattered notes were organized by the Hieromonk Andrew.

"Whose Side Are You On, Priest?"

WHEN YOU FIRST get to the camp you count the days, then the weeks; after the second year, there comes a time when the only thing left for you to do is await death. Exhausting labor, chronic hunger, fights, beatings, the cold, and being away from home all dull you and make you think only of your unavoidable death. This is why most of prisoners were deteriorating morally.

For most of us political prisoners, and for all the criminals, our mood swayed depending on circumstances, be it a visit of the supervisor, stolen bread, a fight, especially heavy work assigned to the brigade, the punishment cell, a frozen finger or the death of a neighbor in your barracks. Your thoughts became primitive and focused only on such occurrences. The great majority of prisoners only dreamed of eating an enormous meal, sleeping for two days, or finding a half-liter of vodka, drinking it all and then gobbling down another meal. But, of course, all of these were pipe dreams.

A very small number of political prisoners tried to stay human, kept themselves apart, supported each other, and did not want to lower themselves to the level of the criminals. They tried to live in a dignified way as much as camp life allowed it. These people gathered in a corner of the barracks, presented lectures, read poetry or memoirs, and even sometimes wrote things on scraps of paper they had found somewhere. Heated arguments would often arise on some topic, but the hottest were the arguments about politics. Even criminals sometimes joined in these discussions; politicals who had, it seemed, lost interest in everything occasionally showed some interest. People argued passionately, with hatred for their opponents. Father Arseny never participated in these arguments. But once he was pulled in against his will.

Usually the prisoners were afraid to express their thoughts, but in the heat of the argument, they forgot all fears and forgot about the possible consequences. Some of them even said, "So what, I'll croak soon anyway, but at least I will have spoken what I think."

The prisoners had been counted, the barracks were locked up, and behind their walls the wind was blowing right and left; the snow blocked the windows, it was stuffy and damp, but warm inside. The light bulbs gave off only half the light needed. All this contributed to the gloom and melancholy. And people were tired of being alone.

54

The prisoners met in groups and started talking, arguing, remembering. The criminals played cards or dominoes for money or for rations. Near the bunk on which Father Arseny rested, a group of people had gathered, and there was soon a passionate argument on the subject of the zeks' attitude toward the government. Within some fifteen minutes about twenty people had already joined in, and the argument had heated up. People interrupted each other and became menacing. Among the participants were ex-party members, educated people from different walks of life, a few Vlassovtsy[4] and some others. There were yells: "What are we here for? For nothing! Where is justice? They should all be shot!" Their faces were bitter and irritated. Only four or five of the ex-party members disagreed and were trying to explain that what was happening was an enormous and tragic mistake which would be corrected sometime. According to them, it was possible that all this was the result of some enemy infiltration which Stalin himself knew nothing about, and that he was being fooled.

"Fooled, while one half of Russia is in camps. It's planned destruction of personnel!" shouted a voice.

"Stalin does know—it's his own order," agreed another.

One of the prisoners, who had been arrested for disorderly conduct and for having plotted to kill Stalin, was especially angry. His face was distorted, and his voice trembled. A few Vlassovtsy were shouting, accusing everything and everybody.

"Those party members should all be hung, shot!"

An old man, a hard-core Bolshevik since the year 1917, was arguing fiercely and slugging it out with a man who had served in the German army.

"You are a traitor," he shouted. "You should be shot, and here you are, still alive! I myself shot and hanged people like you, lots of them. I am only sorry I did not come across you then. I am here for my mistakes, but to think that you, a traitor, are here to die with me."

"Me, a traitor? Me, a traitor? I supported the Soviet Government!"

"You can say 'me? me?,' but here you are, in camp as a traitor. This is where your 'government' brought us to."

4 The Vlassovtsy (singular: Vlassovets) were Russians who, under General Vlassov, joined the German Army to fight Communism from the outside. They were later sent back to Russia by the Allies; most were hanged, and others were sent to camps.

People on the outskirts were laughing, but the argument continued fiercely. Someone suddenly said, "They destroyed churches, they trampled the faith." At this point someone noticed Father Arseny sitting nearby. "Well, Piotr Andreyevich, tell us how the Church looks on the authorities?"

Father Arseny remained silent, but they pulled him physically into the circle of those arguing. Father Arseny's friends were worried. It was clear what Father Arseny would answer. He had suffered so much in the camps.

The Vlassovtsy who were led by Jitlovsky kept themselves apart from everyone else. They were afraid of nothing; they knew they had been arrested for a reason, they knew their end was near. One of them said, "So spill it, *Priest*. Spill it!"

Father Arseny stopped for a moment, and then said, "You are having a heated argument. It has turned sour, even fierce. It is truly difficult to live in the camp and we all know how it will end for us. That is why the argument has become so bitter. It is understandable. Only, no one should be destroyed or killed. All of you are blaming the authorities, the orders, the people; you have pulled me in to draw me into one side and irritate the other.

"You say that the Communists have arrested the believers, closed churches, trampled on faith. Yes, it does look that way, on the surface, but let us look into this more deeply, let us glance at the past. Among us Russian people many have lost the faith, lost respect for our past, we lost much of what was precious and good. Who is at fault? The authorities? No, we are at fault ourselves, we are only reaping what we ourselves have sown.

"Let us remember the bad examples set by the intelligentsia, the nobility, the merchants, and the civil servants. We in the priesthood were the worst of them all.

"Children of priests became atheists, and revolutionaries, simply because they had seen in their families lies and a lack of true faith. Long before the revolution priests had already lost the real right to be the shepherds of their people, of their conscience. Priesthood became a profession. Many priests were atheists and alcoholics.

"From among all the monasteries of our land, only five or six were real beacons of Christianity. Valaam Monastery, Optina Pustin with its great startsy,[6] Diveyevsky Convent, and also the Monastery of Sarov. Others became communities with almost no faith in them.

6 "Strartsy" is plural for "staretz," an elder to whom people come for guidance and advice. The Optina monastery is famous for its tradition of startsy.

"What could the people learn from such monasteries? What kind of an example was set?

"We did not raise our people right, we did not give them the basis of strong faith. Remember all this! Remember! This is why the people were so quick to forget all of us, their own priests; they mainly forgot their faith and participated in the destruction of churches, sometimes even leading the way in their destruction.

"Understanding all of this, I cannot point a finger at our authorities, because the seeds of faithlessness fell on the soil which we ourselves had prepared. And from there comes the rest: our camp, our sufferings, the wrongful deaths of innocent people. But I will tell you in all sincerity: whatever happens in my country, I am its citizen. As a priest I always told my spiritual children that it is our responsibility to defend and support our fatherland. What is happening now must end: it is a huge mistake that will sooner or later be corrected."

"So, our Pops is a commie," said someone. "You should be squashed for a sermon like that. You pretend to be saintly, but actually you are a double- crosser, you are spreading propaganda. You must be working for the authorities." And he rudely pushed Father Arseny out of the circle of arguers.

The argument continued as heatedly as ever, but several people began to leave the group.

After this event some of the prisoners began to persecute Father Arseny. Several times he was beaten up at night; someone poured urine all over his bunk, others stole his food ration. Those of us who were his friends tried to protect Father Arseny from that other group, as we knew they were lost people and thus capable of anything.

One evening one of the men, Jora Grigorenko from Kiev, came to take Father Arseny to Jitlovsky—the leader of the Vlassovtsy. Jitlovsky was reclining on his bunk and was chatting with his buddies.

"Well, Pops, are you going to be on our side or with the Communists? You're working for the camp authorities. You hear confessions and then you report them. We're going to do you in soon, but meanwhile right now we are going to beat you up to make an example of you. Let's go, Jora. But, first, let's listen to what 'Pop' over here has to say."

Jora Grigorenko was hated by everyone. He was stocky and broad-shouldered, with no neck under his head, and his face was marked by a large scar which deformed it and and made him seem constantly to be smiling. All this made him repulsive. Rumor had it that he had worked as an executioner in the German army, although he was in the camp only for having been a member of the Vlassov army.

Father Arseny calmly looked at Jitlovsky and said, "Only God can decide on the life of people. Not you. I am not going to join your group." And sitting down on the bunk opposite Jitlovsky's, he continued, "Do not try to frighten me. I am familiar with yelling, beatings, threats of death. It is God in whom I believe unconditionally, who has assigned to each of us our portion of suffering and our time on this earth. If my life is cut off here, that will mean it was the will of God. Neither you nor I can change this. And all of us will finally have to stand before God's judgment where we will be held responsible for all our deeds.

"I believe in God, and I believe in people, and I will believe until my last breath. And you? Where is your God? Where is your faith? You talk a lot about protecting those who are persecuted, but so far you have only persecuted, killed and humiliated. Look at your hands, they are covered with blood!"

Jitlovsky raised his hands and stared strangely at them; then he looked at Father Arseny. He dropped his hands onto his lap and screeched, "Don't try to talk me into anything!" and again glared at Father Arseny.

From the top bunk Grigorenko called out, "Arkady Semionovich! Pops seems to be on a talking spree. Why don't we finish him off right now?"

"Shut up, Grigorenko!" answered Jitlovsky. "Let him say everything he has to say before we do him in. It is their profession to talk, just like the Communist propagandists."

Father Arseny continued. "Somebody once said to me that you were a believer. But what do you believe in? You have tortured and killed people in the name of what? I remember you talking about Dostoevsky – you said he was your favorite author and the soul of the Russian people. I am going to quote the words of the starets Zosima from *The Brothers Karamazov*. This is what he said on his deathbed to those surrounding him. 'Do not hate atheists, teachers of evil, materialists, even the evil ones, for some of them are truly kind, especially in our day. Love the people of God. Believe, and hold high the standard of faith. Do good to all people and help them bear their suffering.' Meanwhile, *your* life is spent in hatred and anger. Each man has the time to rethink his life and to correct it, and you do too."

Having said this, Father Arseny stood up and started walking towards his bunk. But Grigorenko jumped down from his bunk, caught up with Father

Arseny and started choking him. At this moment, pushing his way through those who were gathered, a tall and strong prisoner appeared, whose nickname in the barracks was "Sailor." In fact, he was a sailor from Odessa who had been sentenced to fifteen years in our camp for "politics." He was a reckless man, always cheerful, and a good friend, and somehow he never lost his healthy appearance in spite of the fact that he lived like all of us.

Pushing the others away, Sailor grabbed Grigorenko, lifted him like a sack and threw him into the crowd of Jitlovsky's friends.

"Hey you! You forgot that here you are not among Germans. You are in our own camp." And turning to Jitlovsky he grabbed him by the arm and said in an Odessa dialect, "My dear, you'd better calm your friends down. If you don't we'll cut all your throats. All of you!"

Jitlovsky's group seemed shaken; a large group of prisoners had appeared, ready to support Father Arseny and Sailor.

Sailor walked up to Grigorenko and said, "Don't you dare touch Piotr Andreyevich. If anything happens to him, I will personally kill you, and before that, I'll beat you to a pulp." He then called to Father Arseny, "Let's go, Piotr Andreyevich! We are just irritating them now. My respects to you all. Hope to see you again some better time."

In about three weeks Jora Grigorenko was transferred to another barracks. After this day Jitlovsky was quiet, and became gentler towards people. There were still arguments, but Father Arseny was never pulled into them. But what he had said about one's responsibility in what had happened in Russia lived on in the barracks for a long while.

Sazikov

TIME PASSED, AND Sazikov became more and more attached to Father Arseny; he took care of him, and told him much about himself. He talked to him about his childhood years. He had been born of an educated family in Rostov, graduated from the Rostov Industrial Institute and became an engineer. Then by chance he had joined a group of "friends," after which his whole life went tumbling in decline, and for almost twelve years Sazikov had walked the path of a criminal. As he walked this path, he sometimes would look back and start wondering, but he was never able to get back on the right path.

He told one version of his life story to the camp administration and his friends, but to Father Arseny he revealed his true life, hiding nothing from him. He had been baptized Seraphim in honor of Saint Seraphim of Sarov. His mother was a believer and taking him with her to church until he was fourteen, she educated him in her religion. She died when he was 22. His father had abandoned the family a long time ago. Seraphim found himself, as it were, caught in a whirlwind; as always it started with petty crimes, and then armed robberies, drunken parties, beatings and murder. There is no stopping. Once you start on this path there is no stopping. If you step aside, your "friends" will make sure you return to them.

He forgot what his mother had taught him; real life was an entirely different realm. He never thought about God. Where can you find Him in a criminal world? And besides, there were too many other things to worry about.

Occasionally he had had dealings with Graybeard. He was a strange man, so cruel, but sometimes he would suddenly show his true soul, such a complicated nature.

Sazikov had worked on big jobs where they stole big money. He would get himself employed in big companies, large stores or any such place where big money was handled at pay time or at times when the company received a big shipment of cash. As he worked he would study the way the place functioned. Women would help him because he was tall, handsome, well-spoken and well-dressed. His work was so impeccable that his superiors complimented him; his working papers were always in perfect order. He knew a lot; he had been educated as an engineer. He also had some knowledge of economics, which was why he was invaluable to department stores where he was considered a specialist. And this is how he did it: he studied the place, found out how things worked there and then stole large sums of money.

Most of the times things ended well for him, but he did do long stretches of time in prisons and camps. He tended to be caught for minor robberies; they never knew about the big heists. But then, under the pressure of an interrogation, a friend told the authorities about Sazikov participating in a very big job. He was sentenced to be shot, but instead they sent him off to die in this special camp.

"I met you, Father Arseny, and you amazed me," said Sazikov one day. "Everything you do is for other people. At first I thought you must have something to gain from it, or maybe you were feeble-minded. But then I watched you, and you started to remind me of my mother. Many of the things she told me when I was little came back to me. You amazed me when you called me Seraphim. I thought maybe I had told you my name when I was ill, but then I saw that this kind of thing happened to you with others as well.

"I kept a careful watch on you until I understood clearly: you do not live for yourself, but for others—in the name of your God. I started looking back at my own life and began to see that I have always lived only for the moment with never a thought about the future. And now I think: where did that get me? I have no real friends, only pals. Nobody needs me, and if they do something for me, it's only out of fear.

"You've touched my heart. You've won me over with the example you set. I've decided to be done with my past. But it's very hard to do—when you turn away from them your own friends will finish you off. By the way, Graybeard is also watching you. In camps the criminals are lost souls, especially in the special camps. They are afraid of nothing since they know they are going to die anyway. In our own barracks we have established some kind of order, but that's not easy to do with the kind of people we are dealing with. I know that I will end my life here, but I want to take your path, I want to believe."

The Confession

ONE DAY SAZIKOV came in, remained standing, seemed at a loss for words, spoke about this and that, and suddenly said, "Father Arseny! If you allow me, I would like you to hear my confession. I can see that my end is near, I will never leave this camp, and I carry a heavy load of sins, a very heavy load."

It is difficult to have an hour or two to yourself in camp. They watch you all the time, which is one reason that this camp is called "special." But Sazikov still managed to come to Father Arseny for confession. They were alone, the two of them. There were about two hours left until the next roll call. If they were found alone together both would be sent to the punishment cell for at least five days. This they both knew.

Seraphim knelt; he was moved, he was lost. Father Arseny put his hand on the man's head and started to pray. He was entirely absorbed in prayer. A few minutes went by. Seraphim started to speak, at first inconsistently in fits and starts. He was very tense. Father Arseny stayed silent. He did not direct Sazikov, did not help him, but listened and prayed, knowing that a man must find himself without help. He had heard the confession of many people during his stay in this camp, but hearing the confession of an experienced and "hopeless" criminal was certainly a rare event.

Most of the criminals who had come with their confessions were people who had lost everything, whose soul was desolate, empty. Conscience, love, truth, faith in anything had already been long gone. They were smashed, stained with blood, cruelty and debauchery. Their past gave them no joy, but it scared them. They were unable to tear themselves away from the company of those like themselves and therefore they lived to their final days in cruelty and anger with no hope for anything in this camp. Before them lay only death or a successful escape.

Their confessions, when they occurred, were always alike. While their childhoods were different one from the other, all the rest was similar: robbery, murder, revelry, debauchery, and above all, the fear of being caught. Depending on the person, the depth of his fall did differ. Some understood what they were doing but could not stop, and sank deeper and deeper; others were proud of what they had done and continued living in violence and blood, considering their lives right and heroic; they delighted in making others suffer. Other criminals, as they aged, started to think about their lives, but could not decide what to do. Seraphim had seen the depth of his fall and had tried to stop it, but could not find a way out of the world of criminals.

Father Arseny knew this.

Sazikov spoke, but his confession did not flow. On his way to his confession he had thought about what he would say and how he would say it, but now he forgot all of that; he was confused. He wanted to be absolutely sincere, but he could not speak from the soul. His confession lost contact with his soul and became a story. Father Arseny saw this and understood it, but he wanted Seraphim to win the battle himself, through his own effort. He had to win the battle over his past, and by doing so to open a path to the present.

Nervous, agitated, and sobbing openly, Seraphim spoke, but his confession still did not flow from his soul. There was such a battle between his past and the present that Father Arseny felt that Seraphim needed help, he needed that proverbial straw which, in spite of being thin and fragile, can save the drowning man who grasps at it. And Father Arseny held this "straw" out to him by saying, "Remember how this woman was begging you to take pity on her, and you did not; and remember how later you were ashamed of yourself."

And in a flash Seraphim understood that Father Arseny saw and knew everything about him. He did not have to choose words to show himself. He simply had to be unafraid to open his soul and Father Arseny would see, understand, and weigh everything. He would then say if it was possible to forgive Seraphim.

Seraphim finished his confession, having surrendered his whole soul and his very self into the hands of Father Arseny. He was still kneeling and his face was wet with tears. For the first time in his life he had opened himself up fully, he had shown his whole life, and was awaiting the verdict, the punishment, the blame.

Bending over Seraphim, Father Arseny prayed and could not find the simple words he needed to cleanse and give light and direction to this man in his newly-realized life.

The confession had been so sincere and the awareness of his sinfulness so full, yet he had committed so many horrors, his crimes had made so many people suffer and had caused so much misery; all of this was mixed together and Father Arseny had to measure, weigh, separate things one from another, evaluating the weight of it all.

The priest Arseny who could forgive and absolve this sinner in the name of God, was now at war with the man Arseny who was unable as a human being to accept, acknowledge and forgive all that Seraphim had done. "O Lord, my God! Give me strength to know Thy will. Help me show the way to Seraphim, help him to find himself. O Mother of God! Help both of us sinners. Help us, O Lord."

As he prayed he understood that he should say nothing, he should weigh and decide nothing. The confession of Seraphim, a man who had lost his ties with God, had been so deep and sincere, had bared his soul and had shown that this man was not only moving towards God, but had found Him and from now on would walk towards Him. For all his evil deeds, Seraphim would answer directly both to God at the last judgment and to himself, in his own conscience.

Father Arseny stood up and, pressing Seraphim's head to his own chest, said, "I, the unworthy Priest Arseny, by the power bestowed unto me, do forgive and absolve you from all your sins, Seraphim. Do good to people and God will forgive many of your sins. Go and live in peace, and God will show you the way."

Having finished hearing the confession and having embraced Seraphim, Father Arseny, as if foreseeing the future, pronounced, "I will not leave you as long as you live, Seraphim. God will help us."

After this, invisible ties united Father Arseny and Seraphim Sazikov forever.

"I Will Not Leave You"

DURING ONE OF their conversations Sazikov said, "Father Arseny, I can see that you pray from memory since you do not have any church books. We have learned that we can get you some books. Graybeard talked to his pals and they said that this was possible."

"In God's name, I ask you not to take books away from anybody. The sin will be on my soul."

"Of course not, Father Arseny, what do you think? All will be done without hurting anyone. There is a place where the administration keeps everything that has been confiscated from the prisoners, the new ones, as soon as they arrive. We found out from reliable sources that there are some books there. They have been there for a long time. The guys decided to lift the whole cache, and I said they should also take the religious books. I told them which ones to take."

Father Arseny was worried. How could he accept this? He prayed at night; then, as if dozing off towards morning, he saw a monk-elder walk in, bless him, and say, "Do not be afraid, Arseny! Take what you need, and pray to Metropolitan Alexei of Moscow. God will not leave you." He blessed Father Arseny again and walked out calmly and majestically.

About two days later there was a big disturbance in the barracks, in which all of the barracks were searched. People were called in to the special sector for interrogation. It turned out that the cache of confiscated objects had been stolen by the criminals.

Ten days went by, and Sazikov gave Father Arseny two small books: the Gospels and a Book of Services. Father Arseny received them with awe, went to his bunk, opened the Gospels and trembled at God's incredible mercy. On the inside of the binding there was inlaid a little piece of silk—a square of about two inches on each side; the silk was yellowed and old. Below it was an inscription: "Antimens,[7] relics of Saint Alexis, Metropolitan of Moscow, 1883"; next to this a little oval silver icon was cut in, the size of a twenty-kopek piece. Father Arseny prostrated himself before such a holy object and thanked God: "O, Lord, I am alive by Thy mercy, and marvelous are Thy works." And he cried with joy.

7 The Antimens is an icon painted on a piece of silk, with the relics of a saint sewn into the middle. In order to serve the liturgy the priest must always have an Antimens on the altar table.

"Father Arseny, each time as you finish praying with the help of these books, give them to me or to Graybeard. Nobody will find them on us, but, they will find them immediately on you and take them away. Do not worry, we will desecrate nothing, and everything will be preserved in safety."

Days of great joy followed for Father Arseny. He would finish his work, and at night, he could read the Gospel by the light of a flickering candle and serve regular services. When it was time to get up, he would give the books to Sazikov.

Some two months went by, the searches died down, and Father Arseny could sometimes keep the Gospel during the day, but he always hid it behind a board in the wall, a secret place made for this purpose by Sazikov. He felt that this was a safe place even during day or night searches. Once, after Father Arseny finished his work in the barracks and everybody else was still at work, he took out the Gospel and started reading it. As soon as he started reading, the door flew open and a group of guards rushed in for a search—the lieutenant, three soldiers, and the supervisor (the Fair One). Father Arseny did not know what to do. He put the Gospel in the inner pocket of his padded cotton jacket, and stood praying.

The soldiers turned everything upside down in the barracks, removing any floorboards that moved even a little. They removed the boards from the walls, and shook all the possessions of the prisoners out of their bags. They came to Father Arseny. The lieutenant from the special sector gave orders to the Fair One: "You search the priest, Comrade!," and went away with his soldiers.

The Fair One started frisking Father Arseny and immediately felt the Gospel, held his hand on it for a little while, then pulled it out of Father Arseny's pocket and put it into his own, and then continued frisking Father Arseny. When he was finished, he reported to the lieutenant.

"I found nothing."

"You searched him too fast! Strip, *Priest*! We will search you our own way." Father Arseny undressed completely, the soldiers checked all his clothing, they checked all the seams, threw on the floor everything that was in his pockets, and of course they found nothing. The lieutenant grew very angry, swore rudely at Father Arseny and left.

Father Arseny got dressed. He prayed and cried in gratitude for this enormous joy—faith in a fellow man. He picked up all his things, sewed up the seams that they had ripped and began cleaning the barracks after the search.

In an hour and a half the Fair One came in and asked Father Arseny, "Is there anyone in the barracks?"

"They are all at work," answered Father Arseny.

The Fair One looked all over the barracks, even under the bunks and, suddenly returning the book to Father Arseny, said, "This Gospel is one of the stolen books, is it not?"

Father Arseny was silent.

"Answer me, where did you get it from?"

"It is one of the books that were taken," answered Father Arseny.

"Are you crazy? You've got to think! If you take a Gospel, you've got to hide it. If the lieutenant had found it, he would have beaten you to death." And then he whispered, "I am sorry, Father! It is so difficult here, in camp. It is difficult not only for the prisoners, but also for us, for those of us who have the least bit of conscience left. I know, Father Arseny, I know everything! I know how hard life is here for all of you. But please remember that we are forced to work in this hell-hole. It is not because we are cowards or weaklings. I will help you, I will even try to send you somewhere where life is a little easier, but all this takes time. I must do what I can in secret, and in front of others I will be especially fierce. You will have to pardon me! Please forgive me!" Having said this, the Fair One left without looking back.

Father Arseny gazed after the departing supervisor and felt ashamed that he had not trusted in God's great mercy, in His inscrutable ways. He understood once again how varied and rich the human soul could be, and that one could find God's spark and love in each and every soul. He started praying, "Have mercy on me O God, according to Thy steadfast love, according to Thy abundant mercy. Lord, my Lord, great art Thou and glorified in Thy deeds. These are the helpers about whom Thy Mother spoke to me. Could I ever have thought that the supervisor would be the one sent by Thee to help me? Could I?"

And remembering the name of the Fair One, Andrew, Father Arseny started to pray for him, and in his prayer, he saw the whole life of Andrew and he understood what kind of a person he was. He was a good and generous man.

A Hard Trek

SOMETIMES THE FACT that Father Arseny knew what others were thinking or had done amazed people who came to him, and even frightened them, but he himself could not understand this and did not think that God had given him a particularly deep knowledge of the human soul. I was constantly at Father Arseny's side, and I saw that he sincerely believed that an understanding of the soul was absolutely natural for a priest. He was convinced that in knowing the thoughts of a person he was not reading his mind, but that the person himself had shared his thoughts with him. He had an enormous and surprising influence on people who were in contact with him. Those who were with him often and saw how he lived were amazed at the depth and strength of the insight that God had given him. Avsenkov told me about two occurrences that had moved him deeply, which he had witnessed when he was just beginning to believe in God under Father Arseny's influence.

"One evening, just before the last roll call, a large group of new prisoners was thrown into the camp. The administration started sorting them out by barracks to fill the empty bunks.

"Something like 25 people were assigned to our barracks," Avsenkov told me. "You could see that the trek had been very arduous. The prisoners were pushed into the barracks. They looked more like shadows than like people. They could barely stand, their life was oozing out of them. Outside it was freezing; they had not been fed for two days, and they had not slept for three nights.

They were mostly intellectuals, "enemies of the people," engineers, agronomists and doctors, along with a few criminals.

"They had arrived just before last roll call, after the evening meal of bread and meager soup. The administration had left or was getting ready to leave for the day.

"At first, the guards thought they should give the new arrivals some bread and some soup, but then decided it was too bothersome. 'We would then have to keep the fire going,' they thought. 'Heat the soup, unlock the storage rooms, cut the bread and then write reports on how much of what was given out...'

"It certainly was bothersome, very bothersome. It was decided that the men could wait until tomorrow, there would be time. The commandant of the camp pronounced: 'After all, these aren't masters to be served, they're enemies of the people. They will survive.' So this was what was decided. Of course they understood that many would die that night, so they would have to report the deaths over the period of a few days so as not to be blamed for so many deaths upon arrival. The deaths would by then be the camp's responsibility.

"So the new prisoners entered the barracks. New people are never welcome anywhere. It all starts in school when kids make fun of new kids, then at work when people sneer at new employees, and even more so in camp. So we just looked at the—they didn't even look like people, they looked like human leftovers; they couldn't even stand on their own. We didn't understand how they could have walked to the camp. They were leaning against the walls or holding on to bunks.

"The prisoner responsible for the whole barracks said to them, 'Go and lie down on the empty bunks.' Now, everybody knew very well that the empty bunks were those furthest from the stoves. It was cold there, and the new prisoners would never be able to get warm.

"The more senior residents of the barracks were getting ready to turn in. Some of them were already lying down, while others still played cards. The criminals glanced at the new arrivals, saw that there was nothing they could get from them, and forgot about them.

"Father Arseny was lying down and praying. When the men walked in, he got up, looked them over and went to the criminals' leaders. Their word was law for the criminals as well as for the politicals; if you didn't listen to these criminal leaders, anything could happen.

"So Father Arseny went to these leaders, the 'serious cases', and said, 'We've got to help the new arrivals. They are cold and hungry, they are exhausted. If we do not help them, many of them will die during this night.'

"The 'serious cases' knew and respected Father Arseny; they had lived with him for several years, and they loved him in their own way, but now one of the criminals spat, swore and said, 'Let 'em croak. We're going to die soon too, and I'm not ready to share my ration. Got it, Popkins?'

"The others kept silent. Who is it that really wants to give away something that belongs to him, especially in this place where the law is that you help only your friends? Everyone looked at Father Arseny and at the 'serious cases': how would it all end? The newcomers stood in a close group and listened.

"Father Arseny looked calmly at the criminal leaders, made the sign of the cross and said, 'So, we are going to put the new arrivals on the bunks near the stoves; we ourselves will take the colder ones. Whatever each of us has for food, let's bring it here and put it on the table. We are going to heat some water—the stoves are still hot. Let's do it all quickly.'

"The 'serious cases' stood up in silence and started moving people about and brought to the table whatever food they each still had. The other occupants of the barracks did the same, of course. Some of the criminals tried to hide part of their bread, but the rest hit them so that they remembered it for a long time.

"Crumb by crumb they collected enough food to feed the twenty-five new people in the barracks. Water was heated on the stove in tin cups. Father Arseny divided what had been collected and distributed it among the new arrivals, and the prisoners placed them in the warm bunks. They all survived, but you could not say the same about the poor people who had been sent to other barracks. In some four days the new people were strong enough to be sent to work.

"I was stunned at the calm and concentration of Father Arseny when he said, 'Let's do it quickly!' He said it to people who had nothing to spare. He said it and they did it. As if it had been an order.

"I often thought," said Alexander Pavlovich Avsenkov, "Where did Father Arseny's power come from? Was he able to appeal to the conscience of people or did he simply order them in the name of God to do their inevitable duty?" And Avsenkov decided that Father Arseny's power was that he requested all this in the name of God.

"I Order You to Stop!"

ANOTHER OCCURRENCE RETOLD by Avsenkov was perhaps even more impressive to him.

"Before the barracks were locked up there was always a roll call. All the prisoners were driven outside, where they had to stand in line until the roll was called. It could be -30° F, it could be raining cats and dogs, or mosquitoes could be attacking everybody, but nothing would change the rule—the prisoners had to run out to be counted.

"This time, everybody ran out as usual and stood in line. It was cold, but they had to count a second time—one man was missing. People were freezing, the administration was getting angry, and they started counting a third time. Suddenly a man ran out of the barracks—he was about 25 years of age and tried to find his place in the line. He did not have the time to get in place before the supervisors started kicking him with their boots. The young man tried to explain himself, but he was beaten mercilessly. Everyone looked on in silence. Everyone had dark faces, angry faces, but nobody dared say anything.

"I was standing with Father Arseny and suddenly I saw that he took a step out of the line, made the sign of the cross, blessed the supervisor who was hitting the young man and said in a clear voice, "In the name of the Lord, I am ordering you to stop! Stop this!"—and having blessed everybody with a wide sign of the cross he returned to his place in the line. The supervisor stopped the beating immediately and got busy counting the prisoners again; the young man unsteadily found his place in the line.

"Later I asked the man who was next to me in the line, 'Did you see what Piotr Andreyevich (Father Arseny) did when they beat up the young man?'

"'Did what? He was standing as still as a statue.'

"All this impressed me enormously; I saw the power that God gave this man—Father Arseny. Could it be hypnosis, I thought, and the answer came to me: 'No, of course it could not be hypnosis. Father Arseny does not do all this for himself, but only for the sake of others.'"

You could see so many very different people in camp. Some were fanatics, in a crazed way. In their own conviction they were absolutely sincere, and as a result they looked at everyone else as if they were stray sheep. They were afraid to give up even unimportant details of their belief. Often these fanatics would help people, but you had the feeling that they were doing this for their own salvation, not for the sake of others.

Father Arseny was loved. Some people tried to convince him that his faith was wrong, to which Father Arseny would always answer, "Am I trying to convince you that your faith is wrong? Believe what your soul dictates you, then you will find the truth. Remember the words of the Apostle Paul: 'Bear each other's burdens, and so fulfill the law of Christ.' Only by goodness can you win over evil."

And I always felt: *yes,* the very fact that he was bearing the burdens of others allowed him to bear his own suffering. It attracted people to him and gave him the strength of spirit which compelled others to do what he had ordered in the name of God. Both cases I just recounted are examples of this.

A Joy

THE CAMP LIVED its heavily regimented life. People died, others came to replace them, only to die themselves; all were awaiting their time. From this special camp almost nobody was ever freed. There were a few cases where especially famous scientists or people who had been powerful in the Communist Party and had worked in Federal Organizations were freed. People said that in the past three years perhaps ten people had been set free, and of those one had died of a heart attack when he heard the news of his liberation.

In 1952, Father Arseny was called in to the special sector of the camp for interrogation. First he was received by the Lieutenant and then by the Major. The Major met him joyously: "Good morning, Father Arseny, good morning, Piotr Andreyevich! I have good news for you. Alexander Pavlovich Avsenkov will be set free. His friends arranged this with great difficulty. I will call him in tomorrow to tell him the news. But I am afraid that the news might stun him. He has a weak heart, so please warn him about it gently. I am going to tell him this in front of the officer responsible for the camp, so I will be rough; he does not have to worry. He is not only going free, but he is also being reinstated into the Party. Stalin ordered this himself.

"As for you, it looks bad. You are a church person. Your file has a special stamp on it: "To be kept in camp indefinitely—until death." I would like to help you, but I am unable to. From this camp of ours, people like yourself are freed only under instruction from Berya[8] or his equal. I can do nothing for your case. If I set you free without their permission, someone will report it immediately and I will be sent to camp as a prisoner myself. If anything changes, I will do everything I can to obtain your freedom, and now Alexander Pavlovich will also be able to help.

"I am also being transferred back to Moscow. They 'forgave' me, if I may say so. I am becoming a general again and they are sending me back to work in the Secret Service.

"I have loved my country and protected it my whole life. During the last war, I worked on reconnaissance and managed to save thousands of lives, and then, when I got in somebody's way, they denounced me to Stalin; they decided to get rid of me and have me shot under the pretext that I had established 'contacts with Germans'...

8 Berya, a cruel man, was Chief of Secret Police under Stalin.

"Stalin ordered that my file be looked over and had me sent to this camp. When I got here, I was horrified. I can't help anyone in any way because they watch my every step. I could never have imagined that I would see the things that I see: people destroying other people. I don't have the authority to do anything at all. One time I halted some injustice and immediately a report was sent saying that I was 'obstructing justice.' It's frightening. What is all this happening for? It can't be understood now. Piotr Andreyevich, do tell me whom I must try to help before I leave. You tell me, and I will do it. I am only sorry that I cannot help you."

Father Arseny looked pensively at the Major and said: "Thank you, thank you. I know you cannot help me; when the time comes, God will help me. Meanwhile help Sazikov to leave this camp; help the student Alexei Nikonov, the doctor Denisov and the ex-criminal Trifonov. Have them transferred to a regular camp—life there will be easier for them and there they can be helped from the outside."

Father Arseny did not name Graybeard. Looking at the Major, he added, "Sergei Petrovich! When you come to Moscow, do everything you can not to work for 'State Security' anymore. Ask to be transferred or else you will burn out. Having seen what is happening here, you have become a new man. Save your soul."

Abrosimov looked at the old man and thought that he himself was not clear about his own life in the future, but that Father Arseny probably knew a great deal about his past and future life. And again childhood memories came to him. Yes, a man like Father Arseny was a true Christian. Sometime in the past he had read about such people.

A feeling of great sadness came over Sergei Petrovich. He got up, came closer to Father Arseny and, very moved, said: "I do not know if I will ever see you again, but you have left an indelible imprint on me. I see things differently now. I trust you, I trust Vera Danilovna and my own wife. I understand everything. I know that you pray constantly. Do not forget me, Piotr Andreyevich—Father Arseny, do not forget me!"

Father Arseny got up from his chair, came to Abrosimov, embraced him and said: "May God keep you, Sergei Petrovich! Do not forget other people, help them, do good wherever you are. Help people. We shall meet again you and I."

He bowed deeply and left. He went out in such a manner that Abrosimov had a feeling that it was not he who had called Father Arseny in for a talk, but that Father Arseny had invited him.

Abrosimov never forgot his meetings with Father Arseny. When he saw him for the first time he had seen an old man in a patched-up padded cotton jacket, exhausted, tired, and he thought that the old man was broken, emptied out. But when he looked him in the eye he understood that Father Arseny was full of life, faith, and an unlimited love for people. He was neither broken nor emptied. He was burning with an inner strength which he was generously giving out to others, making their suffering easier to bear and chasing from them the feeling of fear and desperation. He was carrying his faith to other people.

Abrosimov understood that if this old man only wanted to be freed or to do anything else which he felt was indispensable to him, it all would happen as he wanted, so strong was the power of his spirit, which was enriched and nourished by his faith.

Here in the special camp, although he himself was living the same hard life as others did, he was carrying out his Christian podvig (ascetic task), giving help and the light of God to all people.

The work that Abrosimov was doing was awfully difficult, his whole life had been hard, and as a result his connection to God had been lost. Meeting Father Arseny shook up his soul, made him rethink everything and reevaluate his past. Abrosimov still had to walk a long path to God, but the first step on the path of faith had been made with the help of Father Arseny. Many years later Abrosimov recounted, "My return to Moscow was difficult. Everything was given back to me—my title, my job...but, something came between my old life and my new one. I ended up rethinking my life and left that kind of work. I will be straight with you: I had done many terrible things, many frightening things and while I was doing them I was sure that I was doing the right thing.

"Alexander Pavlovich Avsenkov helped me. He helped me untangle things within myself. When I realized all I had done, I became certain that there was no forgiveness for me; but then, Alexander Pavlovich gave me a note from Father Arseny who was already free by then. The note said, 'Remember and have no doubt! The God who can punish us for our sins is also capable in His limitless mercy of absolving us from our sins. There is no heavy sin or curse that cannot be redeemed by deeds and prayer.'

"In the course of my life Father Arseny helped me very much in understanding the faith. Of course I did not become as good as many of his spiritual children, but I tried and worked on walking towards God.

"Father Arseny, to whom I told all my doubts and hesitations about the faith and its rites, would always answer me, 'If you look at your life, your long wanderings with no ideology, with no inner axle, it is natural that you have doubts and hesitations. But is this what is important? You understand, you feel that God does exist, you know the way to Him. Believe and all that is unimportant will simply disappear.' A remarkable man he was, Father Arseny. A true Christian."

Now Father Arseny returned to the barracks. He was overjoyed for Alexander Pavlovich, for Sazikov, Alexei, Denisov and Trifonov—that they were going to leave the special camp and finally go free, but a feeling of sadness darkened his soul, his friends were going to leave...

He would have fewer helpers and fewer friends. He did believe that God was not going to leave him alone and that new people would appear and replace those who had left. That same evening he told Avsenkov the news of his liberation. They talked the whole night, and in the morning they said goodbye. Father Arseny and the camp had completely overturned the way that Avsenkov had been thinking, and the way he had seen others. When he had arrived at the camp he had wanted to commit suicide; he had become helpless and lost his will. Now, he was leaving spiritually enriched, with a strong spirit, a strong and stable faith in God, and a new understanding and respect for other people's sufferings.

That night they prayed together for a long time. Embracing Father Arseny, Avsenkov repeated, "Do not forget me, Father Arseny, I will meet with your people, who are now mine too. Pray for us!" In the morning Avsenkov said goodbye to Sazikov and to Alexei—he knew that when he was told he was free, he would not be allowed to return to the barracks.

About four weeks later, Sazikov, Alexei, Trifonov and Denisov were each called to the special sector; they never returned to the barracks. The prisoners were trying to guess what had happened to them. Major Abrosimov, now a general, had kept his word.

Life Continues

LIFE IN THE camp went on. New prisoners were systematically brought in to replace those who had gone to the camp cemetery. Death visited the camp daily and took away new victims. Tomorrow brought no surprises; it was hungry, tired, heavy, full of demeaning remarks, it lasted many, many hours. Dullness, indifference, and a desire for death were common among the prisoners. Father Arseny continued to live his ascetic life of devotion.

He missed Alexei the student, Sazikov, and Avsenkov. He had come to love them, had gotten used to them and to their support of all his doings. New people would appear with whom he grew close, but then they would be transferred from barracks to barracks, die or be transferred to some mining pits in other camps.

As he had before, Father Arseny helped those around him, bringing them physical support and spiritual consolation. He was indispensable to many. Somehow he unnoticeably entered the life of others, bore their pains, lessened their difficulties and by the example of his own life showed them that one could survive in camp by knowing that God always stood behind you and that you could always call on Him.

Then the criminal nicknamed "Graybeard" fell seriously ill. He had pains in his digestive system. When the pains became unbearable, he went to the camp doctors. They gave him aspirin, then rhubarb (known for its purgative powers). Nothing helped. They never really looked at him, never examined him. When they finally did, they said it was a longstanding cancer of the liver which had metastasized.

Graybeard was dying a difficult death. They did not take him into the hospital. He had terrible pains, but he still had to get up from his bunk for roll call and to go to the latrine. Father Arseny patiently cared for him and tried to help as only he could. He even went to the doctors to ask for some pain killers, but they gave him nothing.

Graybeard was angry at everybody and everything, but he accepted Father Arseny's care meekly. He liked it when Father Arseny came to him, and would ask him to sit on his bunk. When Father Arseny was near him Graybeard would begin to tell about his life and sometimes could forget his pains.

About two days before he died he said, "I am dying and I am suffering because I deserve it. I have brought pain to many people and I killed many. I started my life the wrong way. I do not want to repent since I've done so many bad things that I can't even count them. I know that it's impossible to forgive me, and besides what for? I barely believe in God. I have some superstitions, but I know and I feel that God exists because you, Father Arseny, believe in Him and live by Him.

"I come from a priest's family. My father was a deacon. He didn't believe in God; he served to be paid because he could find no other job. He served as a professional.

"When I was growing up, I saw lies and fraud around me. They drank vodka, they grabbed women, they made fun of God and the rites of the church, and at the same time they hid behind this same God. My father said one thing and did another. Sometimes he would come home after a service and count the money—then he would send someone to buy vodka, make fun of everything sacred, and swear in a dirty way. He would tell everyone else how he had taken money from the collection plate and how he had tricked a simple woman.

"I didn't believe in God although I studied at a seminary. When I finished I started to steal and went to prison several times. Then came the Revolution, with its troubles and disorders; I started drinking, robbing, feasting. Rob, kill, there is no God, you are your own boss. I found some 'appropriate friends'—and it all started. First it started small, then grew bigger and then I shed human blood... and then there was no stopping me. This is how it was, Father Arseny!

"I spilled much blood. I was always planning the next venture, the next fun with women, or planning ways to avoid prison. There was no time to think 'Does God exist or not?' To be honest, I didn't even want to think about Him. I met you in this camp; I thought you were some kind of fool or else perhaps you were trying to benefit somehow from your behavior. Then I saw how you turned around the souls of Avsenkov and of my buddy Sazikov, and I understood: you sincerely believed in God. And I understood myself that there is a God. How could it be otherwise if even the church where my father was serving was always so full of people. I saw all of this when I served in the altar as a little boy.

"Now, I know that God exists, but I have no path open to him. The things I've done can't be forgiven.

"I am dying, but I'm not afraid of death. Still there is one thing that is scary: and I don't know what it is. I thought for a while that I would ask you to hear my confession. But knowing you, I thought you couldn't forgive me for my sins. But, as a matter of fact, I am not sorry. What happened, happened.

"But there are two things which I often see before my eyes when I can't sleep: I also sometimes dream about them. In the 30's I had to kill a kid aged seventeen; it was a silly little thing. He was begging me on his knees, he was begging and he was crying—I'd had some vodka and wanted to show off in front of my friends so I made fun of him. All I have to do is close my eyes and there he is, the kid, his face covered with tears.

"And then, there was this woman. She won't leave me in peace. She appears in front of me two or three times a week, and now she appears every day. This is how it was: we wanted to rob an apartment, which we thought was empty, everyone was supposed to be at work. So we went in, and someone was there—a beautiful woman, tall, well built—a beauty, as they say.

"As we walked in, she understood it all. She ran to the window. We locked her up in a room. There was lots to take in this apartment; there was even some gold. We started gathering the stuff together. Then it was time for us to leave, but...this woman had seen us. We had to kill her. There was no way out—she could recognize us later. My friends didn't really want to do it – they had never killed yet.

"I went in. I opened the door, she looked at me and she understood her fate. Her eyes were big with fright. I grabbed her, looked at her and decided to have her. I told my friends to go to the next room and there it started. She hit me in the face, and then, suddenly becoming very dignified she told me calmly, 'You are not a man, you are an animal. Get it over with quickly!' In her eyes I saw hatred, but this enhanced her beauty and I raped her. Then I reached for my knife... She stood next to the wall waiting for the blow. She turned toward the corner where there was an icon, made the sign of the cross several times, and said, 'Now kill me. God is with me. O Mother of God, do not abandon me!'

"I did feel pity for her, but what could I do? We had taken a lot of stuff from this apartment, so I stabbed her under her breast with my knife; she started sliding down and crossed herself hastily whispering, 'God have mercy!' This is how she appears to me every day now."

Father Arseny listened to Graybeard and prayed constantly. But the horrible details he was hearing sent chills throughout his body. Such cruelty, anger, cynicism and complete heartlessness were not often seen even in this camp.

Graybeard was dying, his face was disfigured by sufferings or perhaps by anger towards all living people. When he died his face remained unusually angry.

〜

This story about Graybeard was written up in 1965, from the words of Father Arseny. It was recorded by A.R., who at that time lived in the same barracks with Father Arseny, Graybeard, and the other criminals.

The Interrogation

AFTER MAJOR ABROSIMOV left as Head of the special camp, two other heads worked in the camp, each for a short time; finally a stern, middle-aged man was assigned. He brought in many of his friends. The rules of the camp became even stricter than before, so that the life of the prisoners became simply unbearable.

Many were called into the special sector for interrogation. Threats, beatings, and the punishment cell became even more frequent occurrences. It would seem simply absurd to try and get anything out of these prisoners, who were practically condemned to death, but the interrogators still tried to obtain rewards from Moscow by "unveiling" new crimes.

The special sector was working overtime: new accusations were created, "plots" were uncovered, people's files were reopened, new decisions were made, many prisoners were shot. In March they called Father Arseny in for interrogation. His interrogator was Major Odinzov. He was a man of medium height, bald, red-faced, with colorless eyes, whose thin lips cut his face. He was always neatly dressed in well-pressed clothing; he was always polite in the beginning, but then he struck panic into those he was interrogating by the cruelty of his questions. Nobody knows why he was nicknamed by the prisoners the "Gentle One" or even more often, "So, why don't we start?"

Father Arseny entered the office and stood at the entrance. The interrogator was busily looking at some papers and paid no attention to Father Arseny; then he looked at him casually and said, "I am glad to meet you, Piotr Andreyevich! I am very glad! You have probably heard about me—my name is Odinzov."

"Yes, I have heard about you, comrade interrogator," answered Father Arseny.

"So this is good, Father! Now, why don't we start. With me you have to talk and admit; if you don't, you will bathe in your own blood. I am famous for my ways. Let's start! So: admit your crimes."

"What should I talk about?"

"Tell me, silly priest, about the organizations that exist in this camp to plot the death of comrade Stalin. We know everything: people have informed on you. You won't waste my time if you have heard about me."

Father Arseny became a knot of nerves. All his concentration was on prayer. He begged the Mother of God not to leave him. He begged her to give him the strength to bear this interrogation. "O Lord, my God! Do not forsake me a sinner. Give me strength, O Mother of God. My spirit is weak."

"I know nothing about any plots or conspiracies and I have nothing to confess."

"You know what, *Priest?* I won't play games with you, since you are already half dead and you don't care if you do die. But for me it is extremely important for my future that a plot be discovered. So you are going to sit and write what I am going to dictate to you."

"Comrade interrogator, permit me to ask you a question."

"No question is ever asked of me; people only answer my questions. But do ask, since you are half-dead anyway."

"Comrade Interrogator, please check my file, and you will see that I have never denounced anybody in spite of beatings, severe beatings."

Odinzov got up, walked around the table, and gave Father Arseny a sheet of paper and a pen saying, "Who interrogated you, I don't want to know. But with me, you will write whatever I say."

"No, I will not write anything. There is no conspiracy in this camp. You just want to start a new case and have many innocent people shot, people who will soon die here anyway."

Odinzov came closer to Father Arseny, his lips trembled and grimaced, his colorless eyes came alive and, almost stuttering, he said, "Oh, my dear, you have no idea what awaits you right now."

"Lord, help me." Father Arseny had barely had time to think these words, when a strong blow hit him in the face. He fell from his chair and lost consciousness from the unbearable pain. He understood that it was all over, that Odinzov was going to beat him to death. During some spurts of consciousness, he felt blows. He was kicked in the face by boots, and beaten with the metal beltbuckle. In those short moments when he came to, he prayed to the Mother of God, but then he fainted again, and finally was absolutely still.

He came to for a few seconds and understood with some surprise that he was being dragged to his barracks. He came to a second time on his bunk and felt that someone was wiping his face with a wet rag; he heard someone say, "They beat him to death even though he is an old man; he will not live until tomorrow!" And they swore with hatred against Odinzov, the "gentle" interrogator.

Father Arseny came to yet a third time. Only half conscious, he thought that he was being interrogated again because he felt as if his head was being cut off. He wanted to call on the name of God, but having snatched at the beginning words of a prayer, he would lose them immediately. An unbearable pain was tearing him apart; he thought he was going to be beaten again, and so, he awaited death.

Father Arseny awoke perhaps ten times altogether. Whenever he did, he tried to pray, but was unable to enter into prayer: his mind was clouded because his pain was so strong.

During one of these periods Father Arseny was afraid that he would die without prayer, without repentance. Then somebody was turning his head, something was burning, something was pricking and suddenly Father Arseny heard these words, "Quickly, give him two shots of camphor; be careful when you use the iodine, not to get it in his eyes. Suture the cuts. Shave his head carefully!"

Father Arseny felt that somebody's hands were turning his head very gently, and that he lay on something very hard, that he was naked.

Then he passed out again. Later people told him that he had stayed unconscious for three days on a bunk in the camp hospital. When he came to, he tried to understand where he was. Was he at the interrogator's? in his barracks? or where? Then he realized he was in the hospital. He tried to pray again, but fainted again. This battle between prayer and unconsciousness continued for several days.

Each day he managed to snatch, precisely to snatch, a few more words of prayer and finally the prayer won over everything else.

His eyes were bandaged, but he constantly felt the touch of some gentle and caring hands. He heard someone talking to him with love, and lovingly feeding him.

The voice had a Jewish accent. "It is all right! You are alive. I did not think you would make it. Tomorrow I will remove the bandages from your face. I myself have survived a few of their interrogations. I know these 'conversations.' But we fixed you up. You are as good as new!"

Soon the bandages came off his eyes and head. The doctor, whose name was Lev Mihailovich, busied himself tenderly around Father Arseny, gave him advice, and calmed him. "Hush, hush, let us look. My dear! Your face will have almost no scars! This is good! I am happy for you."

Two nearsighted eyes in thick glasses were looking at Father Arseny. The face was gentle and meek. "I will keep you here as long as I can," said Lev Mihailovich. "I will keep you in this hospital so that you do not encounter this animal again. Pray to your God, for otherwise that man will kill you."

Father Arseny stayed in the hospital for more than forty days. When they had to say goodbye both Father Arseny and the doctor cried. The doctor was a good man and an excellent doctor. Hugging Father Arseny, Lev Mihailovich said with conviction, "This cannot go on. It will end, and we will both be out of this hell. We will meet again." And in fact, they did meet again in 1963.

When Father Arseny came back to his barracks almost everyone he had known had been transferred somewhere. They told him that Major Odinzov had been transferred as well.

About three months after he had been let out of the hospital, Father Arseny was called again into the special sector. He was met by a heavy man, with a severe face, who looked Father Arseny over and said, "You are a survivor. Even Odinzov did not finish you off! This is good. I have orders from Moscow not to finish you off. I don't know why, but they are probably checking on something. So, all right, go ahead and live; I will give instructions not to send you to harsh labor."

From the time of this conversation until the death of Stalin, Father Arseny was never again called to the special sector. Scars on his body and head remained as mementos of his interrogations.

⌒⌒)

All this was told by Father Arseny to his friends and spiritual children.

Major Changes

THE NEWS ABOUT the death of Stalin reached the camp only three days after it happened. It came by chance, through the guards. For some unknown reason the administration of the camp did not want to reveal this news.

It was March and the weather was freezing; snow storms swept over the camp, covering it and sometimes cutting off all contact with the outside world. Along with the news of the death of Stalin an uneasy feeling was creeping into the camp, an aching feeling of concern, of worry but mostly of uncertainty. Each prisoner thought to himself, "What is going to happen? Will everything continue as before or will things change? Change for the worse? Will all the prisoners be shot?" Each one was silently waiting; something had to happen.

During the first two months after the news life in camp continued as before, but after that something started to seep in imperceptibly. It felt as if somebody had thrown sticks or stones into a functioning mechanism. They all worked just as hard, they were still badly fed, they still died but no new prisoners were brought in. You could feel a note of uncertainty in the behavior of the administration, the guards sometimes even joked with the prisoners.

About one year after Stalin's death some more changes were distinctly felt. The prisoners were better fed, there was no more swearing, no more beatings. The supervisors were even polite to the prisoners. Inspectors came from Moscow. Numbers were removed from hats and sleeves and the prisoners were called by name, not by number. Cases were reopened, new witnesses were interrogated; some prisoners were even sent back for retrial to the towns where their case had been opened. Letters and even parcels were allowed to prisoners. Prisoners were paid for their work and were given better clothing and food.

A commission came for the first time, interrogated several hundred prisoners, and left. About two months later another commission came, settled in and started interrogating each and every prisoner. First they freed the military people, then the members of the Party, the scientists, and the important land owners.

More time passed and then all the criminals among the prisoners were pardoned: a massive amnesty for them was declared. The camp was no longer "special," but became a "regular" one. Now only the former members of the police, members of the Vlassov army, the criminals whose past was too heavy, and the politicals whose freedom posed a danger for someone somewhere, remained.

Within a year and a half, nine-tenths of the prisoners had disappeared. Many barracks stood empty; the supervisors were half as numerous as before. It was decided to shrink the size of the camp. The towers with their guards and lights were moved, the barbed wire was moved to form a smaller circumference. The barracks that fell outside the protected zone stood empty and were finally burned down. During this time Father Arseny was moved from one barracks to another. None of his friends were there anymore. He prayed continuously and still helped everybody around him. He now could write letters to his spiritual children and anxiously awaited their answers. The other remaining prisoners were embittered and eternally angry. It was difficult to befriend anyone. Two or three priests and several believers whom Father Arseny knew felt as though they were trapped or persecuted and had no hope of being freed. They wrote many letters to the authorities, and many complaints, and for some reason kept to themselves, communicating with no one.

This was perhaps the hardest time for Father Arseny. Around him was emptiness. Only prayer remained and this is what he lived by, but it was difficult. It was especially difficult because he was burning with the desire to help, to do good, but could not find anywhere to apply his efforts.

In mid-1956, Father Arseny's status changed; he was granted permission to leave the camp from time to time in order to go to the nearby village; he was freed from heavy labor and transferred to a barracks for ailing prisoners.

By March 1957, the camp was almost completely empty. It had been reduced in size several times. Many barracks had been burned down and you could see beyond the barbed wires the dozens of chimneys blackened by the fires; rolls of rusty old barbed wire lay everywhere, pieces of glass glittered in the sun; leftover bricks from the foundations lay everywhere.

He received many letters, and this was a source of great joy for Father Arseny. First he received letters from Vera Danilovna, then from Alexei, Irina, Seraphim Sazikov, and Alexander Avsenkov. Then, by a most complicated means, there was brought to him a note from Abrosimov—who was now a lieutenant general. Abrosimov wrote, "I remember! I have not forgotten anything. I am trying everything, but so much stands in my way. I remember and I remember you! I trust that we shall soon meet under other circumstances. Don't lose hope!"

Father Arseny answered all the letters. He was deeply involved in what was happening in the lives of his spiritual children. Often the letters of people he had not seen for many years told him so much that he felt the person was right there with him.

The supervisor they had named the "Fair One" had been transferred from this camp, and Father Arseny missed this man and his simple soul.

A certain number of criminals were brought to the camp again for new crimes they had committed. These criminals were especially aggressive and insolent; they were unafraid of the guards. The head of the camp was suddenly replaced, and everything changed. The work requirements became more strict, but food became better; punishment for disobedience was fierce but there was no more violence, no cruelty, no insults.

Life continued; Father Arseny accepted the will of God.

This was the last barracks he would be assigned to before he was finally freed. He had no friends left in it. They were all free, transferred or dead.

Leave-Taking [9]

THE YEAR WAS 1957. I was no longer under strict surveillance and was allowed to leave the protected areas for short periods. When I finished my work I would leave the camp, and walk slowly to the nearest forest or to the boggy little stream; I would sit on a dry log and begin to pray. My voice carried into the sparse forest, into the branches of birches and willows that bent down into the water, into the pine trees and into the grass. Here, in the forest, it was so peaceful to pray, and so easy: the roughness of camp life disappeared and was replaced by the possibility of uniting myself with God in prayer. At such times it felt as though my spiritual children and my friends who were free were gathered with me. I remembered the deceased whom I loved along with those whom I had accompanied on their last path after meeting them by chance in exile or in the camps.

It was warm; mosquitoes would buzz, forming a gray cloud trying to get under the netting. A sudden gust of wind would carry all of them away, but in a few seconds the wind would quiet down and the cloud of mosquitoes would again surround me. I would immediately forget the camp, the barracks, the criminals, and the constant supervision. There was only the limitless blue sky, the forest, the swaying grasses, birdsongs, and prayer which united it all with God and the whole world created by Him.

It was not often that I was allowed to leave the camp. This day was such a day. I left the protected zone and walked deep into the sparse forest that lay beyond the camp. There, when the special camp was still filled with the thousands of prisoners who had lived and suffered in it, bonfires had burned constantly to thaw the ground to make it possible to dig the shallow pits in which they would bury the prisoners who had died that day.

The burial ground was enormous; this whole area that had been surrounded with barbed wire was now open. In places the posts had fallen over; the wire was broken and hung pitifully. The graveyard now looked like a huge abandoned vegetable garden with its uneven and unkempt rows of dirt. On these there had once stood sticks with numbers on little plates of tin nailed to them. The majority of these markers now lay on the ground; the numbers of the prisoners had worn off and only on some of them could you still see traces of letters or digits.

9 This chapter was written by Father Arseny.

I walked much further on. The ground in places was wet; my feet sank deeply into mud mixed with dead grass and leaves. It was difficult to walk. I had to step over fallen sticks and mounds of earth, and around the bigger mounds or ditches where common graves had been. I walked through the cemetery clutching the slender scraggly trees for support.

The warm spring sun was nearing the horizon. I stopped, looked around me, made the sign of the cross to bless all those who were buried here, and started to pray. My soul was heavy, sad, sorrowful. The wind fell so that the grass, the scraggly bushes, and the young birches and craggy pines were still. It seemed as if the wind was lying quietly near the earth, waiting for something to happen.

I walked slowly in this field, forgetting what was around me and concentrating my attention and praying for those who lay here. They rose before me; memories assailed me—painful, heavy memories.

So many people whom I had known at one time—whom I had accompanied at their deathbeds, whose lives they had entrusted to me in their confessions, people I had befriended—were now here under the ground in this field of death.

I remembered their faces, exhausted, lost, sad, full of sorrow, praying, or with dying eyes burning with hatred. Each one of them had had a life; I had touched their lives and, being a priest, had taken upon myself a part of their lives when hearing their confessions.

Memories came and went, only to be replaced by others. I prayed aloud and the beautiful words of our funeral service were carried over the cemetery, tearing my soul apart.

Thousands, tens of thousands of the people lying here had been killed by the fierce conditions in this camp, killed slowly, brought to death by other people. Young people, old people, thousands of believers, fighters for their country who had given it their blood, and ordinary people who had been sent to the camp because somebody had informed on them for no real reason. All were here, under this swampy ground.

Here too, under the same ground, were people who had been traitors, murderers, executioners, secret police and fierce criminals.

Somewhere in the distance you could hear the sound of the bulldozer that was flattening out the mounds and ditches so that nobody would ever know or remember who was lying here.

Somewhere here had been carelessly thrown the bodies of Bishop Peter, the Archimandrite Jonah, the righteous Monk Mihail, the Monk Theophil from Optina Monastery, many, many righteous and prayerful men; also Doctor Levashov, who had helped so many people, Professor Gluhov, the carpenter Stepin who until his last breath had done good to others, and many others whom I had known at one time or another.

Remembering the departed I prayed; but suddenly the words of prayer drained out of me, and I found myself on this field lost, crushed by memories, doubts and an unfathomable emptiness. What remained of those who were gone? A rusty marker with a number on it, a bone sticking out from under the ground, a torn piece of fabric.

Burials here had always been hasty; the burial pits were frozen and very shallow and many people were thrown into the same grave.

In the wintertime bodies had been covered with snow mixed with earth; in the summer a special brigade had been assigned the job of covering the arm and leg bones which stuck out from under the ground. Even now you could smell a hint of putrefaction.

It was stuffy, humid, quiet. The sun warmed the ground and above the field you could see a light, almost invisible steam. The air trembled and it seemed as if something particularly light and large was floating above the burial ground.

"Lord, O Lord!" I heard myself exclaim. "Are these the souls of the departed floating above the place of their suffering?" An extraordinarily painful anguish caught and squeezed my heart and soul. I felt a lump in my throat, tears covered my eyes and my heart felt tighter and tighter, almost ready to stop. A feeling of absolute hopelessness, heartsickness and a deep despair came over me; I felt overwhelmed, I was so utterly despondent that I felt lost and unhinged inside. An unbearable soul-rending pain tore out of me with a groan. "My Lord, why didst Thou allow this?"

Suddenly I heard a long drawn piercing cry which was carried over the field. At first it was a low, vibrating, moan like the sobs of a human, sometimes louder, sometimes quieter. This moaning, a wavering moan, was tragic and long. It covered the whole limitless field, filling my soul with a sadness unknown to me before. The cry stopped, only to start again a few moments later with the same intensity.

I felt compressed, my nerves stretched to their limit; I was utterly filled with painful sorrow. It had become dark and oppressive outside. I felt broken, smashed.

"O Lord, my Lord, show me Thy mercy!" I exclaimed and made the sign of the cross.

And suddenly the wind that had been hiding in the forest and the grass was free again; it gave life to grasses, shook the trees and blew insistently into my face; suddenly everything changed, came awake, came alive.

The sad moaning stopped. I heard the birdsong, the stuffiness disappeared, and the air was light again.

The feeling of confusion, of oppressive sickness at heart and despair left me. I stood up straight, shook off all fear, and felt in the blowing of the wind the movement of life. The wind brought me coolness, the smell of grass, of trees, memories of early childhood, of exceptional joy.

⊹

It turned out that the moaning sound that I had heard above the field was nothing but the vibrating sound of a large circular saw that was working in the saw-mill of the camp. The wind was picking up, the air was good and pure. A lark flew up in bounds and its song was sometimes quietly, sometimes clearly heard in the sky, and I realized that life went on and would go on in just the same way as it had before the death of all of these people.

Life will continue, and will always continue. This is the law of God, and the world created by Him follows His design. The feeling of despair and unfathomable sadness had been brought on only by my insufficient faith.

I clearly understood that the Priest Arseny had given in to a feeling of despondency and sickness of heart. I knelt down on the mound that remained of a grave and, leaning against a young birch tree to gather all my strength and will, started praying to God, the Mother of God, and Saint Nicholas the Wonderworker.

Gradually, real peace embraced me, but at first prayer came with great difficulty. As before, in front of me lay a field of death, mounds eroded by rain, ditches full of dirty water, tin and wooden name plates, fragments of human bone, a broken spade that had been used to dig the ground. As before, under this ground lay tens of thousands of dead prisoners, many of whom were forever enclosed in my heart. As before, my soul was full of human grief for the departed, but the obsessive feeling of despondency and despair that had overwhelmed me, had disappeared with the return of prayer.

The long period of prayer cleansed my soul and consciousness, and made me understand that God, the creator of life, does not call us to let despondency and grief possess us; He wants us to pray for the dead, He wants us to do good in His name, in the name of His Mother and in the name of all the people living on this earth.

I finished praying and slowly left the graveyard. The winter sun was slowly setting on the horizon behind the forest. The line of the forest climbed the gentle hills, and suddenly ran down them in a way that made it seem as though the treetops cut the sky with a gigantic saw. The wind hid again in the woods and grasses, and now you could only hear complete silence over the graveyard. Now and then, from very far away one could make out the grumbling of a tractor; the circular saw was silent.

From the edge of the forest one could hear the sad song of a cuckoo crying over the departure of her fledglings. This one stopped singing and another started from far away. Whose remaining years of life was she counting?[10] Was the bird singing for those here in this field of death who had found their end and no longer counted time? Was the song for me who still lives in this camp? But the time of the end of my life is known only to God.

Full of memories I walked back to camp. Every once in a while my thoughts were pierced by the voice of the cuckoo, so that distant memories of my childhood passed before my eyes. I am walking with my mother in a forest; she is telling me about the trees, the flowers, the grasses and the birds—a cuckoo was singing then as well. I remembered my first confession, my friends who are long gone now, my church where I served for many years. Did I ever think then that I would be hearing the voice of a cuckoo in a graveyard of some harsh regime prison camp where so many people—most of them innocent—were buried, whose deaths I had witnessed? Did I ever think that I would be involved in everything that went on here and that, just as they had done, I too would walk the difficult path of suffering and humiliation?

What is all this for, O my Lord? What did all these people suffer and die for? All of them: believers, non-believers, righteous ones, criminals whose crimes are impossible to weigh in human understanding? Why? And the answer came to me:

This is one of Thy mysteries, Lord, which we people—the slaves of sin—cannot understand. This mystery is Thine. Thy ways are inscrutable. Thou alone knowest the path of each human life; our duty is to simply do good in Thy name, to walk in the statutes of the Gospel, and to pray to Thee. Then the forces of evil will be overcome. For where two or three are gathered in Thy name, there also

10 Russian folklore has it that a cuckoo sings "cuckoo" as many times as you have years left to live.

shalt Thou be. Have mercy on me O Lord, according to Thy abundant mercy, and forgive me for my despair, my weakness of spirit and my wavering.

Turning in all four directions, I blessed with the sign of the cross all those who were resting here, and bowing low I took my leave of them. Grant rest, O Lord, to the souls of Thy servants who have fallen asleep.

Until the end of my life I will remember those who remain under the ground here.

Bringing to my mind the names of all those whom I had known, I prayed for them, prayed for their peace, and as I prayed each of their faces appeared clearly before me..

⊹

The year was 1957, the camp was getting emptier every day. Somewhere nearby a village sprung up where free people came from all over Russia to work, to replace the many prisoners who were now gone. Streets appeared, squares, rows of houses. People came who knew nothing of the existence of our "special" camp and of the boggy, swampy graveyard where so many people were buried...

The past was being lost to the memory of people.

"May their memory be eternal!"

Departure

THE END OF 1957 was nearing; Father Arseny had six more years before the end of his "term" because in 1952 his sentence had been lengthened by ten years. He was called in by the Administration several times. They called him in, they interrogated him, they wrote protocols, filled out forms, asked for instructions from somewhere, and finally in the spring of 1958, Father Arseny was told that he was freed because of the general amnesty; he was told this now, in spite of the fact that all the other prisoners concerned had been freed due to the same amnesty several years earlier.

They informed him of this casually, as if Father Arseny was being told that he had a parcel from somebody, and not that he had been in camp for the past many, many years without any reason. Only one person, a member of the responsible commission said, "Look at that, the old man is still alive, so we have to free him!"

So, they dressed him, gave him travel papers, the money he had earned for these latter years, a document allowing him to receive identity papers when he would arrive at his destination. His destination? Where was it now for Father Arseny? They asked him where he was going when they gave him the travel papers. Father Arseny named an old little village near Yaroslavl where a long time ago he had gone frequently, living there at times while studying antiquity. He was not used to freedom any more, he could not imagine life outside the camp, and at this point it made almost no difference to him where he was going.

Exhaustion, unfathomable tiredness, weighed heavily on him. "Everything is in the hands of God," he decided. "God will take care of everything."

He needed to rest, to gather his strength, to be alone and find peace and oneness within himself in prayer, and only then would he be able to see his spiritual children again. At this time he had no strength left; only prayer sustained him.

The northern spring began suddenly, warm winds melted the snow from the hills and the roads. It was dry, mosquitoes were not attacking yet, early birds returned from migration, the air carried energy and hope. With a bag full of his meager belongings, in new shoes, black pants, in a new padded cotton jacket and a typical hat with ear flaps, Father Arseny walked out of the gates of the camp. A warm, joyous spring wind blew, tousling his hair, adding a special life to the morning, lightly carrying the dust of the road.

Having passed by the sentries, he turned his face towards the camp, bowed deeply and blessed it with the sign of the cross. The guards watched him with surprise: a very old man was leaving, an old man who had lived here for so many years.

He walked away from the camp, went up a hill on the road, turned again towards the camp and looked it over. The sight was miserable. The few towers and the barbed wires encircling the barracks was all that was left. Beyond the barbed wires you could see piles of bricks, half-burned barracks, posts fallen to the ground, and half-rotten remains of guard-towers. Father Arseny remembered this "special camp" when it was full, when it was enormous and so many people were living there their terrible, painful life.

Father Arseny stepped off the road and prayed remembering the many, many people who had died here, and also those God had brought to freedom. Many tormented years had passed since Father Arseny had first come here—very long years, but God had never left him, and had saved Father Arseny, giving him the possibility to see so much beauty in this sea of sorrow. He found here people who showed him everything a true Christian soul should search for and work towards.

Here, surrounded by human suffering and sorrow, he had learned to pray silently surrounded by people; here the example of so many righteous people or very ordinary people had taught him that he must take on himself the sufferings of others and carry them, and that this is the law of Christ. Praying, Father Arseny thanked God, the Mother of God and all those who had lived here and had helped and taught him.

A truck gave Father Arseny a lift to the civilian village nearby where the supervisor they had called the "Fair One" now worked as a regular employee. It was easy to find his house.

The whole atmosphere of the civilian village was difficult to get used to, though. There was no screaming, no criminals, no schedule of the day, no swearing.

The "Fair One," now called Andrei Ivanovich, together with his wife, accompanied Father Arseny to the train station. The two days Father Arseny had spent with Andrei Ivanovich had given him a chance to truly believe that he was free. The Fair One paid a supplement to the ticket Father Arseny had, so that he could travel in more comfort. Father Arseny was given the lower bunk. He put his bag under his head, lay down and closed his eyes.

The train clanked on each rail joint, the wheels knocked regularly, outside the windows passed the taiga, the rocks, the rivers and lakes of Siberia. Before his closed eyes appeared people and more people in a continuous file. Most had died, but some had survived and Father Arseny would see them. His new life appeared nebulous for him; nothing was known to him. But there was God, and with His help this new life had to start somehow. His distracting thoughts stopped, and Father Arseny started to pray.

Suddenly he heard, "We'd better watch it. There's someone here from a camp. He could rob us!" And another voice answered in a whisper, "I can't understand why they free them. They should all be shot to death." Father Arseny opened his eyes and saw opposite him a young couple...

The train was moving. They passed stations, rivers, cities. On the platforms people walked and talked freely. Life was being lived.

Father Arseny prayed for his newly starting life and for all those who had stayed in camp forever.

Spring was more and more evident as they headed further south. Closer to Moscow everything was blooming with many colors. The terrible past connected with the special camp had disappeared, never to be lived again. The era of awful suffering that had been imposed on Russia had come to an end.

Looking through the window, not seeing anything, Father Arseny prayed and thanked God and His Mother and all the Saints for the mercy and help he had received, and asked for help for all those he knew and loved. The train was nearing the city where Father Arseny was to start his new life and continue to serve God and His mankind.

II

❧THE PATH❧

The Vladimir Mother of God.

Introduction to Part II

IN THIS PART I have gathered together memoirs and stories told to me about Father Arseny, and also about people who in one way or another were in contact with him and were influenced by him. Some of these are people of importance, some are just plain folk. You will meet people here whom you will recognize from the first part, but you will also meet new people. Some of these are spiritual children of Father Arseny; others, having met him, came away with a firm faith in God and an understanding of what it is to be a truly believing person who brings goodness, joy and help in all life's difficulties to others.

Father Arseny knew how to take upon himself the troubles and sins of other people, and how to teach them to pray in such a way that they could find a path to God; he brought the faith out in these men and women and made them understand the joy of helping others. We will never know how many people received his help and support, nor will we ever know how many people he brought to God and helped on their path to Him; we only know that these people were many, very many. Reading the memoirs brought together here, you will see and understand the life of Father Arseny and also that of the other people who are an example to us. We must profoundly thank Father Arseny's spiritual children, friends, and acquaintances who agreed to write about him and about their own connection with him.

Reading these memoirs, stories and notes, you cannot but feel the exceptional, holy love and veneration Father Arseny felt for the Mother of God, to whom he was constantly praying for all of us sinners.

Most Holy Mother of God, pray to God for us!

I Remember

THE TRAIN STOPPED and Father Arseny stepped out of it. It was the spring of 1958, a passionate, happy, cheerful spring. The morning was bright and clear. On the ground were still patches of unmelted snow, and blue shiny puddles reflected the spring sky.

Father Arseny walked along the platform and came out onto the square in front of the station. He looked around. The clean, transparent air allowed him to see so clearly the far away bell towers, and cupolas of churches, their crosses bent or missing.

In his padded cotton jacket, his hat with its ear flaps and his bag of clothing on his back, the slight, gray-bearded Father Arseny at first sight looked like a farm worker who had come to the city to buy food; but if you looked more carefully you would notice details of clothing, gait, and speech that told you he had just come out of a prison camp.

The town was the same as it had been some twenty five years ago, but it looked even shabbier, and had become dirtier and sadder. Even the spring weather did not bring it to life; on the contrary the happy light only accentuated the unpainted dreariness of houses in bad repair, the chipped stones paving the streets, the garbage in the ditches along the streets, the miserable look of the stores and kiosks as well as the oppressive lack of any color anywhere.

Father Arseny pulled out of the pocket of his jacket a note with an address on it and went to look for the house of Nadezhda Petrovna. Everything felt unfamiliar to him: the people, what they said, what they talked about, their behavior and the little town itself, the little town he had once known so well, visited often and even lived in for long stretches of time.

Monastery Street, River Street and so on were now Engels Street, Marat Street, Soviet Street, Lenin Street...

Father Arseny walked all over the town, asking for instructions as he went, and finally the street he was looking for appeared in front of his eyes, at the top of a hill. He found the house, came to the gate, pulled the bell, and waited.

He rang several times, but although he heard the tinkling of the bell inside the house, nobody came out. Father Arseny looked around helplessly. He did not know what to do. It was getting cold, he was tired from his traveling, his emotions, his uncertainty about his future. He felt lost, he was overwhelmed—he was so used to the strict routine in camp; he was suddenly faced with the bustle of freedom. All this made him lose his concentration and his peace. Standing here in front of the closed gate Father Arseny felt lost. Where could he go? What could he do? He did not know anybody in this town; he did have a second address but he was unable to find it even after he had searched all his pockets. It was critical that he find a human being who could help him find a room to rent. He had to rest, he had to live alone for a little while in order to understand his new life and get into this free life he was not used to anymore, after all these years. Only then would he be able to write to his spiritual children and friends. What could he do? Perhaps Nadezhda Petrovna did not live here any more? Next to the fence was a bench; Father Arseny wiped it with his mitten and sat down on it, exhausted.

"I started thinking," said Father Arseny later. "I understood that I had succumbed to pride. I'd thought I could manage my new life by myself without my spiritual children and without my friends. I thought I would get used to this life. But God showed me otherwise; He showed me my mistake. Everything that surrounded me was frightening, was unknown to me, was foreign. My only hope was in God."

Not many passersby walked along this narrow street. The old bent-over man with his patched up cotton jacket and his bag of clothes was sitting on a little bench, his back to the fence and looking as if he was daydreaming. The little town, the street had fallen away from him; only his prayer to God and His Mother was present to him. Father Arseny asked to be forgiven for his pride, for his insufficient faith in the help of his own people.

Time passed. About three hours later a woman stepped out of the neighboring house and asked, "Who are you waiting for, citizen?" Father Arseny looked at her in amazement and suddenly saw himself on this little bench in an unknown street faced by this unknown woman. When he realized where he was, he dug the note out of his pocket and answered, "I am waiting for Nadezhda Petrovna," but the questions still came thick and fast. "Who? Where from? Why? Have you been in this town for a long time?"

Father Arseny answered evasively. "I am a friend. I have come to visit her, since I haven't seen her for a long time." It seemed impossible to stop the nosy questions, but just then a woman arrived and Father Arseny understood that she must be Nadezhda Petrovna.

This is how Father Arseny came to this little town and this is how he met the very Nadezhda Petrovna in whose house he was to spend the fifteen last years of his life.

✤

Nadezhda Petrovna's story was an unusual one. A teacher's daughter, at age sixteen she joined the Communist Party. She took part in the revolution, became active in the administration of the Party, completed the Institute of Red Professors, and started working on the so-called "ideological front." Her articles, brochures and books became famous. She worked with noted Communists and was elected as a delegate to several meetings, but in 1937 she was suddenly arrested, sent to a camp, and was set free only in 1955, at age 55. Out of her three children only her daughter Maria was still alive. When Nadezhda Petrovna was let out of camp, Maria had already been married for a long time to an army doctor. After her son Yuri had spent a number of years in an orphanage, he was mobilized into the army and killed at age nineteen. Her youngest son, Sergei, died in this town's orphanage. Nadezhda Petrovna did not want to live in Moscow and decided to remain in the small town where her little Sergei was buried. Her convictions, love, interest in life, her past, everything had been taken from her, erased by interrogations, by humiliations, by her stay in camp. Her soul was full of unending pain. Her daughter and her son-in-law had bought her this small but comfortable house with its pleasant little garden.

In 1952 Father Arseny had met the husband of Nadezhda Petrovna in camp. His name was Pavel. Pavel was very seriously ill, but had worked until the end in very difficult conditions. Pavel became Father Arseny's friend and had asked him, if he ever got free, to find his wife and to tell her about him. He also asked Father Arseny to help Nadezhda Petrovna in any way he could.

At the end of 1958, while still in the camp, Father Arseny wrote to some of his friends asking them to find Nadezhda Petrovna. They found her with great difficulty; she was then already living in the same little house where Father Arseny later found her. He wrote her a long and detailed letter telling her everything he knew about Pavel—about his camp life and his last days. She answered and offered to let Father Arseny stay with her when he was released from the camp.

Nadezhda Petrovna welcomed Father Arseny. He would be able to tell her about the life of her husband, his stoical behavior, the thoughts he had expressed before dying. Father Arseny told her a great deal. She listened, sometimes in tears, sometimes in anger, repeating the same sentence again and again: "What a man he was, my Pavel! What a man! They destroyed him. They planned his destruction! The bastards!"

Father Arseny stayed with her for several days but felt that to remain there would be difficult for him, because everything felt foreign to him. He felt shy when he prayed. He felt like a guest, despite having his own room.

Meanwhile he had found the second address in one of his pockets. He thanked Nadezhda Petrovna and took himself to Maria Sergeyevna, who was a long-time acquaintance and a spiritual daughter from Moscow.

"About ten days later, I went to pay a call on Father Arseny," said Nadezhda Petrovna. "And what do I see? The house is old and decrepit, Father Arseny is living in a room as small as a closet and sleeping on a broken folding cot under a threadbare blanket; Maria Sergeyevna is so old that she can give Father Arseny no help and needs care herself... In other words the lame leading the blind. I began begging him to move back to my house.

"He looked at me humbly and said, 'Do you really think this is possible? You know that I am a priest; I pray for long times at a stretch and I hold church services at home. You do not believe in God, you are an atheist. Besides, friends of mine will be visiting me, and not just a few: many will be coming. I wouldn't be a good lodger for you.'

"I could see," wrote Nadezhda Petrovna, "that Maria Sergeyevna also disapproved of him moving back to my house. But for a reason I could not understand I felt enormous pity for him, so I came back the next day and took him back into my house. I gave Father Arseny a large room, with windows looking onto the garden. It is quiet and peaceful here, and I started taking care of him—you see I live alone. My daughter and her husband visit from Moscow at best once a month, and my granddaughter can come only during her winter vacation. I have too much free time, I read a lot... so this would be something to keep me busy. And I also saw that he was an interesting person, someone special. At first I couldn't figure out what was so special about him. He prayed all day long, all evening, at night, and then again in the morning. He brought a little icon back from Maria Sergeyevna, hung it in the corner, lit an oil lamp and kept it burning all the time. All this seemed strange to me: I couldn't understand it. I thought he was uneducated, perhaps a fanatic whose mind had been scarred by the hardship of camp. But then after I talked to him I realized he was not only very intelligent but also highly educated. I began watching him closely. Sometimes we had long talks and I would see before me a man of enormous knowledge, enormous culture. On top of all this there was something very special about him: he was highly spiritual, and had such a heart as I had never seen before. It took me about a month and a half to come to these conclusions.

"Looking at Father Arseny I noticed that he was still unused to freedom and that life in the camp still haunted him in all its frightening aspects. He did tell me that people would be coming to see him, but nobody did, not even once; he also received no letters nor did he write any. I later discovered that he had asked Maria Sergeyevna not to tell anyone of his whereabouts.

"For the first three weeks he didn't stir out of the house, but after that he started going out to sit on the little bench near the gate.

"I could easily understand his state of mind, because I myself and many of my friends who had spent time in these camps had been through similar experiences: some closed themselves off within themselves; others became frantically busy, but then got seriously depressed.

"I started talking to Father Arseny," said Nadezhda Petrovna later, "asking him about himself, telling him about myself; I asked his permission to join him while he was praying or serving; at these times he became an entirely different person; it struck me that I had never before seen anybody like that.

"I remember one evening, I had a terrible breakdown, I felt oppressed and extremely sad. My children Yuri and Sergei were constantly before my eyes, I thought of my husband and something dark crept into my soul. I wanted to throw myself on the floor and pound it with my head, crying, sobbing for all I had lost, lost for ever. Life seemed pointless and useless. What did I have to live for? What? I paced back and forth in my room, fell on my bed, bit my pillow, got up and cried, with the tears running all over my face. Who could help me? Who would answer for what had happened to me? Who?

"I was so miserable that I wanted to die. I remembered how children suffer in orphanages and the horror of having to say good-bye to my children when I was taken away and I seeing their eyes full of fear, begging me not to leave them, sobbing while the NKVD police were taking me away. Then there was the death of my husband, the interrogations, and my own life in camp; all this kept running through my mind with a terribly painful, terribly cruel precision. I would have liked to run somewhere and demand an answer to my question: "Why did this all happen?"

"I was alone in the house. Piotr Andreyevich, himself exhausted and out of touch with real life, couldn't help me, but there was nobody else around so, crying, I went to his room. A feeling of emptiness and anger possessed me and I walked in without even knocking. Piotr Andreyevich stood in the corner in front of the icon of the Mother of God; the oil lamp was flickering and he was praying out loud. I had walked in rudely, not knocking; he didn't even turn around. I stopped, and distinctly heard the words of his prayer being so clearly pronounced:

"'O my beloved Queen, my hope, O Mother of God, protector of orphans and protector of those who are hurt, the savior of those who perish and the consolation of all those who are in distress, you see my misery, you see my sorrow and my loneliness. Help me, I am powerless, give me strength. You know what I suffer, you know my grief—lend me your hand because who else can be my hope but you, my protector and my intercessor before God? I have sinned before you and before all people. Be my Mother, my consoler, my helper. Protect me and save me, chase grief away from me, chase my lowness of heart and my despondency. Help me, O Mother of my God!'

"Father Arseny finished praying, made the sign of the cross, knelt down, made several prostrations, said another prayer which I do not remember, and got up. I had stood there, holding on to the door jamb, sobbing loudly, my tears pouring profusely, and I could hear in my mind the words of his prayer to the Mother of God. I can say now that I remembered these words for the rest of my life; I could recall them instantly and forever as clearly as I heard them that day. When he was finished, through my sobbing I managed to say, "I feel terrible! Help me!"

"He asked me nothing, he pulled me away from the door and made me sit on a chair. Through my sobbing I started talking, at first in anger, then in irritation, and then finally I was at peace. My whole life, in all its minute detail, was in the front of my mind and I splashed it onto Father Arseny. I told him about myself, about my husband, my children, my grief, my suffering; I told him about my own life, my mistakes, my ambitions, my work. My past appeared naked in front of me in a completely new light. Telling about myself I saw other people, people whom I had made suffer, whom I had belittled and whose death I had perhaps caused. I saw everything in front of my eyes. The words of the prayer that I had just heard were invisibly present even while I was telling everything to Father Arseny, and shed light onto my path, onto my pain.

"I spoke for a long time, for several hours; Father Arseny, his hands on his desk, listened to me without moving, without interrupting me, without correcting what I was saying. When I had finished, I was amazed that I had been able to say all I did. Father Arseny stood up, went to the icon, checked the oil lamp, made the sign of the cross several times and started talking. He probably did not talk for long, but what he said made me understand my suffering in a new light, a way I had not seen before. I saw that I also had suffered because of all the deeds that I had done; I realized that other people had suffered because of what I had done, but that I hadn't thought of them, I had forgotten their pain. Why should I be better off than they were?

"Father Arseny said, 'It is good that you told me your whole life, because full openness is the beginning of the cleansing of human conscience. You will find yourself, Nadezhda Petrovna.' He blessed me three times. I didn't immediately become a believer, but I did understand that there was a great deal, a very great deal that I had pushed away from myself and had not found before; that is what I finally discovered with the help of God and Father Arseny.

"I first had to get used to him; then I got fond of him and saw in him a totally unusual man who carried within himself a deep spirituality, faith, and goodness towards others. I could never have imagined that the emaciated, exhausted man who came to me in his camp-issued cotton jacket would have such an influence on me and that I would become a believer—I who had refused God and persecuted other believers.

"This conversation brought us closer. Father Arseny felt less shy in front of me, he thawed, he got interested in what was going on around him, and by the end of the second month he had already written several letters and, probably three or four days after that, several people came. I must admit that these people looked somehow strange to me, but only at first; then I understood them and probably became just like they were. I befriended many of them and simply loved them.

"In five or six months I became Father Arseny's spiritual daughter, I went to confession to him," Nadezhda Petrovna said. "But there was one event which happened early on that had perhaps the biggest influence on me."

⁜

"My husband and I had a very close friend named Nikolai. He was arrested at the same time as my husband and was given the same verdict. In 1955 they let him out, rehabilitated him, and returned all his privileges.

"He was going to Kharkov for business once, with a stopover in Moscow, and decided to come and visit me. I hadn't seen him after camp; we had only corresponded. He came! I asked him about himself, told him about myself, why I was now living in this little town, and I told him about my children. He told me about his arrest, his stay in camp, the interrogations and he remembered who had denounced him with an invented case. He asked me about my daughter, and suddenly he asked, smiling: "Natalia, did you get remarried? When I hung my coat I saw a man's coat and hat. Whose are they?"

"I answered him abruptly, but then caught myself and said that I have a lodger, someone who knew my husband during his last year in camp. Nikolai asked, 'Who is he?' and I answered, 'A priest, Piotr Andreyevich Streltzoff; you cannot know him, because for the last four years you and Pavel were in different camps.'

"Nikolai jumped in his chair and shouted, 'What? Father Arseny! Here? Where is he?'

"He ran into Father Arseny's room and I heard him shout, 'Father Arseny! Father Arseny!'

"I walked into the room behind Nikolai and saw how he was embracing Father Arseny. To my enormous surprise, he was crying, saying, 'O Lord! What a joy to meet you again. I asked about you, looked for you through my friends, but nobody could tell me where you were. Please, give me a blessing, in the name of the Lord.'

"They sat down and started talking, forgetting all about me. I left, to make some tea. I was at the stove and I kept thinking, 'What could have happened to my Pavel and to Nikolai? Why are they both so crazy about Father Arseny?' I brought them tea; they didn't even touch it. In the evening Nikolai came back to see me. While he had been with Father Arseny I kept pondering. Yes, all right, Father Arseny is a very good man, but for Nikolai to ask for his blessing, this I couldn't understand.

"What they talked about for all that time, I did not know; only much later, a few years later, Nikolai told me that Father Arseny had heard his confession.

"When Nikolai walked in to talk to me again, he looked enlightened; for the first few minutes he said nothing, but after that he spoke to me for the rest of the night, and only about Father Arseny. At first this irritated me. He had come to see me; he hadn't seen me for years and then suddenly he goes and abandons me for hours on end. All right, Father Arseny is a good man, but Nikolai should not have left me, who had suffered so much... It really was inconsiderate. He could have waited and talked with Father Arseny later. So I said coldly, 'Listen, Nikolai! I can see for myself that Father Arseny is a very good man, but why would you respect him so much, why would you ask for his blessing, why would you leave me and run to see him? You haven't seen me in such a long time!'

"Nikolai looked at me with some surprise and started telling me about Father Arseny. He spoke for a long time and I began to see Piotr Andreyevich in another light.

"I remember him telling me, 'Camp, Nadia, showed me life in a new way: I began to see opinions, people, thoughts, events, even my own past—totally differently than I had ever seen them before. You know this just as well as I do, you were also in camp. When he is free a person is good, faithful, a real friend and you can trust him. The same person goes into a camp, and you see that he is self-centered, can inform on anyone, he can be a traitor—in a word, he is a scoundrel. He wouldn't even take pity on his own father and mother. We saw people like that, and it is thanks to such people that we spent so much time in those camps, and lost our loved ones in them.

"'This person, Father Arseny, Nadia, saved hundreds of people from suffering. How did he save them? By a good word, by care, by helping. You know as well as I do what moral support can mean when you are in camp. It is essential, even more essential than food.

"'In camp we all tried to regroup with people like ourselves: the party member with other party members, the educated person with other educated people, farmers with farmers, a thief with thieves, criminals with other criminals. If by some chance we were ready to help someone, we would only help people from our clique; and let's admit it, we didn't help often... Father Arseny helped everybody. For him good people and bad people did not exist; they were simply people who needed help. This is how he found me and your Pavel. We were desperate, we wanted to escape, and you know that this would have meant death for sure. We said nothing to anybody. The day before we were set to leave he came over to us and started talking to us.

"'Stunned, we looked at him. How could he know? We were puzzled. We felt scared. He convinced us not to attempt the impossible, but he did it so gently and with love. We agreed peacefully.

"'When I heard in the barracks that he was a priest, I started despising him, because he didn't look impressive. But after I had lived in the same barracks with him for a year or so, he had become a guiding light for me and for Pavel. Look at him carefully, Nadia, and you will end up asking for his blessing also!'

"The story Nikolai told me impressed me very much. By that time I myself had become attached to Father Arseny, but I had simply gotten upset and jealous because Nikolai had left me alone."

Notes of a Woman Named Tatiana

I WILL NOW be the one to tell the story of Father Arseny in Nadezhda Petrovna's house.

* * * *

The room that Nadezhda Petrovna gave to Father Arseny was large. The windows opened onto the garden, where there were apple trees, cherry trees, mountain ashes. The neighbor's garden was not visible, although in the winter you could see it a little through the bushes that had lost their leaves.

Early in the morning a rust-colored rooster would fly onto the fence and crow arrogantly. This was the time at which Father Arseny would get up and begin his morning prayers. Then he would go back to bed to get up at seven, at which time he would start serving until nine. From seven till nine all his spiritual children who were there would pray with him. Sometimes Nadezhda Petrovna would join them. After the service he would talk with those who had come, or he would write letters. Sometimes when he didn't feel well he would dictate his letters. He read many books about art and wrote articles.

Very many people came, yes, very many.

Vera Danilovna was one. Tall, white-haired and serious looking, she seemed unapproachable but was in fact an extremely good person. She was perhaps the closest friend Father Arseny had and was a spiritual daughter who had come to him very early in his life. She was a medical doctor, and almost all of us were her patients. Two other doctors also came; they were Ludmilla and Julia, who were the same age.

A beautiful woman named Irina, aged between 45 and 50 and also a doctor, came with her husband and children. They all looked after Father Arseny, took care of his health and sometimes succeeded in taking him to Moscow for a stay in a clinic. Father Arseny always protested that he didn't want to go, but the pressure was so great that he had to give in. At these times Nadezhda Petrovna would help gather his things together and Father Arseny would be "pushed out" of the house. When he was leaving, he would always say the same thing: "I am perfectly healthy, this is just your imagination..."

Irina was a very special person, gentle, feminine, unusually good-hearted. No one could ever have imagined that she was a famous doctor, a professor with an important chair at the university. I didn't know Irina's story, but I observed that Father Arseny seemed to respect her.

I remember the visits of the engineer Sazikov, who was handsome and elegantly dressed and who simply adored Father Arseny. He would walk with Father Arseny in the garden and talk. Sazikov was witty, clever and seemed cheerful, but he had a constant sorrow in his brown eyes. He came often. During one of his visits he talked to me, and told me that he had been in camp with Father Arseny and that he had been a thief, an infamous robber.

I was surprised and answered that he was probably joking, but Sazikov said "No, I am not joking. I am a former criminal whom Father Arseny removed from the criminal world." Sazikov looked like someone who was entirely absorbed in his faith and in his work. I hadn't known who he was or what kind of a person he was. Father Arseny taught us never to question anyone. Four years after we first met, I happened to meet Sazikov in Moscow and he became a regular visitor in our home, in our family. That was when he told me and my husband about his life.

✛

I remember another visitor, a man with white hair and a powerful face. He walked like a military man and had sharp eyes. He went directly to Father Arseny and silently greeted everyone who was in Nadezhda Petrovna's room.

Father Arseny welcomed everyone who came to see him with joy and cordiality, but this person he welcomed especially warmly and intimately. Who he was we did not know, and of course wouldn't ask anything about him.

One day Father Arseny called me in and said, "Meet Ivan Alexandrovich Abrosimov.[1] When I am gone, do not leave him."

I wanted to protest, but Father Arseny said insistently and clearly, "Do not leave him! Do not leave him! You, Ivan Alexandrovich, be friends with Tatiana, be a good friend. When I am gone, find another priest."

This is how we became acquainted with Ivan Alexandrovich.

✛

Alyosha came often, Alyosha—the student from camp. I don't have to talk about him; now we know him as Father Alexei who serves and takes care of the parish that used to be Father Arseny's.

---

1 Ivan Alexandrovich Abrosimov was the major who ruled the special camp for a while and passed on a letter to Father Arseny.

Still I cannot resist and I will write about our Father Alexei.

While Father Arseny was still alive the pleasant, radiant, blue-eyed Alyosha was his support and his hope. Gentle and good-hearted, he was responsive to people's suffering and gentle with everyone; he knew the services very well and prayed deeply. Who could have thought that Alexei would end up becoming the spiritual father of so many of us?

I remember how Sazikov met Abrosimov at Father Arseny's; I also remember how they met Alexei. These greeted each other in the special way that can exist only when there are deep bonds, much deeper than simple friendship; I don't know if even beloved brothers could meet the way they did. Sazikov and Abrosimov adored Alexei's son, Peter. They showered him with toys and other gifts.

Sometimes a farmer would come, sometimes a writer, or a poet, or another time a simple lathe operator would appear. Educated and sophisticated old ladies came, an old scientist with his wife came from Leningrad. Again sometimes the old and frail Bishop Jonah would stay a while; he was retired, but had retained a sharp mind and memory; he knew the services very well and specialized in Church History.

So many people came that it is impossible to write about each and all, but I do want to remember Nadezhda Petrovna, who helped so many of us, who saved so many of us and took care of us during the time Father Arseny was still in camp.

A passionate and impetuous woman, Nadezhda Petrovna was always very active. Once I watched her while she was talking to one of Father Arseny's spiritual daughters. I cannot remember now what they were talking about, but I kept looking at her hands. Her bony hand would form a fist, then would open again so that her fingers were drumming on the armrest of her chair; she drew designs on the table, pulled the tassels on the tablecloth—you could see that the nerves and tendons of her hand were joined with her thoughts and tried, by its movements, to clarify for the listener what she really meant and to convince him of what she considered to be the most important point. When the conversation became passionate, her hands would transmit the power of her thought, the fire in her soul. I couldn't hear her words, but could understand what she was saying, could guess what the argument was about and how important it was for her. Sometimes she would raise her hands to the sky—this meant the listener didn't understand her; gradually her hands became more calm and came to rest on the armchair, and I understood that the argument was over and that Nadezhda Petrovna had convinced her interlocutor.

People came in and out, wrote, received answers and carried away peace, faith, hope for something better and a piece of the soul of Father Arseny himself. I often observed that Father Arseny himself received something from each person who came and he awaited their return eagerly.

"Each person you encounter enriches you, brings you a piece of light and joy. Even if he brings you his grief you will find in everything the will of God. Seeing that person come to terms with his grief, you rejoice together with him. But there are some among my spiritual children who renew me every time I meet them. They are my light and my joy!"

Many times I prayed with Father Arseny. We stood in the twilit room. The oil lamps would be shining on the icons, Father Arseny would be serving. He read very clearly, you could hear each word; he would be entirely into his prayer and you, you who had just gotten off the train and were still carrying the bustle of the city with you, could slowly join in with him, forgetting everything around you, seeing only the icons of the Mother of God, and hearing only the words of the prayer. Somewhere inside you would light up with the joy of being united in the great mystery of God's service.

On his knees Father Arseny would quietly read the prayers for priests. Meanwhile peace and quiet would enter inside you and you would start to pray to God for His mercy towards you; you would ask Him for forgiveness for your sins; you would beg him to grant your petitions. The room no longer exists; you are in the middle of a church, where the oil lamps are lit, the holy faces of the icons of the Mother of God of Vladimir and of Kazan look at you as if embracing you in their forgiving mercy. Father Arseny leads you in the light-giving and warming light of prayer. To be able to pray with Father Arseny was always a great joy for all of us.

⁀

These recollections were written by T.P., who met Father Arseny in 1959 and feels that she does not have enough words to tell everything she should about Father Arseny.

We Meet Again

PIOTR AND I were almost the same age. He was one year older; we went to the same school, but were in different classes. We were just acquaintances, becoming good friends only in senior high school, after which we each went our own way. He went to Moscow University to study art and I went into engineering.

Piotr was always a very serious and very good man; he read avidly, loved art, theater, paintings, and music, but I never noticed any inclination towards religion. I lost track of him for a few years and only after I finished my studies did I find out that Piotr had graduated from University and written a book that was the result of his research. Then suddenly, a few years later I was told that he had become a monk and a priest, which utterly amazed me.

Madly in love, I got married, but a year later my wife left me and married a friend of mine. This was so sudden, so unexpected that I was losing my mind. I couldn't come to terms with what had happened to me; I considered suicide, I was casting about for help, and sometimes even took to drink.

I recalled the Church; I went to talk to a priest, but this didn't satisfy me. I remembered Piotr and decided to seek him out. I found out where he was serving, so I went and found the church; it wasn't big, but it was very old. I remember entering this church. I went in and stood to one side. Piotr was serving the liturgy; there were many people in attendance and praying, and most of them were intellectuals.

The liturgy came to an end. Everybody went up to kiss the cross and receive a blessing and I saw that they all kissed Piotr's hand and that he spoke with love to almost all of them. This all seemed strange to me because I wasn't used to it, and it also was hard for me to connect all this with the Piotr I knew.

Having blessed everybody he went back into the altar. A few minutes later he came out again in his cassock, having removed his vestments, and came directly over to me; it felt as if he'd known all along that I was standing there.

There were still many people in the church. That morning I'd had a drink, and it probably showed on my breath so that people avoided me, but I didn't care.

"What's happened?" asked Piotr.

This question (and the fact that he was sure that I was in this church because something terrible had happened to me) irritated me and I answered, "Nothing, I am here by pure chance." The answer was obviously clumsy and foolish.

113

Piotr did not leave me. He asked somebody to call Father Ioan, another priest who was in this church, and told him, "Father Ioan! Would you please serve the prayer service? I can't today." And turning to me, he said, "Let us go to my house."

He lived close by. We walked in silence. As soon as we were in his house I told him everything; he did not even have to ask me; my grief, my pain just poured out of me. I spoke and sobbed, maybe partially because I wasn't sober.

Father Arseny—I knew by then that he was not Piotr any more—listened to me; he did not interrupt me nor did he attempt to console me. People walked in as I was talking and tried to speak to him, but Father Arseny told them that he was busy.

When I finished my long and confused story, Father Arseny simply and casually said, "You are guilty of this. You pushed your wife away; you forgot her soul, her ambitions, her desires." He spoke for a very short time and all of a sudden I was embarrassed because of his words; it was as if a curtain had fallen from my eyes—I suddenly understood things I hadn't noticed before, hadn't wanted to notice, and I was almost relieved. I stayed with him for three days and left in peace. I had found God, the faith and the church.

Since then, my old-time friend has become my spiritual father and my advisor.

Years have passed and my life has changed; I got remarried, I loved my new wife, I received honorary titles and was successful, more successful than I really deserved, but whenever I came to see Father Arseny, I always felt like a young, inexperienced student before a renowned, white-haired professor. And at the same time he was my best friend.

Camp and exile tore him away from us, but he was always present in our hearts. When we discovered after his stay in the special camp that he was in the little town of R., I went regularly to visit him and I would like here to tell about these visits.

✤

Today I am going to see Father Arseny; as always I am restless and excited. I look forward to this meeting with enormous joy.

The train is just drawing near the station, so I get up to be the first out of the train. The little station is busy and noisy. People are carrying heavy suitcases, bags, packages, and baskets full of edibles bought in Moscow. I believe I am the only one carrying just a briefcase containing a few books and some candies which Nadezhda Petrovna had asked me to bring.

The little town is clean, cozy and cheerful. The cupolas on the churches are not in repair but rather consciously neglected and add to the charm of this little town, giving it a fairy-tale-like appearance.

I left the station and hurried to Father Arseny. The morning air was cool, the wind-borne smell of the distant forest and fields gave me a special feeling of energy and joy. I walked, a little anxious, expecting something mysterious and joyous. I knew this meeting would bring me something new and would force me to live a better life.

Here is his street, a familiar and pleasant street. The little house where Father Arseny lives is now my main goal, the source from where I will carry away the "water of life" without which there is no faith, no hope and no human love.

The windows are shining, visible behind some trees. Light white curtains gave the house a mysterious and attractive appearance, so cozy that you can hardly wait to go in. At the same time I am sometimes afraid to walk through the door, because I carry doubts within myself as to the virtue of my actions.

Here is the gate with its big iron ring held by a lion, a miracle executed by our blacksmiths. I open the gate and walk up a little path strewn with river sand. I ring the bell, open the gate, it squeaks in its familiar way, and I smell the sweet scent of fallen leaves, dead grass, and warm earth. The mountain ashes planted along the fence bear red clusters of berries which hang in the air, and it seems that I am no longer in the small town where I had just arrived twenty minutes ago by a modern train, but that I had wandered into the charming and unusual kingdom of a long-awaited joy.

I take the few steps up the path, stop at the door, and wait for Nadezhda Petrovna to open it. I hear her steps, I hear her talking to her cat who is always right under her feet so that she is afraid of stepping on him. The door opens, Nadezhda Petrovna's face is stern, but she immediately lights up with a smile and welcomes me warmly. I walk in, take my coat off, so happy in anticipation of my meeting with Father Arseny; I am excited and joyous. I keep thinking: now I am going to see the person who is the closest to me in the whole world, and in a few minutes I will confide in him all my doubts, my sins, my thoughts, my dreams. No one, no one is closer to me than Father Arseny; and in spite of this I am tense.

If when I arrive somebody is with Father Arseny in his room, I wait, sometimes for quite a long time. If he is alone, Nadezhda Petrovna knocks gently at his door and tells him that I have come; then in a few seconds the door opens and he, my Father Arseny, walks toward me, joyous and full of light. I ask for his blessing, then we hug and kiss each other several times. We sit and he asks me about Moscow, about the friends and acquaintances we have in common, about newly published books, and about the news, mainly connected with the state of the Church. He asks question after question and I answer. Sometimes when he hears something funny, he laughs contagiously.

We talk, and I look around at the familiar room, the familiar sofa and the desk with its armchair, the icons of the Mother of God in the corner, the oil lamps lit. I see familiar portraits on the walls and many books—books everywhere: on shelves, on his desk and on the floor. Everything is as usual, and at the same time it is always new, beloved, precious, in spite of the fact that I have seen it all dozens of times.

I share with him all my news and then am silent. No, no, there is more to tell, but I am afraid I will tire Father Arseny, I will take too much of his time. He is silent and looks intensely at me and at somewhere above me. This look of his makes me uncomfortable. I begin to see all that has happened to me lately; and mainly I see my bad deeds.

At this particular moment Father Arseny would say to me, "Why? Why did you hurt this man? You and I are both Christians, we must not act this way!"

I had been expecting him to say these words and that is why I was anxious when I was on my way to him, because I was ashamed of my deeds: I did what he had taught me never to do. I began to tell him what had happened, trying to find excuses for my actions, to find reasons for acting that way, but as I listened to myself I understood that I was in the wrong.

When the time came for my confession, I felt embarrassed. Father Arseny became almost angry, his eyes darkened. I wished the ground would open and swallow me up because I realized how awful and sinful I had been. We prayed for a long time together. He prayed very easily, very lightly; praying with him was always cleansing, elevating and uplifting. He was teaching me, showing me the right path of faith, and he never ceased to be my closest friend to whom I could tell anything and, of course, about the most important thing: faith and the way of life of a believer.

He told me much about his own life, about himself, about people he had met and who had left him enriched somehow. This taught him to love every one, to pray to God. Father Arseny loved people unconditionally, seeing in each the image of God.

After my confession we would sit and talk; from these talks I would draw knowledge of the faith and found in them spiritual strength and guidance.

Renewed, I left him and lived from one meeting to another by the advice he gave me. I had a feeling that he was so remarkably caring and thoughtful only with me, but of course this was a naive thing to think!

So many of his spiritual children and so many of his friends came. With each of them he was as loving and attentive as he was with me. Each one felt that surely Father Arseny was his own very special friend. Much was said about Father Arseny. People recounted miracles that had happened to him. I remember that once, during one of our conversations I asked him about these miracles.

He grew sad, and becoming pensive, he said, "Miraculous? Miracles? No, nothing ever happened to me that could be called a miracle. Every priest—hearing the confessions of so many people, giving communion and accompanying the dying, guiding his spiritual children—every priest has remarkable spiritual experiences. The same things can happen to lay people, to any believer, but very often we cannot see the magnitude of what is happening and do not see the will of God, His hand, His providence, His leadership. Yes, what happened to me and what I saw around me shook me up, made me tremble so that I clearly saw the will of God. I didn't stop to think whether it was a miracle or simply the result of amazing coincidences in my life. I have always believed and I still firmly believe that God brings us to everything that happens and therefore whatever way we take, we must recognize only His will in everything.

"And it is only by understanding things in this way that a man can see the will of God. Many events in which I participated amazed me and I said to myself, 'but this is a miracle.' But then when I realized my own nothingness I understood that it is not for me to see a miracle.

"Everything in life is a miracle: the main miracle is that by the will of God man lives on earth. Believe in this!"

I saw that my question had disturbed Father Arseny. Another time I asked him, "Father Arseny! We, your spiritual children, often talk about the fact that spiritual fathers frequently have the gift of prophecy or mind-reading, and I am sorry to say we talk about the fact that we think you have this gift as well, and..."

Father Arseny interrupted me sharply saying, "Don't continue! You don't know what real prophecy or mind-reading is. A priest who deals constantly with people, hears their pains, their difficulties and their joys naturally knows the human soul. If he is sincere in his love for his children, if he remembers what he knows about them he unwillingly begins to notice and to observe each movement of their souls, because he knows them and because he is in constant contact with them.

"Take the mother of a small child, she sees and notices all his actions and she can foresee what he is going to think or do because he is her child and she loves him. In this same way a priest notices everything in the person who comes to him, and therefore can tell what that person wanted to say. All this isn't prophecy or mind reading; it is a kind of spiritual observation which is common to many. True prophecy and mind reading is given by God to a few chosen people, people like Father John of Kronstadt, but certainly not to us sinful people. Let us stop this conversation, it is useless," said Father Arseny.

I always left Father Arseny peaceful and joyous, but it was always difficult for me to say goodbye. During the several days I would spend there, the house, the street and the little town would become my own and Father Arseny's room would be like a monastery. But I had to leave. I would hug him and he would give me his blessing; I always knew I was losing something, but I always lived in anticipation of our next meeting.

Letters: Excerpts from the Memoirs of O.S.

I CAME OFTEN and stayed near him for long stretches of time, so I came to know his way of life well.

Father Arseny received very many letters. These brought him people's joys, their tribulations, sufferings, longings, grief, passionate cries for help, heartaches, their doubts and their deep faith. In each letter lived a person; his soul was reflected in it. Some people opened up their lives to him completely, some preferred to find excuses for themselves, some tried to open up their souls in phrases and unfinished sentences, others only reminded Father Arseny about themselves, sure as they were that he knew what worried them and what they should start doing from now on.

These letters almost never came in the mail; most of them were sent to friends in Moscow who in turn entrusted the letters to Nadezhda Petrovna when they came to visit Father Arseny. Letters came from different towns, as many of Father Arseny's friends had spent time in camp with him and were scattered all over Russia after they had been set free. Each and every letter was read attentively; each sender knew for certain that he would receive an answer, an answer on which he depended to determine the direction of his life.

I often observed that while he was reading a letter Father Arseny would embrace in his inner sight everything he knew of the life of the person who had written to him. This person would become present in Father Arseny's room, stand next to him and continue to tell about himself even events that he had not written about in his letter. Having read the letter Father Arseny would be pensive and centered, sitting at his desk, sometimes looking at the branches of trees swaying outside his window. It seemed he was listening to the author of the letter telling him what was on his mind.

With his mind cut off from the rest of the world, Father Arseny would write his answers; sometimes crossing himself, he would pray sitting in his armchair and then go on writing.

For Father Arseny there were no "ordinary" letters; every one of them was important, and he saw behind each a suffering and worried person.

Sometimes Father Arseny would make several attempts at starting an answer—he would put the letter away, then pick it up again—you could see that he was worried or in doubt. Sometimes he would sit thinking and praying for a long time. The room would be lit by the oil lamps which stood before the icons, and by his desk lamp which tore out a circle of light from the darkness of the room; the light would fall on the unfinished letter. Father Arseny wouldn't notice it when somebody entered the room, so absorbed was he in the person he was writing to. He would pray for that person, begging God to send him or her His help, and all of a sudden Father Arseny's face would light up. He would get up, stand before his icons, bless himself several times, and then sit and just finish the letter that had come together for him.

Through his love for his spiritual children he would obtain from God and the Mother of God help for them. You cannot count the hours, the sleepless nights he spent praying for all of us. He was rich in love: there was enough of it for all who came to him. But this love did not come easily to him. It was through his years of work, prayer, difficulties in camp, imitation of the Fathers of the Church, and the advice and experience of people of deep faith that Father Arseny obtained the all-encompassing gift of love for people! The grace of the Lord was with him!

Once I came in as Father Arseny was writing a letter. It was obvious that the letter did not come together as he wished. He blessed me and said, "Forgive me, I cannot talk now, I am upset! God is punishing me: I am unable to write this letter, and I must. Please wait!" He started praying. I sat in an armchair. He prayed for a long time. When he stopped, he sat down and started writing. He wrote one page, then put his pen down.

I had been dreaming or had fallen asleep and awoke to his words: "There is sometimes a duality within me. The man and the priest go different ways, and this must not be. For instance, now my duty as a priest dictates one thing, my human feelings another. The way of a person is difficult and multifaceted. To understand oneself, to evaluate one's own strength is a difficult task and not everyone can undertake it successfully. It is my duty as a spiritual father to weigh what this person is able to do and show at the right time what he or she has to do. If the spiritual father makes a mistake the person is lost, and his soul is lost. To reason or to trust in his own judgment is detrimental to the spiritual father; it is not permissible. He has to trust only the will of God which he can find in prayer and only in prayer.

"For example I just received a letter from a very good man who has led a complicated and beautiful life and who has won many a battle within himself; he is now begging me to give him my blessing to become a priest. But the life of a priest, a real priest, was always difficult, and now it is even more so. Some people think that it means only serving in Church, but no; it is an extremely difficult and all-encompassing way of life. You have to forget yourself completely and give yourself to others. You must take upon yourself the souls of hundreds of people and lead them. Not everyone is strong enough to undertake this way of life. Many people think being a priest is an easy profession. Yes, it is easy if you do not give yourself to others, but it is extremely difficult if you do. It is painful for me to write this man not to become a priest: he longs for it, but it is not for him. He will do more good for people if he does not become a priest. People around him, seeing what a good person he is, push him to become a priest." Father Arseny turned away from me and said, looking at the icons, "I trust, Lord, You will help this man, I trust!" he started to pray.

I remember that some letters brought him joy; he would thank God for them. Sometimes the joy was almost childlike, he would then thank God and the Mother of God profusely.

I myself used to write to Father Arseny very often, sharing with him many useless details of my life, and it was only when I saw for myself how seriously he looked at everything we wrote him did I see how inconsiderate I had been in burdening him with my trivia.

In his answers Father Arseny would pour out his soul, he would tear out a piece of his soul and give it to the other. It happened sometimes that when you received a letter from him you would suddenly realize something about yourself that you had been unaware of. You would be shocked and frightened to be made aware of something that hadn't been clear even to yourself; you hadn't talked to any one about it or you had only sporadically thought about it, or sometimes you had tried to hide it from yourself. Suddenly, his advice would appear to be the only right decision.

Father Arseny never forced his spiritual children to follow his advice. He would gently make a suggestion and then wait for the person to come to his or her own decision. He had a vast memory. He remembered everything each had told him, he remembered their addresses. If somebody did not write for a while, he would worry and himself would write.

I was a witness to the fact that sometimes during the liturgy that he celebrated in his room, he would pray spontaneously for the departed servant of God Sergei, or for the health of the servant of God Antonina. A few days later he would receive a letter that a Sergei Georgievich had died, or an Antonina would appear and tell us she had been very ill. What was this? Was it intuition or was it knowledge of what had happened? We never dared ask Father Arseny about this, but this did in truth happen.

When you would come to confession and start to tell about yourself, he would sometimes interrupt and finish your sentence for you, or he would answer the question you had not even asked yet or tell you his opinion about your actions. Sometimes I would just come into his room and he would greet me saying, "I did not expect you would have an argument with your brother because of your mother, I did not expect this! You are closer to your mother than he is, you are the one who must be understanding." I would just remain standing in front of him, wishing the floor would open and swallow me up, I was so ashamed.

Many of us noticed that Father Arseny was particularly attached to the people he had met in camp. I told him about it once, and he answered, "You are right. I am very attached to many of them. In camp, I saw people in a different light, and I saw the mercy of God in them, I saw things I had never seen when I was free.

"Everything there is naked, acute in the extreme, people's suffering is at its limit, you yourself are condemned to die, each person knows this. And during such a time of lengthy and painful deterioration it is extremely difficult to summon up any faith, or any desire to help others. But such people did exist, I met many of them and they never ceased to amaze me. They were my guides in finding God under awful circumstances; they showed me a powerful faith and a love for His people. These are the people who saved me from spiritual death; they kept me from doubt and despondency and gave me the ability to stay spiritually alive in camp, and they taught me how to pray in the midst of swearing, fighting, and talking. Yes, I am extremely grateful to my friends from camp, and I am grateful to God and to the Mother of God for having sent them to me. Every time I see them, I remember what they gave me, what they did for me and for so many others. They did it all in the name of God and man. I am eternally indebted to them; this is why I feel so attached to them."

He said all this and then sank into his thoughts; meanwhile I was thinking about Father Arseny in camp and about the number of people whom he himself had helped and brought to faith.

In the last year of his life, when Father Arseny was too weak to write himself, I would read to him the letters he received and write the answers he dictated to me. I could not but wonder at his wisdom. It would sometimes seem to me that the answers didn't mesh with the questions expressed in the letters. Several times I even told this to Father Arseny. He would falter and be unable to dictate any more, so that we had to put the letter away for a while. I understood later that I was the one who had been mistaken; in the letters Father Arseny later received, the same people he had written to would thank him for the precious advice he gave them, in spite of the fact that this was not the advice they had asked for. Yes, this is when I truly saw how wise and how insightful he was, and how well he knew and understood human nature.

He was extremely gentle in his ways with people, but absolutely firm in his own chosen way of life. Prayer and living for others were the foundation of his spiritual task.

Returning from the Past

FATHER ARSENY'S HEALTH and his strength came back to him very gradually. Even after three years of freedom Father Arseny hadn't changed much. Rather tall and thin, and always standing straight, he gave the impression of being healthy; his attentiveness and cordiality towards whomever he was talking with made one forget that he was a sick person and that he was tired.

His eyes would only look sad sometimes and it seemed that the grief and suffering of many were still with him. We all knew that he never forgot anyone he had met. Back in the camp of the special regime he had paid no attention to his own illness although he had probably suffered more than most. Here, in freedom, his illnesses became more evident: rheumatism in his joints and sudden attacks of tachycardia sometimes forced Father Arseny to stay in bed for a while. But this did not change his way of life. Even lying in bed he would talk with his visitors. Only the attentive eyes of the doctor Irina could discern his illnesses. Paying no heed to his objections, she forced him to stay in bed. Many visitors came every day and even more on holidays, so that Father Arseny wouldn't have enough time for prayer. Since he couldn't live without it he would pray at night, thus shortening the hours reserved for his sleep.

His friends loved him, but when they came to see him or wrote pages and pages to him, each of them thought that he was the only one to do so. All this resulted in an enormous load on Father Arseny, so that although we loved him, it's possible that we were unintentionally destroying him.

✚

Sometimes it was necessary for him to travel to another town to see one of his spiritual children.

At the end of 1960 Father Arseny decided to go to Leningrad to find the two people whose addresses had been given to him by the dying Monk Mihail. I went with him. We arrived in Leningrad very early in the morning, and since Father Arseny didn't want to stop at some friends' to rest, he went directly from the railroad station to the address he had. I begged him not to do this; he didn't even know if these people still lived at this address. When I offered to go myself to check if they did, he answered, "There would be no point, let's go. They do live there."

We got off the train and as always in a new town things felt unfamiliar and seemed complicated. He refused to take a taxi, found out where the bus stop was and pulled me there. We rode in silence. Father Arseny looked very attentively at the streets, at the people, at the houses. We got off in the middle of the Nevski Prospect and took a cross street. The building where we came to a stop was big, about six stories high, with two impressive entrances. One of them was flanked by large bronze plaques inscribed with names—a sign that at some period or other it had been occupied by important scientists or professors. We took the elevator to the fourth floor. The door bore a plaque with the name of the person we were looking for. I rang the bell.

The door opened and a woman about 45 years old asked, "Who are you looking for?" Father Arseny gave the last name, the first name and the patronymic of the owner of the apartment.

Wiping her hands on her apron, the woman said very kindly, "Please come in," and we entered the vestibule. "Wait just a moment, please. He will be with you in a minute." She opened a door that stood ajar and said, "Sergei Sergeyevich! There is somebody here for you!" Almost immediately a man came out. He was tall, with a handsome, refined face and a black beard. His big black eyes were strikingly lively and attentive. He looked at us and said, "How can I help you?"

"I am here with a message," answered Father Arseny.

He answered "I am very pleased, so pleased. Do take off your coats."

We squeezed our coats into an already full armoire and entered the large room out of which Sergei Sergeyevich had just appeared.

An enormous desk near the window occupied about one quarter of the room. Antique furniture stood along the walls. The walls were covered with beautiful paintings mixed in with antique icons. Heavy shelves were loaded with books. There were books everywhere—on the desk, and even on some of the armchairs. In the middle of the room stood a table covered with a white tablecloth. This whole room ended up imprinted on my memory and made evident what kind of a person the owner was.

"So, what can I do for you?" Sergei Sergeyevich asked again and asked us to sit down. The woman who had opened the door for us was also in the room and stood next to the desk.

"In 1952, God gave me the opportunity to meet a man named Mihail Terpugov. I met him in a special regime camp from which I was set free only in 1957. In the course of his confession Mihail gave me your name and address and asked me to be sure to see you; he said that it would be indispensable for you and for me. He asked me to ask you not to forget him in your prayers and he also wanted me to tell you about his last minutes on this earth."

Sergei Sergeyevich almost leapt from his chair; he tensed up, his eyes became even darker than before, and he was clearly worried. He looked at Father Arseny for a few minutes, then he suddenly rose, saying icily, "I apologize, but you have made a mistake. I am not the one you want, you want to see someone else. You probably have the wrong address!"

The woman who stood next to the table took a step forward and almost moaning, tearfully said, "Sergei!"

"Let it be, Liza; they are mistaken. They have come to the wrong address. I am sorry! I cannot ask you to stay! There has been some mistake. . . ." He was speaking in a distraught way. We rose and hurriedly started to leave. No one spoke. I put on my coat and gave Father Arseny his. The woman had stayed in the room, but then she ran up to Father Arseny, took him by the arm and said, "Tell me who you are! What is your name?"

"Piotr Andreyevich Streltzoff—Hieromonk Arseny," he also said my name. "We came from R. especially to see you!"

"Wait, don't leave, come back and sit down! Wait 20 minutes. Sergei, don't get angry!" The woman rushed out of the room and started telephoning someone.

We were still standing in the vestibule, uncertain what to do. From within the room we could hear the woman's voice. "It's me—Liza! I beg you, drop everything and come over here immediately. It is urgent. You will understand everything, you will help us!"

Sergei Sergeyevich looked absentmindedly away and sat down at his desk. The woman ran into the kitchen and five minutes later reappeared with a teapot, cups and some cookies. For a while we were all silent, so that the atmosphere was embarrassing and heavy. In an attempt at being casual I started talking about the paintings on the walls. Sergei Sergeyevich made an obvious effort and naming the artists told us about two or three of the paintings. Meanwhile Father Arseny got up and walked over to an icon of the Mother of God. He looked at it for a long time and said, "An excellent icon, such art and such spirituality—such a combination of the human and the divine in the face of the Mother of God you only seldom encounter."

"Sergei also likes this icon, but he cannot determine for sure when it was painted. Do you know anything about icons?"

"I know a little," answered Father Arseny. He came over to the icon once again and studied it carefully. "May I take it off the wall? I would like to hold it in my hands," he asked Sergei Sergeyevich who, looking unhappy with the request, took it off the wall himself and started showing it to Father Arseny. Father Arseny wanted to take the icon in his hands, but Sergei Sergeyevich took a step back, obviously not wanting a stranger to touch his treasure. But, after a close look at Father Arseny, he handed the icon to him with tremendous care.

The woman and I looked at Father Arseny in great surprise. His hands, the bent of his head and his whole appearance were so prayerful that it was as if he had been handed a chalice with the body and the blood of Christ, and of course Sergei Sergeyevich also saw this.

Holding the icon in his hands Father Arseny went over to the window. He looked at it with care and attention. His look was utterly serious and prayerful and it rested a long time on the image. He looked at the face in the daylight, and then he slowly turned it over and studied the way the board had been reinforced. He did not return the icon to Sergei Sergeyevich, but carefully laid it on the table.

The light from the window fell onto the white tablecloth and onto the icon. I almost cried out—so amazingly beautiful did the face of the Mother of God appear in the sunlight. Where it had hung on the wall you could not see this. In the arms of His Mother, the Son sat freely while she pressed Him against herself and looked at her child with eyes filled with tenderness and love. At the same time, you could read in her eyes a deep sadness, because she knew the destiny of her Son; she knew what she had to raise Him for. She knew that death on the Cross awaited him. It seemed that maternal love and divine knowledge came together in her with the life of her Son and His future suffering. Her face was full of motherly joy, and at the same time, of sorrow.

Father Arseny was silent while Sergei Sergeyevich looked at the icon in a state of ecstasy. He had never seen it in such a way.

The tender golden thread running in the dress of the Mother and of the Child underlined and augmented the impression of beauty and unearthly glory. There was mercy in the soft half-smile of the Mother. It said, "Come to me all who labor and are heavy laden and I will give you rest" (Matthew 11:28).

Tearing my eyes away from the icon, I looked at Sergei Sergeyevich. He was stunned, looking at the icon and seeing what he had never seen before. He slowly raised his head to look at Father Arseny and I understood then that he trusted in him and really wanted him to be the man who had known Mihail.

Father Arseny had straightened up, and looking at the icon he said, "Is it really so important to know when this icon was painted and by whom? This sort of thing is only important for art historians. Just look at the faces of the child and the Mother of God and, if you are a believer, you will understand that a man could not have painted such an icon without the help of God. Just look!

"When was it painted? In the beginning of the seventeenth century. Where? Who was its iconographer? God alone knows, the God who inspired the artist. The board is very old and has been painted over many times, one icon on top of the other. This last icon was restored, but a very long time ago. All this is totally unimportant, because the spirit of God lives in this icon. Look! What peace radiates from the faces of both the Mother and the Son. The icon painter was full of love and faith in Christ, so that he increased his talent by faith and love. That is why the face of the Mother is so spiritual and so real that it consoles all who are oppressed by sorrow and sadness, those who are deprived, naked, orphaned, imprisoned, those who have almost lost faith in human justice, those who are weak. It gives life to such people, it restores their hope, it reminds them that there exists another life, free from horror and fear, from blood and the evil of this world. The face of the Mother calls us and gives us the hope of salvation."

The door bell rang in the vestibule. Elizaveta Andreyevna (as she was later introduced to us by Sergei Sergeyevich) ran to open the door. We could hear whispering in the hallway. Two women were talking and one of them was taking her coat off. Sergei Sergeyevich was tense and you could see that it would be a tragedy for him to find out that Father Arseny wasn't the man he said he was.

The door opened and Elizaveta Andreyevna walked in followed by another woman, who ran to Father Arseny, saying, "Father Arseny! Father Arseny! How wonderful it is that you have come. My God, why didn't you announce your arrival? Liza says that Sergei Sergeyevich thought you were an agent. I had been telling Liza about you, and thank God she thought of calling me. I have wanted to bring them both to meet you for a long time! This is remarkable! Please give me your blessing."

Everything changed immediately. Father Arseny stayed at Sergei Sergeyevich's for four days. I found Mihail's second friend and he also came to meet Father Arseny.

On the way back home Father Arseny said to me, "The ways of God are mysterious! How much beauty this meeting has given me, it gave me so much of what I needed." After that, for many years I would see Sergei Sergeyevich and Liza and the other friend of Mihail visiting Father Arseny.

1967

I Remember

I REMEMBER! YES, I will never forget the "special camp." Even now, many years later, life in camp is still vividly present in my memory. I remember every minute detail, and at night I have recurrent nightmares about it.

My arrest; the numerous interrogations with tortures; the prison cell; the long trek to the camp, on foot surrounded by guards armed with sub machine-guns and trained dogs, in a freezing autumn rain, hearing the constant shouts: "Two steps to the side and you'll be shot without warning!" All this was terrifying, but there was hope that when we got to camp, life would be easier. Finally we got to this long-dreaded camp, and only then did I understand that all I had lived through until then was nothing compared to what I had to live here, in this camp. Eight months in this "special camp" proved to be an unbearable ordeal for me.

It is night and the barracks are locked. Along the rows of bunks you can see electric bulbs that barely give out any light at all. It is dusk and sometimes through the windows blocked by snow you can see the passage of the searchlights. Outside it's freezing, -50° F, and the wind is hitting the windows and moaning in so many different tones. Although many people are in the barracks, you are alone, absolutely alone. You are a stranger to all, and everybody is a stranger to you. An endless night surrounds you. Sounds disappear and a dead silence stands next to you and a hopeless horror doesn't leave you all night. In their sleep some prisoners scream, others moan, still others swear, but all this makes the silence even more tragic—so that you feel separated from life itself. Sometimes you feel that it would be possible to touch the silence around you with your hands, a silence that sticks to your thoughts and surrounds them with despair and fear. The past day was an awful memory; death was always so near: death accompanied by beatings, degradation, hunger and destruction of the human soul.

"You rotten nothing, I will send you to the punishment cell! I'll have you shot," screamed the guards with angry faces. "I'm going to kill you! I'm going to strangle you," screamed the criminals. We all knew that these were not just threats but real deeds that happened all the time before our eyes. You never really rested during the night, because the night was in fact exhausting and depressing and made you suffer even more than the day that had just gone by. You never knew when your stay in this camp would end. As soon as you seemed close to freedom, you got a few years added to your time, for no reason at all.

At one point I was transferred to another barracks. On the fourth day of my stay there, I noticed while going to the latrine a man who was continually standing by his bunk. What was he doing standing all night? People said he was praying. Sometimes criminals going past him made fun of him.

We have to die here anyway. Why is he praying? What for? When I was still free I had heard that some people believed in God and that they got exiled for resisting the authorities. In my own family, religion and superstition were considered a sign of a lack of culture and intelligence. What could faith give to anyone? And what is there to believe in here, in a camp where everyone must die? Despair took hold of me, so that I decided to commit suicide. I was already considered dead by my family: when they inquired about me in Moscow I knew the answer must have been, "He is not on our lists." My decision was made. I want to die not when the guards or the criminals so decide, or when hunger or cold become unbearable. I want to die now. I have suffered enough—I am going to put an end to it all. Is this cowardice? No, it is a necessity. When there is hope, it is possible to fight for life. Here in this camp there is no hope—only the certainty of a martyr's death. One night I walk to the latrines, and nearby I see a beam that had been used by many others for the same purpose. I steal a piece of rope which I carry on my own body. Let me end things quickly. I will not live any longer—this is what I want.

As I walk amidst the bunks, I pass the old man. There he is, standing and praying as usual. Everybody else is sleeping. The old man does not seem to notice me, he is so deeply in prayer. I want to pass him quickly and end everything. As I am walking, suddenly the old man turns around and walks with me along the bunks. He takes me by the arm and says, "Sit down! You are not alone here. There are many of us who feel the way you do, but God is with us!"

I sit and he talks to me in a whisper, calmly, deeply and with love. I listen to the old man and I find myself unexpectedly answering him. At this point I hate him, because he is in my way and what I decide to do with my life is none of his business. He starts talking about my life and he knows it in such detail that it scares me. How does he know it all?

He is calm; yes, he understands that it's hard for me. I am sick, exhausted, hurt, despised, hungry. Yet all this can be vanquished—must be vanquished—and, if I so choose, victory will be mine.

I am very angry and I want to hurt him. I tell him unpleasant things about himself and try to leave—he holds on to my arm and continues to speak. I interrupt him, but he keeps talking quietly and peacefully. He tells me that man has no right to destroy his own life and must fight to keep it. I begin to listen to the old man and also to understand that in some mysterious way he is already helping me. Nothing has really changed for me, but I am not alone any more.

He doesn't push his God on me, but only mentions Him. At this point the old man simply helps me. I feel that he has some special inner power which I don't have. I feel that this man takes upon himself all my desperate grief and all the heaviness of my life in this camp. He will bear everything together with me. And I do not go to the beam as I had intended and remain with him forever. It is only later that I find out that he isn't really old at all, but has simply lived in this camp for a few years. Some people call him "Piotr Andreyevich" while others call him "Father Arseny." I will never forget this name or this image of him and his life.

Father Arseny opened up a new life for me, he brought me to God, and he recreated my inner self. This is why now I want to say what is essential about him. One can talk about him endlessly, because his deeds have no limits, and these deeds boil down to *God* and *love*—the love he feels for people in the name of the Lord. I remember his words: "Before dying, each person must leave something behind, must leave a trace of some kind. Be it a house built with his own hands, or a tree he has planted, or a book he has written—but whatever it is it must have been done not for himself but for other people. Whatever your hands have created will be the mark you leave after your death. People will look at what you have made, or at what you have planted and you will live again in bringing them joy, and they will remember you and ask the Lord to bless you. What you make is not the important thing, but what is important is that what you have fashioned becomes better than what it was before. It will contain a spark of yours, if you have made it in the name of God and of love for others. "The most important thing," said Father Arseny, "is to help others, alleviate their sufferings, and pray for them."

This is how Father Arseny lived, and this is what he taught all those who came to him. He gave away what was most precious to him: the warmth of his soul, his faith, and his experience in living his faith. He taught us how to pray and transformed into fire the spark of God in each of us. How can anyone who knew him forget his deeds? So many came to him and carried away with them all of this, so much joy and peace did we take from Father Arseny.

I experienced all this myself. I saw it and I saw how people were changed, renewed and strengthened. They left as believers and carried away with them the warmth they had taken from him. Remembering what had happened to me and seeing what I myself had become, I was able to pass on to others the light of faith, the love and goodness I had received from Father Arseny.

Many people who had lived alongside him died, but didn't leave this world angry or desperate, but instead illumined and lit by faith in God, and their awful life in camp didn't appear like an unfair suffering to them but like a kind of unavoidable test, a way towards God.

Often these same people, before leaving this life, had a chance in their turn to give light to others around them. If people met Father Arseny on their deathbed, he was able to alleviate their suffering so that they passed away peacefully into another life. The gift Father Arseny received from God and which he multiplied through his works was one he shared so generously with others. He never became poor because of it, but on the contrary he only became richer without knowing it. When he spoke to you, you realized that he knew more about you than you did yourself. He knew what awaited you. His eyes were attentive and gentle. Looking into his eyes you acquired strength and peace; when he spoke, his voice was so convincing that you trusted him and just knew that he was right.

He was courageous and strong in everything, he wasn't afraid of anything. God, God and only God was his strength, his refuge and his hope. Strong in this he stood strong amidst all difficulties and all sufferings.

When he had become a monk he was given the name Arseny. Arseny means "courageous." What an appropriate name.

I was freed from camp a few years before he was, and wrote to him always. When he was freed I searched everywhere for him and met him again at last in the small town where he lived.

The little house, the room where he lived the last years of his life will never be erased from my memory. The many happy days and hours I spent there, obviously can never be erased from my mind.

✠

When you entered Father Arseny's room, the first things you saw were icons of the Mother of God of Vladimir[2] and of Kazan, the icon of Jesus Christ, Not-Made-by-Human-Hands,[3] and the icons of St. Nicholas and of St. John the Theologian. The icons were old and excellently painted. Two oil lamps constantly burned in front of them: one red and one green. Next to the icons was a crystal glass holding a few fresh flowers. On the same little table, covered with a white napkin was a Gospel, a Psalter, and a service book as well as the Menaion proper to the time of the year. On his desk near the window were many books—theology, art history, ancient architecture, poetry by modern and classic poets, as well as technical works about atheism.

Along one wall stood an armoire full of books, along another was an old sofa on which Father Arseny could rest during the day and sleep at night. Three comfortable old armchairs completed the furnishings of his room. On the wall hung paintings by famous contemporary artists who had given them to Father Arseny. Almost all these were paintings of nature. One represented a woman next to a camp barracks. The face of the woman was beautiful and attractive; exhausted, tired to grayness, but in her eyes you could see life, conviction, strength and an unyielding will.

The background of the painting was another gray barracks, and the woman was dressed in a gray-green vest, an old brown hat with ear-flaps. The effect was that of a desperate situation, but again if you looked into her eyes you saw that she was alive, unbroken in spite of her suffering, her imminent death—you knew then for sure that nothing would ever break this woman, she would not give in, she never would renounce what she believed in. She may be crushed by the difficulties of life, but the spirit of God lives on in her and will never die—her eyes looking at you from her portrait told you this eloquently. The portrait was painted by a famous artist, a friend of Father Arseny's.

We didn't know who the woman on this portrait was, but we knew she was a spiritual daughter of Bishop Makary who had died in camp.

✠

When Father Arseny returned from camp he no longer served in a church. The first months after he left the camp he lived in solitude, but then a whole

2 The Mother of God of Vladimir is a particularly tender depiction of the Virgin Mary and her son, Jesus Christ.

3 According to tradition, the face of Christ was imprinted on th cloth given to him by Mary Magdalen to wipe the sweat from his face as he was led to the cross. The icon is a representation of this cloth.

large spiritual family surrounded him, a family which was spread out all over the Soviet Union.

People came, people wrote (actually they did not write to him at his address, since that would have meant endangering both him and them; they wrote to other spiritual children who in turn brought the correspondence to Father Arseny—he received an average of eighteen to twenty letters a day.) Every day two or three people would come, but on Saturdays and Sundays an impossible number of people would come—up to ten people in one day! These days made Nadezhda Petrovna worry about him.

The spiritual children of Father Arseny were numerous and each visited him at least twice a year. In one room of her little house Nadezhda Petrovna set up two beds where visitors could spend the night. When there were more than two visitors, some had to sleep on the floor.

Father Arseny didn't forget his interest in art. He devoted his free time to it, but as a matter of fact he didn't have any free time. Still he managed to write a few articles, though no publisher wanted to print his work because he was a member of the clergy; one of his friends tried to convince some acquaintances to publish him so that the name Piotr Andreyevich Streltzoff would not be forgotten.

✛

Father Arseny would get up every morning at six o'clock, and went to sleep at midnight. He prayed ceaselessly, celebrated liturgy daily, heard confessions and talked to his visitors.

The oil lamps were burning and you could hear his quiet voice praying. It was such a joyous experience to pray with him—the grace of God would illumine you. He prayed so warmly, so spiritually and so majestically to our Lady the Mother of God.

He read the Akathist to the Mother of God of Vladimir in such a way that you forgot where you were and who was there with you. With the final words of the service, "Rejoice, Most Holy Mother of God who has shown us your mercy through your icon," he celebrated the infinite perfection of the Mother of God and begged her to help his spiritual children whom he named individually.

Once a week he would serve a Memorial Service (a panikhida) in which he prayed for thousands of people; these services were extremely moving to us who were present. As he was praying for the departed you could see that he held each one of them in his memory and that he felt the presence of each one. Sometimes Father Arseny would cry, and we who prayed with him could sense how beloved and how *present* the departed were for him.

People who came always carried away with them a reserve of strength, faith, and the desire to help others and be better people themselves.

During the long years that Father Arseny was in camp, his spiritual family became smaller. Some people died, others were too sick, others deserted him for fear of being caught; but the majority stayed devoted to him. New "children" came: he had met some in camps, while others were brought to him by friends—I myself was one of these.

I knew and I remember many of them, but I will mention only those I met when I visited Father Arseny or those I met in camp and came to love; they had all later become spiritual children of Father Arseny.

People have already written about some of them: about the doctor Irina, Father Alexei (who was once the student Alexei), Abrosimov, Sazikov, Avseenkov, and Nadezhda Petrovna, the owner of the house where he lived, as well as many, many others. Such good, remarkable people.

I remember the visit of Bishop N. in 1962. He was a serious theologian, a philosopher and, many said, a very good confessor. He came to have Father Arseny hear his confession. Many spiritual children of Father Arseny were going to the church where Bishop N. served.

He stayed for two days, during which time he confessed to Father Arseny and also heard his confession. They talked about the fate and the future of the Church in the Soviet Union and about what was important for the believers. Looking at Father Arseny's library he pronounced, "The faithful one needs only the Gospel, the Bible, and the works of the Holy Fathers. All the rest isn't worth his attention."

Father Arseny remained silent for a few moments and answered, "You are right, Your Holiness, the most important things are in those books, but we must remember that man as he develops nowadays is very different from man in the fourth century. The horizon of knowledge has become wider and science can now explain what couldn't be understood then. The priests today must know a great deal in order to be able to help believers make sense of the contradictions he sees. A priest has to understand the theory of relativity, passionate atheism, the newest discoveries in biology, medicine and most of all modern philosophy. He gets visited by students of medicine, chemistry, physics, as well as by blue collar workers, and each one of them has to be given an answer to his or her questions such that religion doesn't sound anachronistic, or just a half-answer."

✠

Father Arseny prayed constantly. Whether he was thinking about something, or walking, or going somewhere you could perceive the slight movement of his lips pronouncing the Jesus prayer, "Lord Jesus Christ, Son of God, have mercy on me, a sinner."

He lived to help people in any possible way. Even in camp, where he himself was undernourished and exhausted, he helped others, did their work for them, and cared for the sick, sharing with them his meager ration.

Here, after he was freed, he would go anywhere immediately when he was called for; his only desire was to help, to give himself to others. We often tried to convince him not to give away all his strength, not to let himself get completely exhausted. He never accepted any material help. He felt that his duty was to be self-sufficient. We did try, though, to help him a little through Nadezhda Petrovna—he probably knew about it. You cannot count the people he helped, helped in the way taught in the Gospel: "bear one another's burdens, and so fulfill the law of Christ" (Galatians 6:2).

This is what I know about Father Arseny; others will write more about him, about what he did for them. As for me, I know that he gave me the most important thing: he breathed faith and love into me.

I know that by the way he prayed and by the way he lived he lit up and still does illumine the way for many, many people.

⬿

From the Memoirs of A. R. Sh., 1967-1969.

Irina

DECEMBER OF 1956 was cold and windy. The camp was almost empty and Father Arseny was to be set free very soon. Correspondence was now allowed and this was a big consolation. He received many letters.

One day, a letter came from Irina. It was a spontaneous, joyous, good letter. It seemed that the whole of Irina was in it.

Piotr Andreyevich!

Babushka Liuba told me you were alive. God has saved you. Somehow I knew you would be strong enough to survive all the hardships. You are needed by so many, and to me you are indispensable. The past—the horrible past—is slowly disappearing, and I trust the future will be better.

The children are now grown up. Tania is a big girl, Alexei is in fifth grade. You have not seen him.

For fifteen years I have known nothing about you, and during this time much has changed in my life. As you suggested to me, I became a doctor. My husband is still my best friend. There are sparks of faith within him, and I try to make these sparks become a flame. He knows everything about you and always tells me, "Remember Father Arseny and do not forget what is good. Be with people the way he is with people."

Come soon—though I know that this is not for you to decide. I will meet you and simply force you to live with us. The Mother of God is always with us. She saved Tatiana and is constantly helping me. Your Babushka Liuba has given me so much! My mother died, and she took her place for me.

O Lord, I am so lucky that I met you!

Anna

This short letter filled Father Arseny's heart with memories and gave him a chance to glance with his inner eyes at the past and marvel once again at the ways of God.

☦

Father Arseny remembered:

The year was 1939. A few years earlier he had finished his first stay in camp, only to be exiled to Kostroma, Arkhangelsk, Perm, Vologda. These were distant regions, and this was the only year he had lived near a railroad station. The village was small, but the old woman in whose house Father

Arseny lived happened to be a believer, and she was good and compassionate. She soon became his spiritual daughter.

On the feast day of the Lifegiving Cross, August fourteenth (Old Style),[4] Father Arseny secretly left his place of exile and went to this small town to stay for a short time with one of his closest spiritual children, Natalia Petrovna Astahova.

Only seven people, his most faithful friends, knew of his coming. The apartment of the Astahovs was on the third floor of a large stone apartment building. It was agreed that Father Arseny would not go out into the street. Natalia Petrovna and her husband went to work every morning. Father Arseny stayed alone in the apartment and it was decided that he wouldn't open the door to anyone. If one of "the seven" came, they would ring in a particular way and Father Arseny would then open the door without asking who it was.

His stay was kept a secret from everybody. He was officially in exile in the North. He had come to meet with two bishops to discuss the future of the Church in these difficult times. The meeting was to occur at the house of a famous painter in the village of Abramzevo. It was August nineteenth, the Feast of Transfiguration (Old Style). The whole time that Father Arseny spent in the apartment of the Astahovs, he was writing letters to his friends and spiritual children. He would pass the letters on to one of his seven friends, and they in turn would give them to some of their friends who would make sure that the addressees received them safely. Those who received the letters assumed that they had been written from exile and delivered by friends from there.

The first six days were quiet. Father Arseny served the vespers and matins of the forefeast, heard confessions, and served the liturgy on the feast day, with his friends receiving communion from him.

After this, they all went to work and Father Arseny stayed alone. After the festive service he was joyous and calm. There was no reason to be concerned. He had received no telegram from Marfa Andreevna (they had agreed that she would inform him in this way if people were looking for him). This meant that nobody had noticed his absence. Nor did it seem that there was any reason for worry here. It looked as though nobody was watching him.

Father Arseny knelt and prayed, thanking God for His mercy, for having allowed him to serve a liturgy on this great feast day and to share it with his friends. The apartment was quiet and peaceful. Father Arseny sat at his table to write letters. He wrote on narrow strips of paper, since they were easier to

4 The Russian Orthodox Church uses the Julian or "Old Style" calendar, which is thirteen days behind the civil or "New Style" calendar.

hide. His fine neat handwriting filled the strips and carried so much that was of importance to his spiritual children. They instructed, warned, convinced, ordered, calmed. Each addressee awaited these narrow strips with great impatience, since they carried the light of the words of their spiritual father. Once in a while Father Arseny would get up, walk to the window and look—through the curtain—at the store on the other side of the street. He thought he recognized the silhouette of a woman who had been walking back and forth there for a few days now. She was looking carefully at the windows of the apartment where Father Arseny was staying.

"Are they watching me, or am I imagining things?" thought Father Arseny. He had not left the house; he had not noticed anyone watching him when he arrived and only his closest friends knew he was here. "I am being paranoid," he told himself and he prayed and sat back at his table to write. It was now almost eleven o'clock in the morning. Father Arseny checked the oil lamp and started praying. The light of the lamp leapt and sometimes almost went out. Deep in prayer Father Arseny recited the Akathist to the Holy Mother of God praising her, glorifying her and thanking her.

Suddenly his prayer was interrupted by the violent ringing of the bell. The signal was the one that had been agreed upon: one long, three short, one long and again one short. "Who can it be?" thought Father Arseny. "I'm not expecting anyone today. What has happened?"

The bell rang again, insistently and loudly.

Concerned, Father Arseny went to open the door since only his friends could ring in such a manner. Something must have happened.

"Probably a telegram has come from Marfa Andreevna," he thought.

Entering the vestibule, Father Arseny crossed himself and, placing his hope in the Mother of God, he opened the door. Immediately, pushing the door with her foot, an unknown woman entered forcefully. She was perhaps 22 years old. She almost pushed Father Arseny aside as she went into the living room.

"I am from the Soviet Administration. Here are my papers, see for yourself. You—Streltzoff, Piotr Andreyevich—have been living here now for six days. I have been sent here to watch you during the day. At night somebody else takes over the watch."

Father Arseny was lost: he knew that on his desk were letters from his spiritual children; he was in this town without authorization. He was afraid for the safety of his friends who might suffer because of all this.

"O God, O Mother of God, help me!" he prayed silently. One thing was clear to him: many people would be arrested because of him...

The woman was beautiful, young, and obviously intelligent. She was dressed in very unobtrusive clothing, probably so as to go unnoticed in a crowd.

"You understand, I am from the Administration, I have been watching you from outside. But something terrible happened to me personally: my daughter has fallen seriously ill. I called home, and they told me. She has a fever of over 104, her throat is swollen, she is blue in the face, and she is having difficulty breathing. All this is so sudden. When I left this morning she was in good health, and now my mother says: "Tania is dying." I called my superiors asking them to send a replacement, but they refused. They forbid me to leave my post. But what can I do? My daughter is dying. I have to help her, I have to go find a doctor; my mother doesn't know what to do. Tatiana is dying, and I have to go home. My replacement will only come at five PM. I have a big request to make of you: please do not go anywhere. Give me your word that you will not leave. I beg you, do not leave the apartment: you would destroy me. Another request: if anyone comes to see you, someone may have accompanied him or her, and I must know it and inform the authorities about it. Your people who work for us say that you are a good person and help others. Please, do not leave. Tell me you will not. Tatiana is very sick and I am not allowed to be with her."

Father Arseny understood everything. She didn't need to say anything more. In her eyes he read a great deal more than she could have told about herself.

"Go to your daughter. I will go nowhere, and if anyone comes, I will let you know. Go."

"Thank you, citizen Streltzoff! Thank you. I will be back at three o'clock, and will be at my post again." And for some unknown reason, she added, "My name is Anna."

The door banged closed, and Father Arseny was left alone. The oil lamp was burning, the prayer book was open, and on the table were numerous letters.

The NKVD knew everything: they knew he was here; he was being watched; the others were watched as well. They wanted to identify all those who visit him, later to arrest them. This Anna who came into the house, who knew the signal, who had to go see her sick daughter, though the authorities did not allow it; her awful phrase: "Your people who work for us," the meeting planned with the bishops; the sudden illness of Anna's daughter—Father Arseny read all this as a chain of events sent by God's great wisdom.

The weight of what had happened fell onto Father Arseny and almost crushed him under his thoughts and feelings. He was afraid; he felt his responsibility for the fate of others, for their possible suffering and fears. Yes, of course coming here had been a mistake.

Father Arseny took his prayer book, fell on his knees and began reading the Akathist to the Mother of God of Vladimir, starting where he had been interrupted by Anna's bell. But the sentences were jumping around in front of him, so that he couldn't understand the familiar and beloved words he was reading. Gradually he brought himself under control, forgot all his earthly cares and went deeply into prayer. He prayed for close to four hours. He read the Akathist and other prayers; he served the service of thanksgiving.

What had happened was a proof of God's great mercy and of God's care for Father Arseny and his friends, his spiritual children. The fears and worries left him.

At three o'clock the bell rang again and Father Arseny opened the door. Anna ran in.

"Thank God you are still here," she blurted out.

"I am still here and I went nowhere; nobody came to visit me. Go back to your post, Irina."

The woman was exhausted, but when Father Arseny called her by the name Irina, she trembled and asked fearfully, "Why did you call me Irina?"

"Go, Irina, go!" answered Father Arseny.

Tears appeared in her eyes, and she whispered, "I thank you."

"Lord! You told me to call her Irina. You alone know everything, O almighty God."

On the other side of the street, he could see Irina walking back and forth. At five o'clock she was replaced by a man.

Father Arseny decided to say nothing to Natalia Petrovna or to her husband, nor to their friends who would come that evening. Telling would change nothing, and would only make them all worry. An inner voice insisted that he should wait until tomorrow, that everything was in God's hands.

Father Arseny made his preparations for the worst; he burned all the letters he had written and received and asked Natalia Petrovna to burn anything that could be compromising.

On August 20 he served an early liturgy and, after Natalia Petrovna and her husband had left for work, he started to pray, but his prayer did not flow easily. He was not at peace, but was troubled. At about eleven o'clock he heard the bell, opened the door, and saw Irina.

Father Arseny let her in, sat at his table, and waited.

"I have come to see you. I was able to have Tania admitted to a hospital with great difficulty. I am terribly worried about what will happen to her. Thank you for yesterday. I called the authorities last night and they said nobody had been 'accompanied' to your apartment. Nobody came."

"Sit down, Irina! I was very surprised that you dared to come and see me, the one whom you are watching. You probably consider me an enemy?"

"I have come to talk to you, so you don't need to be afraid of me. Trust me, I have come alone, on my own account, and my daughter's illness is not just a fabrication. Tell me who you are, who your friends are and why you and the authorities are fighting so ardently. Those of your people who keep us informed tell us about all the good deeds you are doing, and the help you give, and the care you feel for each other. They tell us many good things about you, but we are also told that you are a fanatic, an enemy of the people, that you are gathering together a group of church people. They say that your goodness is endangering our government.

"I have three hours now of free time. Nobody will come to check on things until two in the afternoon. Tell me about yourself. I'm going to have a glance at the street and if I see something dangerous, I will leave quickly."

Looking into Irina's face, Father Arseny started telling her about the faith and about believers. He explained why the Communists had to fight against religion, and that believers were not trying to fight the authorities.

While he talked Father Arseny was afraid of nothing; what did he have to fear when he could easily see that this Irina knew a great deal more about him and his friends than he could ever tell her. As he was talking, Father Arseny got so involved in what he was saying that he forgot about the identity of the woman in front of him. He just spoke to her as one human being to another and, knowing he was in the right, he defended the faith.

Irina listened to him carefully although it was hard for her: she knew that the community of faithful was dangerous and that they were the enemy, and here she had this man telling her the opposite. What was the truth?

Over in the NKVD where they knew a great deal, they were waiting to catch all the members of the community, arrest them and send them to camps or into exile. They had to be arrested not for their faith but for their anti-communist activities. But it seemed that there was no such activity, there was only this faith that united people.

"In the state departments we have classes where we are told that you are our enemies. You make everything sound so different, and while watching you I can only see that you are people from another era. In our classes we are told about your organization and about you. They show us your letters, where you only show care for others and speak about God. Is this all a code?

"Several of your people work for us and all of our information comes from them. I am going to tell you their names."

"No, do not give me their names, I don't want to know!" interrupted Father Arseny.

"But I want to give you their names! I don't like traitors, particularly since the same people could later betray us. I was present once at an interrogation. It is a disgusting sight. Their eyes are looking right and left, they contort like eels, they are scared, but they write things down anyway. I listened in, sitting to the side, and it seemed to me that much of what they said was only half-true. The names of the traitors whom I know are Kravtzova, the deacon Kamushkin, Guskova, and Polushkina."

Father Arseny shook and he almost shouted out, "You aren't telling the truth, these people could never betray us." But looking at Irina he knew that she was telling the truth. He started to cry. He wept bitterly.

"What's wrong with you, Citizen Streltzoff? I am telling you the truth. On August 16, I myself accompanied Kravtzova to the authorities. It is all true. Calm yourself, they are just worthless people.

"Perhaps I shouldn't have told you, but I pity you. Don't be upset. I am going to leave you now. I will stop by tomorrow. You will not be arrested any time soon. They want to be sure to have the names of everyone who works with you. I want to make a call from a telephone booth to find out how my daughter is doing. I am sorry I upset you."

Father Arseny was left alone, shaken, crushed.

Tears flowed from his eyes and his thoughts grew heavier and heavier.

Katia! Katia Kravtzova, who was one of the people he felt closest to. She was a steady helper, she had a heart of gold, she was prayerful, and she knew the church services. She knew everything there was to know about their community. Yes, she knew everything. What could have pushed her over the edge into becoming an informer, becoming a traitor? Katia, whom everyone called Katia the White to distinguish her from other Katias. Beautiful, intelligent Katia. What had pushed her: fear? disappointment? hurt? temporary weakness? threats?

Then there was Deacon Kamushkin, his spiritual son and concelebrant in all services, and the other two, Lydia Guskova and Zina Polushkina, his faithful spiritual daughters. Yes! They were faithful, loving, deeply believing and beloved spiritual daughters. What could have happened? How did they fall? Was it just fear? He thought, "Perhaps I myself, as their spiritual father, missed something, perhaps I did not save them from this fall? Perhaps I am guilty in all of this? O Lord! Forgive me, a sinner, teach me, set me straight! It is my fault, have mercy on them and protect all the others."

Remembering their confessions and their conversations, Father Arseny tried to reconstitute the tiny missteps which might have led them to this fall.

Yes! He, Hieromonk Arseny, should have noticed what was happening, he should have stopped their hesitations and their mistakes. Father Arseny fell on his knees and, crying, prayed, begging God and the Mother of God for help. He said, "Lord! Lord! Do not leave me! Stretch out Your helping hand to me, and be merciful. Save my children from destruction!"

On August 21, Irina came again. Her daughter was far worse. There was an abscess in her throat, she now had pneumonia, and her breathing was irregular. The doctors said they felt the situation was hopeless. The authorities would not let Irina off her post. During the day the grandmother was with the child but at night Irina was with her. As soon as she entered his room Irina started crying.

"Calm down! Calm down, God is merciful and your Tania will be all right," said Father Arseny. As he looked at Irina he saw a woman lost, sad, desperate, empty, and left with no hope.

"It's hopeless. Tatiana is going to die. She has two serious illnesses at the same time. The doctors did say that she is going to die, and I cannot be with her during the day," she sobbed with her head on the table.

Father Arseny went over to his icons, lit a second oil lamp and said, "I am going to pray for Tania, I will beg God for her!"

"I will also beg your God, since I am ready to do anything. I only want to save my Tania, but I don't know how to pray, I don't even know God."

The light of the oil lamp flickered and illumined the icons, but mainly sent its light onto the icon of the Mother of God of Vladimir. "Irina, we are going to make the request together, we are going to pray to the Mother of God. She is our protector and we will ask her to cure your Tania." And he started to pray clearly and loudly. While he was praying, Father Arseny did not see Irina; he forgot about her and only remembered an inconsolable human grief. Father Arseny prayed for the child Tatiana with all his soul and with all his priestly power.

(Telling me about this prayer almost 25 years later Father Arseny said, "You know I seldom cry, but here I wept and begged God and His Mother for help. I prayed aggressively and, I am almost afraid even to pronounce the words, I demanded. Yes, I demanded a favorable response to my request, so great was Irina's grief. She had no hope and no faith, but I could see the goodness and love in her eyes. I truly begged to be heard and I asked for the child to be cured and for Irina to receive the light of faith in Christ and hope. Later I confessed my aggressiveness to Bishop Jonah.")

Two hours later, having finished his prayer, Father Arseny turned around and looked at Irina and there she was, on her knees, her face wet with tears, her eyes looking at the icon and her lips murmuring. Father Arseny's heart was filled with pity for her.

He went over to her, put his hand on her bowed head, and said, "You may go, Irina! God will help. We have asked Him, both of us—you and I. The Mother of God, our Intercessor, will not desert us. She will help."

Irina stood up, took a step towards Father Arseny, took his hand and said crying, "Piotr Andreyevich! I will now believe for evermore, I believe in you and in her. She was a mother, and if everything is as you say, she will help. O Mother of God, save my Tania. I will do anything if you will only save her."

Father Arseny prayed until Natalia Petrovna and her husband came home from work. In the evening when two other friends were with them, the telephone rang. Father Arseny arose and picked up the receiver, saying, "Yes, Anna!"

And what he heard was "Thank you! Thank you, all is well. She helped us, and now I am a believer for life. Thank you. I am calling from a telephone booth."

Father Arseny blessed himself, and said, "Yes, this was necessary. God and His mother have shown great mercy, not only to me but also to a newly born person. Nobody can possibly know who I was talking to. There are many Annas." He went back to the icons and started praying again.

(It is worth mentioning here that during the interrogations that Father Arseny was subjected to after this, he was asked many times who Anna was.)

The sudden appearance of Irina changed all his plans. After much thought and prayer, Father Arseny decided not to meet with the bishops and to leave on August 25. Until then he would not set foot from the apartment.

He had to protect those who were faithful from being arrested, and somehow isolate those who were informing the authorities.

Until the day Father Arseny left, Irina would come at eleven to spend time with him and stay until two. She would come, she would ask questions and tell him about herself, but mainly she would listen to Father Arseny talk. For the first time in her life she went to confession and received communion, and she became one of Father Arseny's spiritual daughters. They agreed that Irina would write to him, under the name of Anna. She gave him the address of her cousin (which he memorized), where he could send his replies. So that Irina could learn more about the faith and the Church, Father Arseny gave her the address of Babushka Liuba, who was a convinced believer but not a member of the "community." He sent Babushka Liuba a note saying, "Help her, guide her, never abandon her! Pray together." Father Arseny was able to write Irina a few times a year before he was sent away to the special camp, and from there he was not allowed to write.

After meeting Father Arseny, Irina left her work for the Communist party and started studying to become a medical doctor. When she had finished she started work in a big Moscow hospital.

Father Arseny found all this out when he returned from camp in 1957. Now, in December 1956, as he thought back on the days of August 1939, Father Arseny could remember well his sad thoughts about the deacon Kamushkin, and the sisters Zina and Lydia. He remembered that he had felt no awareness of what they were up to in their conversations with him and in their confessions, so that he realized that he would not have been able to stop them.

Father Arseny also remembered Katia Kravtzova's confession on August 23. When that confession came to an end, Father Arseny waited, because he wanted her to tell him what she had done, but she said nothing. Father Arseny prayed to God. Katia expected the prayer of absolution and could not understand why

Father Arseny was holding off on it. Father Arseny remembered her saying, "Father, I have finished!" and he, Father Arseny, gave her the absolution.

The confession may have been finished, but not the conversation.

"Katia, what made you denounce our community? Why have you been telling the authorities about our activities? Why? You are destroying so many people. You have been my mainstay and one of my most beloved spiritual children, Katia."

Her face expressed shame, fear, horror. Her big eyes filled with tears and she bit her lips fearfully.

"How did you find out? Who told you? Father Arseny, they knew everything even before I told them. They knew that you had come. I only told them half the truth, I..." Her face became serious. "I wanted to save the community, our people, and you. I lied to them, but they knew very much. And now I am all caught up in it."

The conversation lasted a long time and ended with the decision that Katia must leave the community. She did. In a few years Katia got married and no longer saw her old friends. She only met Father Arseny again in 1958.

In 1942, during rigorous interrogations, Father Arseny had the opportunity to see once again how right Irina had been about the identity of the traitors.

The ex-deacon Kamushkin held an important post in the Patriarchate by 1960.

Father Arseny had to leave. He spoke for a long time with Natalia Petrovna and Vera Danilovna. He told them the reason he had come, but he didn't tell them about Irina nor how he found out that he had been denounced. He spoke to them about the deacon, about Zina and Lydia, but he did not talk to them about Katia, Katia the White. He trusted that she had made a mistake and that she was not a real traitor.

Father Arseny understood that his arrest had already been decided on, but it was important for other people's sakes that this arrest not occur here, but in the place in which he had been exiled, and where he was supposed to be. Let them interrogate him, put him in the isolation cell, beat him, show him signed statements of agents—but he would say that he had never left his place of exile, that he never had been in this town. Irina bought him a ticket for the night of August 25 and on the evening of August 24 Father Arseny wrote letters, one of which was to Katia Kravtzova. In 1966 Katia gave Father Arseny's letter to Vera Danilovna and told her how and why she had become an agent.

Here is part of this letter:

I pray to God for you. Strengthen yourself in prayer and ask the Mother of God for help. You fell; now find the strength to get up again. I understand your mistake, and I do not blame you. You are strong, decisive, stoical; when people called you, you trusted that you would be strong enough to resist them. Your mistake was that you trusted in yourself and not in God. If you had trusted in God, then your decisiveness and your strength would have helped you resist evil. Your heroism ended up first as a mistake, and then as evil.

Keep away from your activities. Resist the pressure of evil and you will be victorious. I know that this is difficult. Fight against evil.

Find consolation in prayer. The Mother of God is our protector and intercessor. Let God protect you.

Your spiritual Father,
Hieromonk Arseny

There will be a time when we shall meet again. I pray for you constantly. God bless you.

On August 25 at eleven o'clock, while Irina was at her post, Father Arseny left for the railroad station and stayed there until evening. Irina's mother came to see him off and brought him some food. She was tender, pleasant, and caring.

This departure was painful for Father Arseny. He had lost three of his spiritual children. But he still trusted Katia; he trusted she would come around.

Irina had said goodbye to Father Arseny in the morning and asked him to pray for her and her family. A new person had come to the faith, to the source of hope and of life, and this was a great joy for Father Arseny.

I remember somebody asking Father Arseny, "How could you have believed in Irina straight away?"

He answered, "Because the ways of God are inscrutable and His mercy is inexhaustible."

This was written according to the accounts of Father Arseny, Irina, Vera Danilovna, and Natalia Petrovna. It was edited by a person who participated in all these events, in 1968-1975.

The Journalist

HE WROTE DOWN everything. From somewhere he had obtained rough, gray paper, folded it to the size of a notebook, cut the pages with a knife, and sewed it together. Returning from work, he would swallow a bowl of the awful food he was given, and eat a piece of old, frozen bread; still half hungry and very tired he would sit on his bunk and start to write on the crumpled paper with his tiny stub of pencil. The pencil would race over the paper and leave very neat lines of very neatly written words composed of extremely neat letters.

It might have looked as if he had been sent to report on the conditions of life of prisoners in this camp, as if he were supposed to understand the psychology of the people around him and of the administration and later make his report in articles called "A Special Regime Camp." But it only seemed this way. He was just a prisoner, number K-391, according to the 58th Article of Law,[5] who was to spend 20 years in this special regime camp. In the year he had in this camp, he had found the time to fill several notebooks, describing in them things as they were in reality and in all honesty.

He had decided to leave behind him a complete report on life in this camp, life the way it really was. He would grab each new person he met and question him in detail: "Who are you? Where are you from? What are you here for? Who put your case together?" Although one expected that the next question would be, "What are your impressions about this camp?"—that was a question he never asked. The answer was too obvious. With the help of the "criminals" he managed to hide his notebooks. He had to pay them by giving them part of his ration.

Every so often portions of his notes were discovered and taken away from him. He would be sent to the punishment cell, but this didn't stop him in his determination to write.

He viewed the world with the eyes of a journalist. It is probable that, were he condemned to death, he would be seen jotting his reactions down until he was shot. This is the way he was. In observing the camp, he tried to make sense of what he saw. The barracks and its widely varied occupants were subjects of his analysis. Only a few people had never yet been questioned. Among them was Father Arseny.

5 Article 58, the most strict, concerned all the alleged enemies of the government.

The barracks called him "the Journalist" and he was proud of this nickname. He really had been a journalist when he was a free man and had written for big newspapers like *Izvestia, Pravda,* and *Trud.*

His hurried manner, his nervousness, and his desire to inquire about everything made many people suspicious, but because he was good-natured and easy to talk to people finally accepted him, politicals and criminals alike. But the police, anyone who had collaborated with the Germans in any way, and the Vlassovtsy, were all against him.

After a year and a half in camp he understood more and interviewed people more rarely. When he was writing you would see him spend more time pondering, trying to rethink and reevaluate things.

He met Father Arseny in the barracks. He had heard that he was a priest, an art historian with a university education. He saw that many people in the barracks respected Father Arseny and that he had authority over many. But the mere fact that he was a member of the clergy made the Journalist despise and pity him.

The Journalist was sure that it was only right that Father Arseny was in camp; he had been told that all believers agitate against the government. The Journalist thought that the police officers, the German collaborators and the believers were all part of the same group, so he didn't bother to interview them.

He was sure that he himself had been arrested because of some traitors and was offended in finding himself among "such people." He, who had always been on the side of the truth, was now obliged to live among traitors and priests—whom he had always considered his enemies.

The interview with Father Arseny did occur one day anyway. The Journalist fell sick and was left behind in the barracks to work with Father Arseny, cleaning the barracks and feeding the stoves with wood. They worked in silence. The Journalist didn't talk; he carried logs, cleaned out ashes from the stoves, removed the bark from logs, and made kindling. He was young and strong and did his work faster than Father Arseny. Father Arseny was still carrying logs in when the journalist was ready to light his stoves. He struck match after match but couldn't start the fire. He used up a whole box of matches but the logs wouldn't burn. He went to another stove but couldn't light it either. The Journalist was getting anxious, because he knew the barracks had to be warm by the time the prisoners got back from work.

Father Arseny finished bringing in the logs, placed them in his stoves, put in the kindling and needed only one match to light each one. He noticed that the journalist hadn't managed to start his fires.

He walked over to him and said, "Will you allow me to help you?" The answer was irritated, angry. "I ask you not to get in my way. I don't need any help!" Father Arseny stepped aside, but looked attentively at the way the Journalist was working.

The man was getting more and more anxious. He was losing his temper. He knew perfectly well that when the workers got back they would beat him up for not having the barracks warm for them. They would also beat up Father Arseny. In another twenty minutes, Father Arseny prayed and calmly went over to the journalist, passed him by, took all the kindling and the logs out of his stoves, put them back in the proper way, put a match to them, and the fire took immediately. Father Arseny went to the next stove and the journalist followed him. He said not a word, but looked carefully at what Father Arseny was doing. The journalist was able to light the third stove himself. His face was black with soot but happy. "Thank you for teaching me. I thought it was all so simple, but now I see that this is an art."

"I have lit hundreds of these stoves since I have been here, and I have mastered the art!"

The stoves were burning so that you only had to throw in more logs. They started talking. The Journalist thought that he would be interviewing Father Arseny, but he ended up telling Father Arseny his own life. He was amazed later when he realized that things had turned out this way. He had told Father Arseny his life in all its minute details. He had told his life to a man he didn't know, and for some reason he felt good about it. He felt at peace.

The workers returned to the barracks. It became noisy. The roll was called several times and the barracks locked up. The Journalist lay on his bunk, eyes wide open, and couldn't stop thinking. "How did this happen? Why did I tell my whole life to this man? I told him everything." And Father Arseny had unexpectedly become close and dear to him.

One conversation led to another and little by little, imperceptibly, the soul of the Journalist came into the hands of Father Arseny.

In the beginning he said, "Father Arseny is so strong! His soul is as big as the world—there is room for everything."

And a month later he said, "Father Arseny is a man of great soul and there is so much goodness in him. I understand, I have seen a real believing Christian." He became Father Arseny's friend for life.

The Journalist loved poetry. He knew many poems by heart and would read them every night to himself or to others. He read well, in a beautiful voice whose intonations revealed the very soul of the poet. He read Blok, Brusov, Pasternak, Simonov, Gumilev, Lermontov, Esenin—he loved these poets above all others. While he was reciting his voice would become clear, expressive, giving importance to each and every word and sentence. Even a poem you knew well became different when he read it and was listened to afresh. I remember him reciting "The Unknown Woman" by Blok. We listened and forgot where we were; we forgot the barracks, the cold, hunger, imprisonment—we were transported into the St. Petersburg of old together with "The Unknown Woman."

> Her thick silks
> Remind you of olden times,
> Her hat with ostrich feathers
> And her thin hand with rings,
> She slowly walks, among the drunkards,
> Always alone, without a friend,
> Exuding perfumes and mists
> She sits near a window.

Listening to him, we sat there and saw this woman.

When he recited Esenin he conveyed this poet's unhappy, ailing soul; his deep but exhausted gentleness, the soulfulness of his poetry, his grief and sadness over a life lived without a purpose.

The Journalist recited many different poems, but I remember especially the one by Simonov, "Wait for me, I shall return." Five or six people sat around him, talking. Somebody asked him to read a poem. He spoke for a few minutes, then suddenly stopped, lost in thought—it was obvious that he had remembered something and said, "I will recite one by Simonov. I remember him reciting this poem to me in 1942 on the battle front. It is a war poem:

> Wait for me, I shall return
> But wait and wait well.
> Wait, when yellow rains
> Bring sadness,
> Wait when snows are blowing,

> Wait when it is very hot,
> Wait when many are no longer awaited,
> And are forgotten.
> Wait when letters do not come
> From places far away.
> Wait alone when those who used to wait with you
> Are tired of waiting."

We listened to the first lines almost carelessly, but then the depth of his reading, the warmth of the words caught us. The camp life around us, the hopelessness, the desperation reminded us of our close ones, awakened in us our past—so far gone.

> Wait for me. I shall return,
> Against all and any odds.
> Let the ones who did not wait for me
> Think that it was luck.

His reading voice was loud and filled a good part of the barracks, so that many other prisoners joined the group of listeners.

Each one caught up in his own memories, they scarcely dared to breathe so as not to miss a word. They all thought about their families, their homes, all those who lived in freedom: "Are they waiting for me? Do they remember me? Officially I am dead. I am not on any lists any more."

The voice continued:

> Those who did not wait, will never understand
> How in the midst of fire,
> You saved me
> By waiting for me.
> How I survived will be known
> Only to you and me—
> You simply knew how to wait
> Like no other woman knew.

The Journalist finished, lowered his head and fell into a reverie. Those around him quietly and slowly returned each to his bunk.

A tall man, about forty years of age, unexpectedly said, "I survived the war, I spent time in hospitals, I fought for Russia again. I wrote to my wife: 'I will be back—wait for me!' And here I am, with my wife still waiting for me, but what's the point? We're stuck in this special camp, and that's for good." And unexpectedly he ended with, "Who knows, maybe we *will* get out?"

The Journalist lived long enough to see the death of Stalin. He was freed, and somehow kept his notes, nobody knows how. Now his name is well known and his articles are published in thick magazines and major newspapers. I have read several books where I recognized events we had lived through together, stories of suffering and of meetings with Father Arseny, with whom he remained friends his whole life. I often get together with the Journalist. We recollect life in camp, Father Arseny, and all those who came out of camp and lived. But the most important thing is that we believe in God and that Father Arseny gave us both a new life. Many of the Journalist's notes are being used in this book.

The Musician

ONE DAY HE appeared in our barracks: tall, thin, badly dressed like everyone else, and looking like he had suffered much. His face was gaunt, the skin close to his bones, he seemed alive only through his large black eyes which were deep and sad. They looked somewhere far away and seemed uninterested in what was going on around him. Unable to fulfill his quota at work, he didn't get his full ration of food and became weaker by the day. He would come back from work, eat slowly what he had, sit on his bunk, talk to no one and look through the dull window of the barracks at the sad sight of the camp. At times his face would come alive and you could see his fingers moving swiftly in his lap. It looked as if he was playing the piano.

He said little about himself—actually nothing—but one evening, by chance, everything became clear. This happened after he had been in our barracks for over six months, when everybody had gotten used to his silence and his lack of interest in others.

A group of a few people had gotten together to talk; Father Arseny was among them. At first they talked about life in the camp, but after a while they started remembering the past. They reminisced about the theater, about music, and this was the time when even those prisoners who never said anything decided to join in.

The conversation about music became more serious. People argued about the influence of music on the soul, some feeling there was propaganda in music. Usually Father Arseny didn't participate in such debates, but here he suddenly expressed an opinion that music, music with a deep meaning, could have a positive influence on the soul; it could ennoble the listener by bringing elements of religious influence to his soul.

The normally silent and introverted prisoner suddenly came alive, his eyes shining, his voice stronger, his speech authoritative. He spoke very intimately, professionally, and convincingly, developing on Father Arseny's thought about the influence of music on the soul.

One of the prisoners who was standing nearby looked at the man carefully and suddenly exclaimed, "Wait a minute, but I know you. You are a pianist," and he named a very famous musician.

The Musician shivered and said a little shyly, "If you only knew how I miss music! Yes, if you only knew! With music I could survive even here."

Somebody asked the silly question, "What are you here for?"

The Musician answered, "A friend testified a lie against me; but actually, I am here for the same reason we all are here." He spoke and stepped away, returning to his bunk.

After this conversation, his sadness and lack of interest in anything became even more pronounced. His eyes were empty, and he only answered if called several times. We could see that the man had lost interest in the outside world, and that was equal to a death warrant.

A month went by. The Musician grew weaker and weaker, went to work with great difficulty, couldn't fulfill his assigned work, and therefore received less and less to eat.

Father Arseny tried to talk to him, tried to help him, but all his efforts were unsuccessful. The Musician would give just any answer, whether it pertained to the question or not, and would then walk away. "The man is dying without music. What can we get for him to be able to play?"

One of the criminals who liked Father Arseny said, "I saw a broken down guitar in the red corner.[6] We will try to steal it."

In this special camp there was a "red corner," where nothing educational or recreational ever took place. But there were several dozen books there which no one was allowed to touch, and a bookcase in which there was a broken down guitar. The red corner was always kept locked, but probably in camp reports to the authorities it was listed as a crucial tool in the "political development" of the zeks. It will never be known how, but the criminals managed to get a hold of the guitar and bring it to the barracks. The sounding board had cracked, it had only five of its seven strings, the finish was in poor shape—the guitar looked miserable. Everybody knew that the guitar wouldn't last long in the barracks. It would be found at the first inspection and be taken away; still it was a very welcome diversion—an event.

Somebody glued the sounding board and cleaned up the finish. The criminals hid the guitar for two days while the glue was drying. On the third day, after both roll calls and inspections, they put it on the bunk of the Musician while he was busy on the other side of the barracks.

The Musician came back to his bunk, noticing nothing until his hand touched the strings. He jumped up, grabbed the guitar, looked around not knowing what to think, and started tuning it. At first the strings wouldn't give

6 A red corner was a recreation and reading room set up for political purposes in Soviet institutions.

out a decent sound, so that they gave the impression of being dead; but soon they became taut and the musician started playing.

In five or six groups the criminals were playing cards (using homemade cards), others were playing dominoes, and still others were throwing dice. They were swearing angrily. Suddenly the barracks was full of sound. People were caught by this sound. The swearing stopped, the cards were put down. Something immeasurably big, something dear, a little sad but unusually close to each man's heart had penetrated the barracks.

In these sounds they saw familiar places, fields covered with grass, their wives, their mothers, their children, their friends all lost for ever.

Everything remaining in these people that was bright and good, was stirred and came to stand by them. The rudeness and cruelty of camp life fled. The prisoners stood, lay or sat, very still, lit up by their past. What the Musician was playing was unimportant. It might have been his own composition, but whatever it was the guitar was singing and telling their past.

We were listening and the music was flowing light and pure. You could hear the clinging of icicles, water singing in a stream, calmly pouring at times and at other times passionately battling a stone in its way. The heart of the music was beating in our hearts and gave us light inspite of the surrounding gloom; it gave us life and joy.

The sound flowed, uniting that which otherwise could not have been united. It was among us despite the fact that the dream that had enlivened us was immeasurably far away. A time came when the strings played more and more tragically; they began to weep, to moan, to protest quietly. With all this, the music cut people off from hateful reality.

Suddenly we heard loud footsteps in the passage between the bunks. A tall man with dark black hair appeared, his face grimacing and covered with tears—he was one of the camp's infamous criminals, cruel and pitiless. "Stop the music! Stop turning my soul inside out! Stop, or I'll kill you!" The criminal took a step towards the Musician with his fist raised. At this moment another criminal, who happened to be standing near by, grabbed the first one and threw him out into the passage. Later his sobbing could be heard at the end of the barracks.

The sound of the music told of the suffering, the unbearable grief, the despondency, the treks, the camp. Your heart was tight in your chest but all the sadness seemed to disappear progressively and there came calm, peacefulness.

It seemed the man had found his way. The Musician was telling his life in these sounds, but each listener heard his own life in them. The music stopped suddenly, and the Musician remained silent for a while, motionless. Somebody said, "Sing for us!"

The Musician raised his head and sang with a low, slightly hoarse, but very expressive voice. He sang an old Russian song:

> Why do you hang your heads, my friends?
> She doesn't love me any more. So what?
> I am no longer dear to her;
> But I will love you, my friends.

Everyone came alive and smiled. The voice of the Musician wasn't the voice of a singer, but it was so warm and so expressive that he charmed all his listeners. He finished the song and played a waltz, a waltz they all knew. He played it in a slow tempo. The familiarity of the piece somehow united them and made them feel very close to one another.

They all went to their bunks in silence. The Musician sat on his bunk. He was straight, calm, luminous and held the guitar with the greatest of care.

His big eyes looked into the darkness and expressed gratitude to all for this guitar.

Father Arseny was sitting near me on his bunk. He was pensive and serious. "He is a believer, a deeply believing man. He told us all about this in his music."

The guitar lived in the barracks for two days. In the course of these two days the Musician was totally transformed. He became cheerful, he came alive, he became communicative. The criminals called him "the Performer" and decided to protect him.

The guitar was taken from him during a morning inspection. Somebody had denounced him. The Musician was put in the punishment cell for three days. For a little while the Musician remained calm and even joyous, but then he faded again.

About three weeks later, Father Arseny woke up because somebody was shaking him by the sleeve. "Please forgive me for waking you up! I know it is night, but I just have to talk to you. I know that you are a priest. I've wanted to talk to you for a long time, but I didn't dare. Thank you for the guitar. I know you initiated it. Hear me! I will be brief. Forgive me for waking you up!"

His head was bent over Father Arseny and his breathing was warm and nervous. He spoke very quickly, he wanted to spill all his thoughts. "My God, O my God, I am such a sinner!" he repeated from time to time. It was clear that he had thought about everything he was saying for a long time and had suffered over it.

His tears were pouring onto Father Arseny's hand. "My God, I know I am a sinner, but why did they take my music from me?"

Father Arseny prayed for a long time with the Musician; the Musician prayed with him.

Three weeks later, at work, the Musician's left hand was smashed. In another two weeks he sent a note to Father Arseny from the hospital. The note was carried by a friend. The letter said, "Do not forget me in your prayers. Death is nearby. Pray to God for me!"

This was retold by prisoners who were in the barracks at this time, and by Father Arseny himself, in 1959.

Two Steps to the Side

I HAD KNOWN Father Arseny for a long time—a year was considered a long time in camp. We knew each other, saw each other rarely, but I heard people speak about him very often.

I was drawn to him in 1953.

In the summer we had been temporarily transferred to build new barracks in a place where nobody had ever lived. We also had to build a mine shaft. We had to walk 40 kilometers to get there, not all that far. We had three days, two nights to get there, and quite a bit to carry. The sun was scorching, the mosquitoes attacked and entered any opening in your clothes. We were walking fully dressed, it was sultry and the air was heavy. Our hands and face itched from mosquito bites and sweat.

In the hot summer, treks could be more difficult than in the middle of the winter with its freezing temperatures. We had to walk, our legs as heavy as lead, our loads getting heavier and heavier and cutting in to our shoulders. Our clothing stuck to our bodies, making any movement even more difficult. Each of us had only one wish: to lie down flat on the ground and never, ever get up—whatever might happen as a result. Still, some unexplainable power made us all continue to walk, dragging our feet, each yard a fight, walking like robots.

Everyone was tired: the guards, the prisoners, the dogs. The road seemed endless, in spite of the fact that many of us had already walked it several times. With each step we felt weaker. The file spread out, the ranks becoming irregular. Every so often you could hear orders shouted by the guards: "Close the ranks, don't spread out!" but the order came from a tired man, with a tired voice, a man who was hot and felt the weight of his weapon. He was tired from watching so many people move slowly in the heat. Our feet sank in the reddish leaves that covered the ground. The leaves from alders, aspens and birches fell slowly from their branches, circled lazily above the heads of the prisoners and fell to the ground to be stepped on.

Father Arseny was walking right next to me. I tripped several times and he helped me up with utmost care. Two or three times I looked at him and wondered, "Why is he still walking?" But there he was walking, straight, concentrating on something—you might think he didn't see anything. His lips were moving and I knew he was praying.

The road meandered along hills. The slopes on both sides were covered with fallen leaves which had been brought in by the wind. Sometimes there were a few bushes growing. Just in front of us a Tatar was walking. His face resembled that of an ascetic. His bag was empty, he wore rags and he was dirty. We knew he originally came from Kazan. He could not take the camp and was near his end.

In the barracks his bunk was very close to mine. Seeing that the man was hopeless many of us tried to help him. But it was too late, it was useless. Now he was walking, stumbling constantly, his arms were jerking, he was swaying from side to side.

When would it be time for a break? Sometimes somebody fell, the others would walk around him and the guards would make him get up by kicking him.

The dogs were walking on their leashes and it seemed they didn't see anything, their snouts were so close to the road. Everything was calm and quiet, no one talked; we heard no orders or threats, only the disconcerting rustle of our feet. Our feet hurt, our heads hurt, our bodies ached all over. I could only think about a rest. I was so tired that sometimes I couldn't even see the people in front of me. They would disappear and reappear in the dust.

This is it! I have no more strength. I am going to fall down. Suddenly I hear, "I'm off! I am running!" I immediately came to and saw the Tatar who had been walking in front of us running up the hill, slowly because he didn't have the strength to run fast.

The whole file of people was astir, awakened from their daze. The guards lifted their automatic weapons and started shooting. The bullets hit the ground and raised a small cloud of dust, but the man was still running.

This kind of escape had a special name: "escape to death." It happened when a man could bear it no longer, ran to be shot, not to have to live any longer. The guards understood about this kind of "escape," but they didn't want to give in to a prisoner's desire. With the help of the dogs, they would overtake him, beat him, and force him to get back in the lines, only occasionally killing the man—it all depended on the lieutenant.

The Tatar had great difficulty in climbing the hill. When the lieutenant and his assistant saw that he was losing strength they shouted to unleash the dogs. The dogs would stop him, he'd be beaten, the zek would get a few additional years in camp—but he would live.

Everybody was silent, they were moved to understand that the lieutenant wanted to save the man's life. Then suddenly, we heard the sound of an automatic rifle. The soldier turned out to be a good shot: he hit the Tatar with his first shot. As he fell one might think that he was trying to hold on to the bright blue sky—he stretched one arm towards the sun and fell head over heels down the embankment. The automatic rifle was still firing.

The Tatar lay still, but everyone could see him. His face was destroyed, his clothing was covered with blood, but the man was still shooting.

Tense and emotional the file of zeks walked towards the guards; the lieutenant in charge fired a few shots over their heads and shouted: "All of you! Fall to the ground!"

The men dropped to the road, which was covered with leaves. Above their heads they could hear another volley of shots and the same voice, hoarse from straining so much, continued, "Down! Flat on the ground!" and he swore rudely. Everything was quiet and you could hear the voice of the soldier saying, "Comrade Lieutenant! I got him like a sniper, with my first shot!" and you could hear that the soldier had a Tatar accent.

At this moment you could hear a voice from the ranks: "You dog! You killed one of your own! You deserve death yourself." The Tatar soldier turned around and aimed his gun onto the zeks, but the Lieutenant shouted, "Ibrahimov! Stop it!"

We were all flat on the ground and I suddenly heard someone crying. I turned my head and see Father Arseny, on his knees, above all of us flat on the ground; his face is wet with tears, as he quietly sobs with his lips moving in a whisper. I hit him with the flat of my hand and tell him, "Lie down, or they will shoot you!" but he didn't move. Resting on his knees and looking somewhere far away, he whispered and made the sign of the cross. I pushed him a second time, but he didn't want to lie down. What can I do? He doesn't want to lie down, I can only hope that they will not shoot me. For some ten or fifteen minutes we could hear the guards running around and then someone dragging the body. Then we heard the order: "Up! Stand in line—stay in order. If you take even one step to the side, I will shoot!"

We got up from the ground. We started walking. We noticed that the body of the man killed had been put away somewhere. There was still blood on the leaves. We walked on. The guards were fierce—we all knew that any attempted irregularity will be met with bullets. I look at Father Arseny—his eyes are wet, his face is serious and sad, very sad, but I can see that he is praying. I don't know why, but this made me angry—what a time to pray and to cry!

I asked him, "So, Streltzoff? Are you going to tell me you have never seen anything like that?"

"I have seen things like that, and not only this once. It is always horrible when an innocent man is killed. I see it and cannot help in any way."

I answered him ironically, "Why didn't you call on your God, so that he could help. Or you could have cursed the killer. It would have been useless perhaps, but you could feel revenge."

"What are you saying? Is it possible to curse anybody? God has saved many of us even now. God will punish the killer: the angel of death is already near him. O Lord! I am such a sinner!" he said and continued walking. He was very sad.

The killing of the Tatar somehow relieved the tiredness of our bodies and we walked faster, but no one said a word.

One day later, we came to our temporary assignment. We were to stay there about a month and work fifteen to eighteen hours a day. Our rations were even smaller than in our regular camp. Each day somebody died and was buried. The mosquitoes ate us alive. We were in such a state that people fell down dead while still holding their spades or axes.

The guard would calmly walk over to the man who had fallen, order the next zek to pick up his spade or axe, and kick the fallen man—sometimes the man would be able to stand up after a while, but most of the time he was put on a cart and shipped to a medic who would certify that he was dead and sign a paper. This was the end of this man's sojourn in camp and on this earth.

I started to keep an eye on Streltzoff. He had amazed me during the last trek. I could see that he was an exceptional man. He had been working like all the others for many years in the same camp. He was old and exhausted but he was still alive, he hadn't died. He believed in something, he believed so hard that this was obviously the only reason he did not die, but lived.

I kept an eye on him. What I found amazing was that although he worked as hard as anyone else and was as tired as the rest of us, he was always kind to others, always trying to help everyone. He was attentive to each. Even the guards respected him in their way and tried not to hurt him.

We worked for a month. Six hundred of us came. Not more than two hundred walked back!

The walk back to the camp took us four days. We had to walk slowly, but even the guards understood that there was nothing left of us but our souls. When we returned to "our" camp, they gave us a better ration to eat and let us rest for three days. There are human beings everywhere!

During this month I got very attached to Father Arseny. Everything about him surprised me. He was so warmhearted. He always helped and did it especially when you were close to giving up. He just knew when you needed him most. You would be in despair, ready to give up, and he would walk up to you, put his hand on your shoulder and say two or three simple words, words that would give you light, warmth and an answer to what made you so miserable at this particular time.

Many people like myself received help from him. People died, new people came. There was something like a circle, a special circle around him.

Perhaps you wonder why I started my story about Father Arseny with this terrible trek and the killing of the Tatar? Well simply because what I saw of Father Arseny during this time was so unusual; his care for everyone around him during this hard month amazed even the guards. I remember that many of them called him "Father" because of his helping others.

The Tatar soldier Ibrahimov was killed by someone the day we arrived in camp, when we were all locked in our camp. He was killed outside the camp by his own people—not by zeks—he was killed in an awfully cruel manner, clearly by other Tatar soldiers. We heard about this sometime later. I told Father Arseny about it. I remember how sad he was and how he said, "O Lord! How awful all this is. One more death, a cruel, frightening death. A death before the man had had time to find peace in his soul, before he had repented." He said that and walked away. I could only think, "A dog's death for a dog!"

I was freed from camp three years before Father Arseny, but my whole life was lit up by him. I always thank God for giving me the opportunity to meet this man—Father Arseny. In 1958 I saw him again, when he was out of the camp.

Written by a man spiritually loved and raised by Father Arseny, 1966-1967.

I Am Freezing

PIOTR ANDREYEVICH? OF course I remember him—I will remember him as long as I live. We met, if I may say so, in transit. We left the camp in the morning. It was -22° F and it was windy, but we only had our cotton padded vests to wear. We didn't have very far to go—only some ten kilometers—and this was supposed to take us four to five hours because we each had to carry a bag with our belongings. It didn't take long for the cold to strike me to the bone, and in about two hours I was really freezing. I looked around and saw that everybody else was also freezing, even the guards, although they were dressed in heavy wool coats. The dogs who were watching us were covered with frost. We started walking faster to warm up, but I could feel that my feet and hands were seriously frozen; they felt like wood. We all slowed down. The guards shouted, "Walk faster or you'll freeze to death!" I started stumbling because my feet no longer obeyed me. Suddenly I felt somebody supporting me by the elbow. I look, and I see an old man walking right next to me. I am surprised. What does he care about me? I almost fall, having no more strength. The old man grabs me by the arm and holds me so tightly that I can't fall and tells me: "Don't despair, move faster. It will warm you up. This way you will be able to get where we are going, with God's help." I keep walking for another half a kilometer. I am almost unconscious, I don't see the road, I slip and fall. I try to get up, but my hands and feet don't obey me. My consciousness comes back because of the fall and I realize perfectly well that this will be the end of me. If I freeze, I will die. I see the feet of the other prisoners walking past me. The old man stays with me. I know the routine: after the last prisoner walks past me, the guards will walk over to me; if I don't get up, they will shoot me and then report to the authorities that they had to shoot because I had attempted to escape.

I don't know why, but the old man is still next to me. I see the guard walking over to me, he kicks me and shouts, "Get up!" I understand everything, but am absolutely unable to move. I hear the old man telling the lieutenant, "Citizen, help him! He is going to freeze to death!"

Another guard walks up to us and says, looking at the lieutenant, with a question in his voice, "Comrade! Perhaps I could give him a little alcohol—I have a little in my flask."

The lieutenant gives the order to the others to keep walking and then stays together with me and the guard. The old man asks them again to help me. Why? I am already frozen, it is nothing but trouble to take care of me, it would be so much easier to just shoot me. One prisoner more or less—who cares? The old man looks unafraid. I had only fallen, but he was the one who committed an irregularity—he had stepped out of the file. I am sure they will shoot him. The lieutenant looks at the guard who takes the gun off his shoulder. Well, I think, this is the end. We are both going to die. The guard walks over to us, hands his gun to the lieutenant and says to the old man, "So, granddad, let's pick him up!" They picked me up. The guard took his flask and put it to my lips, and alcohol started pouring into my throat. I felt fire in my body and I swallowed avidly, drinking quite a lot. The guard and the old man started throwing me from one to the other to warm me up. They moved me while the alcohol warmed me from the inside. They dropped me onto the ground—on purpose—and made me get up again. My hands started to burn, my feet began to tingle and hurt, then they came alive. I cheered up. I told the guard, "Thank you!"

"Don't thank me, thank the old man here. He stunned us by daring to stay with you." Turning to the old man he said. "How did you dare stay with him? You know the orders—two steps to the side and I shoot without warning!"

The old man bowed to them and answered, "Why would I be afraid? All people have a soul, and I saw that you would help. God doesn't leave a man in trouble!"

We caught up with the others. People were amazed that they hadn't killed us. I never told them how I had stayed alive. That is how I met Piotr Andreyevich. He was the old man. At first I knew him only as Piotr Andreyevich, afterwards as the Priest Arseny. Piotr Andreyevich—Father Arseny—entered into my life like something enormous, something bright, giving, something joyous in such a way that I not only remember him but I constantly live through him. Remembering many things, I often think, "Father Arseny was right—many people have goodness within them. Sometimes it is hidden. It is our duty to find it, the same way that Father Arseny saw the good in the lieutenant and in the guard."

✢

In 1963, I met by chance in Kaluga the lieutenant who had saved me. He had become a civilian and I found out later that he was working in a factory as a mechanic. I went up to him and said, "Good morning, Comrade Lieutenant," but he didn't recognize me. I reminded him of the incident—he looked happy. We talked about the past and he said, "Those were awful times, it's painful even to think about them!"

I asked, "How is it possible that you didn't shoot us then? And that the guard gave me some alcohol?"

He answered, "We were people too. And then we were amazed at the old man. He knew he might die, but he wasn't afraid to help you. I will tell you the truth, many of us guards used to talk about this old man. He was special, he was good-hearted. They say he was a priest." And he asked, "Where is he now?"

I answered that Father Arseny was still alive. The lieutenant and I kept talking. We went to a cafe to have a little glass of vodka; we talked about our life in camp. This is how it all was. I corresponded with Father Arseny until he died. I have kept all his letters. I just have to tell you: he was a great man!

⬧

Written from the words of the president of a collective farm—an agronomist somewhere not far from Kaluga.

The Boots

———

YOU ARE ASKING me if I remember? Of course; I remember everything.

It has been told thousands of times: the interrogations, the sentence, the camp, hunger, beatings, criminals, death always on your doorstep and the constant longing for your loved ones.

Do you remember the song:

> You are now far away,
> Between us lie vast snows.
> I cannot reach you,
> And death is only four steps away...

It really was that way; death was so near that you could almost touch it with your hand. "Old woman death" was watching us all; she could take on the face of a new sentence, or a killing by a criminal for a piece of bread, starvation, or any of a thousand other faces.

I shared this fate with hundreds of thousands of others like myself. It is no use remembering it all. I am not the only one who had to endure it, so it is no great feat. On the other hand, to be able to find one's calling in prison camp is something few of us knew how to do. Father Arseny found his place in a camp, and he accomplished not only this one feat but hundreds of them.

It is difficult for someone who never was in a prison camp to understand what constitutes a "feat" in camp—how it compares to the heroic deed of a soldier. During the war, you might sometimes have a spurt of craziness and risk your life to save another. In camp you are constantly under the threat of death, and if you help people, it is doubly difficult. It is a true *podvig*.[7]

I met Father Arseny one winter because of... well, because of felt boots. Before that I hadn't had a chance to meet him. In the winter the most important thing is to keep your feet dry. There in camp, however, your boots are always wet, your feet freeze, they hurt and are covered with sores. You cannot dry your boots during the night—if you leave them on one of the stoves, you can be sure they will be stolen. You can't dry them in the evening, because that is the time the criminals dry their boots! In the course of that winter my feet were frost-bitten and I just was no longer able to go to work.

7 A *podvig* is a heroic deed, an ascetic feat, or an ascetic way of life.

The night before, I had come back to the barracks from work, and my heel was stuck to my boot with ice, because I had fallen into a little stream. I stumbled into the barracks, unable to take my boots off; I fell onto my bunk and thought, here it is, tomorrow I am going to croak. There I am, lying down unable to move and suddenly I feel that somebody is taking my boots off of me. My thought was that they have probably decided that I am dying and want to take my boots, but at this point I don't care. This somebody took off one boot, then the other, removed the cloths that were wrapped around my feet, and started massaging them. I was unable to react, but I understood everything that was happening. He restored the circulation in my feet, covered me up and left. A terrible thought came to me: he has taken my boots and my foot bindings[8] and wants to keep them. But why then did he massage my feet and put some kind of balm on my wounds? My feet still hurt, but less now, and I fell asleep.

In the morning the prisoner in charge boxed my ear and asked, "Why are you not getting up?"

I had overslept. I jumped up, my feet were bare, I looked around and I saw that the old man was bringing my boots and my bindings back and everything was dry. I was confused, but I got dressed and went to work. In the evening the old man took my things again and dried them again; he did this several times. That is what saved my life. I kept an eye on him, I finally started talking to him, and I just got used to him. Do you want to know how he got my boots dry? He put them on the stove and stood by all night watching over them. Of course he worked like everybody else during the day. This is what I call a real feat—a *podvig*.

I was very depressed when I thought that I would die there without ever seeing my family again. I know that many other people also felt this way. The old man—by then I knew that his name was Piotr Andreyevich or Father Arseny—simply told me one day, "Everything will be all right with you and your family. You will get out of this camp soon and you will see your relatives." I really don't know why, but as he said it I believed it absolutely.

I was in fact released a year or so afterwards. They had arrested me in 1952, and I had been in a regular camp some two years. In January 1953 they had reviewed my case and added time to my verdict, sending me to the special camp. At the end of 1955 they unexpectedly released me, returned all my rights and gave me my job back, and my relatives were indeed alive and well.

8 These were worn by peasants and by prisoners instead of socks.

Now, every six months or so I go to visit Father Arseny: I arrive with an empty soul, deeply tired. He meets with me, talks with me, hears my confession, removes the froth from my soul. I come to life and impatiently await my next visit with him. I return to Novosibirsk carrying with me the parcel of warmth and of faith which I receive from Father Arseny and I spend this treasure gradually. I am both a Communist and at the same time a Christian; nobody there knows that I'm Christian. I have a responsible job, but I try never to get involved with any work which has to do with atheism or with antireligious propaganda. I just make my way around all that.

So that is how I met Father Arseny. The world rests on people like him. I watched him in camp: he helped so many people and we, looking at him, helped others. I can see that you want to ask me how I could become a believer? I just looked at the way he lived and behaved and, what can you do? I became a believer. Later on, others helped. They told me about the faith, they explained, clearing things up for me—and I found out everything I needed to find out.

I want to come back to what you want to ask me next, the question of the heroic feat—the podvig. Many people nowadays like to use this word. They say podvig, podvig. But what is it really? I lived through the war, where I was involved in many battles. I was a volunteer, starting as a regular soldier and finishing as a major. I received the Cross of Honor, two Crosses of Lenin, a Patriotic War Medal, a Red Flag Medal, I cannot even list all the honors I received. I commanded a patrol of partisans, I was sent to work with the Germans to spy on them, I was wounded four times—all that was easy. I knew what I was doing it all for, I knew I always had friends around me, and I also knew that if I died it would be for my country. Then I found myself in a camp and came to understand what "the depths of misfortune" means. I understood that death for a cause wasn't the most frightening thing. In camp you are alone with yourself, with death, desperate death around you all the time. A painful death slowly creeps up on you. You are surrounded only by people who are also going to die, who are angry, desperate, emptied out. There is no end to their suffering and you are dying for no reason, not in the name of anything.

Even if you attempted to escape, where would you go? You have no more friends, because they are all afraid of you. You are alone. Believe me, the biggest podvig of all is to give help to others under such inhuman circumstances, when you yourself are tired, cold and dying of hunger. It is a podvig to give away a part of your own ration under these conditions, to do a difficult job for someone else when you yourself are half dead. You have to believe me, I have led soldiers to the attack, I have saved friends from fire, people have saved me, but I knew in what name I was doing all this. In camp in what name would you do all this? We were all condemned to die anyway.

Father Arseny saved many of us. He did it in the name of God and of His people. He never took pity on himself. This is a podvig in the name of love for others. He didn't expect any reward for all of this. O Lord, if only all people could be like Father Arseny!

From the words of Andreyenkov in 1966.

III

❧ SPIRITUAL CHILDREN ❧

"O Victorious Leader of Triumphant Hosts!"

I HAD STAYED late at my friend's place. We were chatting away. I looked at the clock and saw that it was 11 P.M. I said good-bye to her and ran to the train station. It was not far; first I had to walk through the village streets, and then nearer to the station I had to go through a little forest—a seven minute walk in all. The moon was young and it was dark, but I refused to be accompanied, and ran off alone. I was a young woman and afraid of nothing. As I walked I thought, "Mother will be angry with me because I will get home late. Tomorrow I have to get up early for liturgy, and then I will have a lot of work to do."

I walked fast, then ran through the streets and entered the forest. It was dark, and of course I was a little afraid, but I was all right—the path was wide, and I had walked it many times before. I slowed to a walk, since I did not see or hear anybody. Then I started running, but felt somebody grab me by the arms and throw something over my head. I tried to break loose and wanted to scream but they bound my mouth with a rag. I fought, trying to tear myself away, trying to kick my attackers with my feet, but they hit me on the head which kept me quiet for a bit. They pulled me off the path and removed the jacket they had used to cover my head, but they did not remove the rag that was keeping my mouth shut. A man's voice said: "If you make a sound we will cut you to pieces!" I saw a knife appear. "Lie down, you idiot! If you cooperate we won't kill you." I looked at the men—one was tall, the other smaller; both smelled of wine. "Lie down!"

They took the rag from my mouth and pushed me to the ground. I whispered, "Take pity on me! Let me go!" and pushed them away. The tall one put his knife to my chest and pricked it. I knew then that nothing could save me. The tall man said to the other, "You walk thirty paces to the side up that path. When I finish with her, I'll call you," and the smaller one left.

Here I am and I know that there is no hope for me to be saved. What can I do? How can I defend myself? I thought about God. "Help me, O God!" I could not remember any other prayer, only the one that suddenly came back to my mind, a prayer to the Mother of God. I knew that she was the only one who could save me. And I started praying: "O victorious leader of triumphant hosts, we, your servants delivered from evil, sing our grateful thanks to you, O Mother of God, as you possess the invincible power to set us free from every danger so that we may sing: Rejoice, O unwedded Bride!"

175

At this moment, the tall one threw me to the ground and started tearing my clothes off. He tore my dress off and bent over me with his knife in his hand. I could see him very clearly, but I did not stop praying, repeating the same prayer over and over to the Mother of God. I was probably praying aloud because the guy asked me, "What are you mumbling?"

I continued to pray and then realized I truly was praying aloud. The guy repeated, "I ask you, what are you saying?"

He suddenly stood up and looked above me. He looked attentively, glanced at me again and then angrily kicking me in the side, he picked me up and said, "Let's get out of here!" Still holding onto his knife and my clothes he led me away. When we arrived where he wanted to go, he threw me to the ground again and bent over me—I kept praying.

He stood near me and again looked up, over me. I continued to appeal to the Mother of God and suddenly felt that I was no longer afraid. The guy looks into the woods and, looking at me, says, "What does she need here, in the woods, at night?"

He picked me up, threw his knife away, and led me into the forest. We walked in silence, I continued to pray and I was no longer surprised by anything. I just knew that the Mother of God was with me. Of course, this was a daring notion, but that is what I thought at the time.

We walked for a short while. I suddenly saw the light of the train station. Without emerging from the woods, he threw my clothes at me and said, "Get dressed. I am going to look away!" He looked away and I got dressed. We kept walking. He bought me a ticket to Moscow, wet a handkerchief in the drinking fountain, and washed my face where it was bloody because of the blow I had received.

We sat down in the train and there were no passengers other than the two of us. We sat, not saying a word. I continued my prayer, silently repeating: "O victorious leader..."

Arriving, we got off the train and he asked, "Where do you live?"

I answered. We took the tram to Smolensk Square and walked to my house. I kept praying, walking in silence and looking at him every once in a while. We came to my house and we went up the stairs. I took out my key and again I was afraid. What is he doing here? I didn't want to open the door, and just stood in front of it. The man looked at me and started walking back down the stairs. I opened the door, ran into my room and knelt in front of the icon of the Mother of God. I thanked her and I cried. My sister woke up and asked me, "What is the matter with you?"

I could not answer, but only kept praying. Some two hours later I washed my face, cleaned myself up and prayed till morning, thanking the Mother of God. The next day I went to the early morning liturgy and told everything to Father Alexander. He listened to me and said, "You received a great blessing from Jesus Christ and His Mother. We have to thank them. He will punish the evildoers."

A year went by. One day I was at home studying. The windows were open; it was hot and stifling. Only my mother and I were in the apartment. The bell rang, Mother opened the door, and I heard her say, "Come in, yes, she is home!" and she shouted from the hallway, "Maria, it is for you."

I thought, "How inconvenient," but I shouted back, "Do come in!"

I got up, thinking it was one of my friends—a student. The door opened and I froze. It was the guy from the forest. If you had asked me a minute earlier what he had looked like, I would have been unable to say, but I recognized him immediately.

I stood without moving: he came in, looked around my room and, paying no attention to me went to the corner where there hung a lithograph of the icon of the Mother of God of Vladimir. We kept all of our icons in a locked cupboard, but this one we had hung on the wall under the pretext that it was a painting.

He went over to the picture, looked at it and said, "She's the one!" After he stood there a minute, he came over to me and said, "Don't be afraid, I came to ask your forgiveness. Please forgive me, I am terribly guilty before you, forgive me!"

I was still standing motionless, like a stone, not knowing what to think. He came very near me and said again, "Forgive me!"

He then turned around and left. This meeting made a big impression on me. Why had he come? What did this bandit want of me? A thought crossed my mind—perhaps I should inform the police, have him arrested. But instead of this I opened the cupboard with the icons and began to pray.

One thought did not leave my mind: why did he say, looking at the icon of the Vladimir Mother of God, "She's the one!"

I kept thinking, "Why did I not look at him before? Why did this bandit ask for my forgiveness? What does he need? He is not as tall as I thought, his eyes looked at me inquiringly and intensely—not at all like those of a bandit."

✠

The war was in progress, the year was 1943. We were always hungry. I was working as a nurse in a hospital and trying to study medicine. My sister was sick but studied in the Institute. My mother was so weak that she could barely walk. Life was very difficult, but I still had the time to stop into church every once in a while. There was fighting near Moscow, in the Caucasus, around Stalingrad—it was the spring of 1943. I had to be on duty two days in a row; I came home exhausted and there was nothing for me to eat. My mother and my sister were both sick in bed.

I took my coat off and started the fire in the stove; my hands were trembling and they hurt. I tried to pray, I began to recite the Akathist to the Mother of God. I heard a knock at the door. When I opened it I saw a lieutenant carrying a big bag. He was leaning on a walking stick. "I am here to see you!" he said.

"Who are you?" I asked. He didn't answer but pulled the bag into the room and said, "I'm that guy! Andrei!"—and I knew then that it was him.

My mother lifted her head from her pillow and looked at him. Andrei opened the strings of the bag, pushed his leg clumsily away and sat down on a chair without being asked, and started pulling things out of the bag. On the table appeared things we had not seen for months: cans of bacon, condensed milk, lard, sugar and other things. When he had taken everything out, he tied up the bag again and said, "I was seriously wounded, and in hospitals for three months. I didn't think I would live. Even now they are working on my wounded leg. While I was bedridden I kept remembering you and the Mother of God. I prayed as you did then. I heard the doctors say that I would die, that I was lost. But I survived, I am alive. These cans of food were brought to me by my brother—he was so happy to find me in that hospital. He is working near Moscow on a collective farm; he traded things for this food and brought it to me."

He got up, walked over to the cupboard with the icons; I had left it open. He venerated the icons, blessed himself with the sign of the cross, walked up to me, and said again, "Forgive me, in the name of the Lord. I beg you! My past obsesses me constantly. I feel terrible!"

I looked at him and at the food and shouted, "Take all this away and leave immediately!" and started to cry.

Here I was standing and sobbing; my mother looked at us from her bed, my sister lifted her head and also looked on. Andrei looked at me and said, "No, I will not take anything back!"

He went over to the stove, laid some kindling and some logs and lit it, stood near the stove for a few minutes, bowed to me, and left. The whole time I could not stop sobbing.

Mother asked, "What is the matter with you? Who was that man?"

I told her everything. She listened to me carefully and said, "I do not know how you were saved then, but whatever it was, I see that Andrei is a good man, a very good man. Pray for him."

During that same year, 1943, Andrei literally saved our family. We didn't see him for two weeks, but then he started coming regularly, sat with my mother for hours on end and talked. He always brought us a lot of food. He came one evening when I was home. He walked up to me and said again, "Will you forgive me?"

I started talking with him. He told me a lot about himself. He told me how they saw me in that forest and why they attacked me. He told me how he bent over me and heard me whispering something. He was surprised, and confused but suddenly he saw a woman next to me. This woman halted him with a commanding gesture. When he threw me on the ground again this woman protected me with one arm and he got frightened. He decided to let me go and brought me to the station. He saw that I was in shock, so he took me home.

"My conscience did not leave me in peace! I suffered constantly, I understood that all of this had happened for a reason. I thought about this woman. Who was she? Why did she stop me? I decided to go to your house to apologize. I was ashamed, I was afraid, but I went. When I came into your room, I saw the picture of the Mother of God and understood that she was the one I had seen then in the forest. When I left you, I asked everybody I could about the Mother of God; I found out all I could. I became a believer. I understood that I had seen a great apparition and that my sin was heavy. Everything that happened had a big influence on my life; I felt more and more how guilty I was before you. I knew there was no way I could make up for it."

Andrei told me a great deal about himself. My mother was exceptionally good-hearted and a faithful believer. Before Andrei came this last time she kept telling me, "Maria! The Mother of God showed this man a great miracle—she showed it not to you, but to him. For you it was horribly frightening and awful, and you did not know why God saved you. You believed that your prayer saved you. But it was the Mother of God herself who stopped Andrei. Believe me, she would not have appeared to an unworthy man. The Mother of God will never leave Andrei, and you must forgive him!" Clearly he had told my mother everything.

My sister Catherine had fallen madly in love with Andrei; as for myself I could not stop feeling disgust and even hatred towards him. I even tried not to eat the food he was bringing. After we talked this last time, though, I understood quite a lot; I saw him differently, and I calmed down. I went up to him and said, "Andrei! You've changed. You have become a different person. Forgive me that I couldn't stop hating you for so long," and I gave him my hand.

He said goodbye—he was being sent back to the front lines after his short stay with the wounded who needed rehabilitation. As he was leaving, my mother took from her chain a small icon of the Mother of God on which there was the inscription "save and protect." She blessed Andrei with it and, according to the Russian tradition, she kissed him three times. He undid the collar of his uniform and my mother sewed the little icon in a seam. When Katia was saying good-bye, she kissed him quickly on the cheek. He came to me, bowed low and said as always, "Forgive me for the sake of God and of the Mother of God. Please pray for me!"

He walked up to the icon of the Mother of God of Vladimir, venerated it several times, bowed to all of us and, without turning around, he left.

The door banged shut. Mother and Katia started crying. I put the light out, lifted the black-out curtain and saw in the moonlight how he left our house, turned to look at our windows, made the sign of the cross several times and walked away.

I never saw him again. In 1952, when I was already married, I received a letter from him at our old address. My mother passed the letter on to me. The letter was short, with no sender's address, but the postmark showed that he had sent it from Saratov.

Thank you, thank you, all of you. I know I was frightening to you, but you did not push me away. At perhaps the hardest time of my life, you gave me support by forgiving me. The Mother of God was a helper and protector for you and for me. You owe your life to her. I am even more grateful to her, because I owe her the faith which gives me life—human and spiritual life. She gave me life and protected me during the war. May the Mother of God save and protect you. I am finally living as a Christian.

Andrei

This was the last news we ever had from him. I retold all this to Father Arseny and he said, "This man received a great blessing and he showed that he deserved it. God was keeping him for important and good deeds."

Father Matthew

THERE WAS A time when Father Arseny really did not feel well, so much so that he spent most of his time in bed. Just during that time a man about 55 years old came to visit him. Father Arseny wouldn't listen to us, got up from his bed, and joyously welcomed this visitor. Nadezhda Petrovna prepared dinner, after which Father Arseny and his visitor disappeared into his room and spoke the whole night long—Father Arseny's bed did not have to be made up that night.[1]

In the morning Father Arseny and Father Matthew served a liturgy at which Nadezhda Petrovna and I were present. They talked the rest of the day. It was hard to convince them every once in a while to stop long enough to eat anything.

During dinner that evening, Father Arseny felt much better and gazed at Father Matthew with particular affection. As for Father Matthew, he calmly sat, talked, listened, answered questions or recounted things. He stayed with us for six days. At the end of the fourth day he told me a great deal about himself. The story of his life after the end of the war, of how he found his family and lost it again, made an indelible impression on me and I asked his permission to write down what he had told me. Below are my notes.

✤

In April 1941 I was suddenly called into the army. I was then 28 years of age and my Ludmilla was 25. I had married her out of enormous love. Living apart was no life for either of us. During the first months in the army I could find no peace. We wrote each other every day. Ludmilla was everything for me; I think my love for my sons even came second after my love for her. She is a very special person: she has an enormous will power, is faithful to her values, always tells the truth, and is goodhearted. I knew that she loved me as much as I loved her. Our love was based not on sexual attraction but on a deep spiritual closeness and attachment to one another.

I was educated as a physicist, while Ludmilla finished the Pedagogical Institute and taught the younger levels of the middle school.

War, like any other tragedy, comes unexpectedly. Right from the beginning I was involved in heavy battles where we had to retreat and I had to fight seriously. I wrote home very often, but I later found out that my letters never

---

1 In Soviet Russia most often people would use a sofa as a bed, as apartments were small and both rooms and furniture had to serve many purposes. The sofa had to be made up each evening when the person was ready for bed.

arrived; as for me, I of course got no news. I was wounded several times, I stayed in hospitals in the Urals and in Siberia, during which time I still wrote Ludmilla often and received letters from her. But as soon as I was back at the front the letters stopped altogether. In February of 1945 I was seriously wounded, and on May 7, when I had gotten better, they sent me to Prague. This is where I heard about the end of the war. My chest was covered with medals, but my thoughts were always at home. I was not the only one to feel this way, I think everybody did. We finished the war—we had saved our country.

Six days after our victory I was arrested. On June first I was condemned to be shot, though my verdict was changed to twelve years in prison. The accusation was dreamed up by my superior officer who claimed that I had led a campaign against my country with the enemy. I tried to convince the interrogator and later the tribunal that this was not true. Nothing changed. They listened only to my superior. I later heard that he had done the same to several of my friends. He was trying to get a promotion.

I was convicted and stayed in camps until 1957.

In one of those camps I met Father Arseny and got attached to him; I loved him. By that time I had already become a believer. Another prisoner helped me in this. He was a good man and a real believer. He really gave me so much in that camp.

I was never able to let my family know that I had been arrested and sent to camp, but I hoped that Ludmilla would find out through the authorities or perhaps through some friends. I spent the last years in the wastelands of Siberia, and was freed in 1957. I still had to labor for three months in Norilsk. From there I wrote to Moscow looking for my family, but received no answer.

I was desperately searching for my family; first I tried to find them through legal channels, but didn't get anywhere.

So I got dressed just as decently as I could and decided to search on my own. I tried to find out what I could through friends. I discovered that Ludmilla had been evacuated to Kostroma and had stayed there. I was very anxious, because I knew that I might see them soon and I worried all the time about how they were. What had happened to them?

Here is Kostroma. I arrived at seven in the evening, and had to look for the street where they lived. When I finally did it was already about nine o'clock. I knocked at the door and a man opened it. He looked at me, shuddered, took a step back, and suddenly he said, "Come in, Alexander Ivanovich!"

I went in and took my coat off. The man stood silently looking at me, then he turned to a door and said, "Ludmilla, somebody has come to see us!"

Ludmilla came in. As soon as she saw me she ran up to me and screamed, all in tears: "Sasha! Sasha! It is you! Where have you been?"

She hugs me, she kisses me. I forget everything, everything in the world. I hug her, I hold her against me, and I kiss her face, her hands and I feel the beating of her heart. How long this lasted, I do not know. But when I glanced at the man who had opened the door for me I saw on his face such suffering and such sincere grief that I cannot even begin to describe it. I asked, "Lyuda, who is this?"

She stepped away from me, she looked at both of us and, with a strange moaning in her voice, she said, "He is my husband!" and only then did I understand that I was finished. I felt helpless, I felt lost. I sat down and I asked, "And what about me?"

They both were silent. I held my head in my hands and started sobbing. I was shaking and I was weeping—this was something which had never happened to me before, but all the years I'd spent suffering and waiting for a reunion were taking their toll. I was desperate. I felt someone take me by the shoulders and say gently, "Calm yourself. Tell us what happened to you during all these years."

I lifted my head and I saw that it was my Ludmilla's husband who was talking to me. He sat across from me, while Ludmilla was still standing. I looked at her, unable to take in what was happening. My thoughts were heavy, angry, unclear. Then all this disappeared and I only saw Ludmilla. Her face was pale, her eyes were enormous and filled with tears and indescribable suffering. There she stood, looking at me and then at Boris—I later found out that was his name.

She was as beautiful as before, my own, my familiar Ludmilla, my wife who now was the wife of another. The Lyuda about whom I had been thinking all these years, towards whom all my thoughts had been directed during all these years. Only the hope of seeing her again had let me survive in camp during those twelve years—I had finally found her and had immediately lost her again.

I looked at Boris and saw the same suffering and feeling of being lost. "Tell us please," he said.

I started telling them everything. I probably talked for a long time. I told them about the army and how I kept writing letters. I mentioned how I had been sent to Prague, how I was arrested, court-martialed, and given twelve years in camp. I told them everything and then fell silent. They were also silent and at this moment, as if out of a dense fog, a thought about God came to me and I silently addressed Him, saying, "O Lord, help us, pronounce your judgment. Only you know what is right."

Ludmilla walked around the table that was separating us. She came over to me and said, "Sasha, forgive me, I am guilty before you. When I did not receive any letters from you, I asked the authorities about you and I waited. The answer was always the same, "missing in action.""

I decided that you had probably been killed. The last letter I received from you came from Prague. I only thought about you, but you see I met Boris, and got used to him. I started loving him and married him after I had known him for four years. Then a little daughter came to join our two sons. Her name is Nina and she is seven years old now. Forgive me, I am the only one who is guilty. I didn't wait long enough. "Forgive me"—she kept talking and cried as she talked. Boris stayed silent.

What was I to do? What was I to do? I did not know, I could not see a way out and neither of them could either. I saw my photographs from before the war hanging framed on the wall. I suddenly saw everything in a new light.

The accusation and irritation that I'd felt disappeared, and goodness and warmth invaded my heart and my soul. She had not forgotten me, she had remembered me and it was true that it was nobody's fault. But what could we do now?

A heavy silence invaded the room. A sad and heavy silence of suffering. "Where are the children?" I asked.

"They went to visit their grandmother. They will spend the night."

I looked at my wife. I knew, I just knew, that if I asked her to follow me she would leave with me. She would take the children and leave Boris. I would then forget her second husband and love her as before. But what about the children? In those last eight years my sons had gotten used to and started loving their new father. There was also his little girl. How would they react to all this? Would they love me? Would they understand what had happened? Would they be able to forget Boris?

I would break apart an existing family, a united family where people loved and understood each other. Did I have anything to forgive Ludmilla for? Why was she guilty? She had waited, she had looked for me, she had suffered alone with our two children. Only after she had been sure that I had died did she get married. I was not forgotten by this new family; my photographs were a witness to that. I was alone and there were three of them. What rights did I have? Neither she nor I were guilty of anything, nor least of all was Boris. I loved (and still love) Ludmilla, but that did not give me the right to destroy a family, just for my own sake. I would sow evil and sorrow and I would deprive my children of the man who had become their father. My sons loved Boris. Did they now love me? What would happen to the daughter whose father was Boris? And again my thoughts returned to God. I do not know why, but I got up and went to the next room.

There were three beds next to the walls. This is where the children slept. At the head of the smallest bed I saw a little icon hanging on a ribbon. I was unable to see which saint it represented, but the thought that Ludmilla, who had not been a believer before, allowed an icon to hang over the bed made me feel happy and warm inside.

In camp, the man who had helped me become a believer had always said that the only way to God is through doing good, through helping other people and denying the enormous, human "I" we are always trying to push forward.

These thoughts came and went. I had only one choice. I had to, I simply had to leave and get out of the lives of the children, Ludmilla and Boris.

Ludmilla looked miserable; she was oppressed with the weight of the unknown. Her face was so sad that I felt ashamed that I had kept them both waiting such a long time for my decision. Boris sat with his head hanging as if a heavy weight was pulling him down.

I got up and went over to Boris and Ludmilla, and said, "I am leaving. This is the only way that is fair to all of us. You are a family, and I belong to the past. You have two sons and a daughter while I have nothing. You love each other. I will leave. This is not a sacrifice, it is the will of God and it is your right."

I got up and started putting my coat on. Boris looked at me with concern. Ludmilla ran to me, hugged me, and said, "Don't leave!" But I sensed some uncertainty in her voice. Boris walked up to me, shook my hand, and said, "It is difficult for her. She suffers for us both and for the children."

I walked out as if the meeting with Ludmilla and the children had never occurred. Only the past remained. I was alone again. The woman I love was lost for ever.

I had waited, full of hope, for so many years, and I was alive only through that hope. I had found her, and now I had lost her for ever. I was walking the streets of Kostroma, it was dark, I walked oppressed by all that had just happened, but I understood that there was no other way out. But still I saw Ludmilla in front of my eyes.

I was sick for about six months. There are many good people in the world, people who helped me. During this time I became very close to the church, and this stopped me from making many wrong decisions and actions.

I found work as a physicist at an institute; I got absorbed in my work, and thank God I got good results. I even became somewhat well known: my work was published and I had enough money, but the memory of Ludmilla and her eyes were constantly in front of me.

The town where I lived was not big; there was only one church left: all the others had been destroyed or simply closed down. The church became my salvation, a place where I could rest my soul, where I felt comforted. In this church I met a doctor, a faithful believer who influenced me and helped me very much.

As far as I remember theirs was the only home I visited where I could feel at home and learn about spiritual life. I did not follow what was happening in Ludmilla's family: this wasn't necessary for her or for me. One time I wrote Boris and asked him to accept financial help from me. I sent him almost all my money through a good friend who lived in Kostroma. Life was very hard for me in those years. I suffered not being able to forget Ludmilla and the children.

About four years later I found out that Father Arseny was still alive. I wrote him, went to visit him, and he became my spiritual father and counselor for many years. Later I became a monk and was ordained a priest. I had wanted this for a long time, but Father Arseny would not allow it. He gave me his blessing only two years ago.

I left my work and started serving in the church. My colleagues were surprised. I am living now in a little industrial town where the church is small, but there are many parishioners, many real, good believers.

I calmed down, my past leveled out, but half a year ago something happened which shook me and stirred deeply.

I came home one day, after liturgy. The owner of our apartment said that a middle-aged man had come to see me. He had not left his name, but had said that he would return about four o'clock. I paid no special attention to all this, but at four o'clock the bell rang. I went to open the door. A man of about fifty walked in. His face was yellow and he looked exhausted, but his eyes were luminous and impressive in their expressiveness and their kindness. He walked in, said hello, and called me by my name. I understood that I had seen him before, but I could not remember where. I looked at him surprised. He noticed this and asked, "Don't you recognize me?"—and I knew at once that he was Boris, Ludmilla's husband.

He started talking right away. "I came to give you some news about the children. I have cancer, they've operated on me twice, and now I get chemotherapy. I have gotten yellow, but my health has not improved. At best I have two months to live.

"But this is only the beginning. I want to thank you for the help. It was really important to the family. You helped us very much. I never told Ludmilla about this, as you had asked me, but I'm sure she guessed. She knew you well.

"Your sons now have children of their own. Ludmilla raised good people. They are both engineers. Our daughter Nina has started university. God is good: all the children are believers. Ludmilla used to not believe in God, but after you left she changed very much in this respect.

"I came to report to you. I always tried to know where you were. I felt this was important because our fates had become intertwined in a complicated and difficult way. I know all of it was difficult for you, but it left a scar on Ludmilla and myself as well. Ludmilla loved you and she still loves you; but she doesn't know where you are. Your departure drew her even closer to you. By sacrificing yourself you showed the power of your love.

"Her love for you was difficult for me to bear. But it wouldn't be fair to say that she didn't love me afterwards. We lived together for many years after that and she never was cold or indifferent to me; she never blamed me for anything. It would happen that I would wake up in the middle of the night and see very well that she was not sleeping, and only made believe she was. I knew that she was thinking about you."

He told me about the lives of the children in detail and finally said, "I do not have long to live—my days are numbered. If there is a second priest in your church, ask him to hear my confession. Help me!"

I was looking at Boris and I realized that after my departure his life had been very difficult and painful, full of doubts and worries. In spite of this he had been able to raise the children, make them believers and make Ludmilla believe. His life had been more complicated and more difficult than mine. It was a truly a heroic feat. He stayed with me for three days.

Father Andrei, our priest, heard his confession and gave him communion. I remember him saying to me, "You brought a good man here; this Boris is a good man. A rare man."

✠

While Father Matthew was telling me his life, Father Arseny listened very carefully. I knew he had already heard all this before. Father Matthew stayed with us for a few days. I never saw him again, and I only remember that some five months after this visit Father Arseny said to me, "Do you remember Father Matthew? I received a letter from him today. His life is difficult and complicated but he has managed, with the help of God, to come to the only correct decision. May God protect him!"

The life story of Father Matthew made a big impression on me and I will never forget it as long as I live.

Father Platon Skorino

IN AN ANCIENT patristics book, I read that the Fathers once said that God gives each person a chance to look back on his life, to see its meaning and decide what his relationship is with God—he can then take a step towards God or push himself away from Him. In the course of our life many events give us a chance to meet God and to draw nearer to Him. We have free choice either to approach or to move away. In surrounding man with chains of events, it seems that God is trying to help the undecided person to come to Him. It is entirely our own fault if we push away our own salvation.

In my own life, I was given the opportunity in several situations to choose the way I was going to go. Twice, if I remember correctly, I turned away from the path of Truth which was put before me, but God was merciful to me and he helped me again and again to turn to faith. Thanks to His mercy I became a believer, a Christian, and later a priest.

On my way to faith I met remarkable people who were true helpers of God, who helped me and taught me a great deal and showed me, through the example of their own way of life, what a true Christian is.

(This is what Father Platon told me. He stopped, kept silent for a while and then continued his story. Father Platon was tall, broad-shouldered, and had typically Russian good looks, with somewhat unyielding gray eyes. His lips closed tightly, giving the impression that he was a strong-willed man who was ready to overcome any obstacle. At the same time his face was extremely kind. It seemed his eyes spontaneously reflected everything that happened around him. I decided, for some reason, that this man would lay down his life for friends if he felt he had to; but that if he was angry, he would be frightening in his anger. These thoughts ran through my mind as Father Platon continued to talk.)

I tell you, when you recount a story, everything seems complicated; in life it is all much simpler. I am from Leningrad, from an orphanage. I finished seven years of schooling and had to take a job as a metal worker in a war factory; because of my line of work I never was mobilized during peaceful times. I never had time to become a party member—I was only 23 years old when the war started. In school I had been a Pioneer in the *Komsomol*,[2] I always wanted to be the head of dances, parties and outings. I can admit now that I was very interested in girls, and they

2 A Pioneer was a young member of the organization of Communist youth called "Komsomol." There was great pressure for students to join this organization.

seemed to adore me. It was fashionable in those day to be an active anti-religious propagandist; I was not among the last in this area.

In 1941 when the war started, I immediately volunteered for the army. I was strong and healthy and they assigned me to an espionage unit. For a whole year I never got a wound or even a scratch—everything was all right. I thought then that I was lucky. When our commander got killed, they replaced him with a young lieutenant. We saw him as an intellectual, because he looked "too clean" to us. He was of medium height, thin; he didn't seem strong, and he spoke without cursing. When he gave orders, they were as precise as if he were making a pencil drawing: he was clear and meant to be obeyed. We all felt that we knew more than he did since we had been in battles for a long time; it was easy for him to give orders from his bunker but how would he behave behind the lines?

From the very first time he went out with us, we were surprised. We say about a good soldier not that he fights well but that he "works" well. That was exactly what the lieutenant did—and he "worked" like an artist. He was fearless, careful, precise. He walked like a cat and could crawl on the ground like a snake. He protected his men, not hiding behind them—on the contrary, whenever possible he went first.

About three weeks after he arrived, we had to go behind German lines, far away. This was a dangerous mission. Six to ten people were usually sent—we knew this from the radio operator—but in most cases not one returned. They were all killed. For this expedition there were eight of us including the lieutenant. While we were crossing the German lines, we lost two men. We found ourselves behind the lines in a forest, and started our reconnaissance mission. This lasted six days. We sent messages every day and we lost three men. There were only three of us left: Lieutenant Alexander Alexandrovich Kamenev, Sergeant Seregin and myself. We received the order to return. It is easy to say "return home." The Germans were looking for us and they would probably catch us. They also knew what they were doing. So we came to the front of their lines and waited for the night. We were lying on the ground, studying the situation. "Where can we cross?" We crawled into no-man's land, and that is when the Germans saw us. We hid in a shell-hole. The Germans started shooting seriously, sending flares over our heads and pouring bullets everywhere. I got shell-shocked. Seregin managed to crawl out of the shell-hole and make it back, so the lieutenant and I were left alone. I kept losing consciousness, the lieutenant had been lightly wounded in the leg. Once when I regained consciousness I thought, "He will do the same thing Seregin did, he will leave me." And I knew that it was the only thing he could do. But the lieutenant pushed me onto a piece of tarp—it was difficult for him to do since the shell-hole was a shallow one. Then, as soon as it got darker, he started dragging me on the tarp. I told him: "Leave me, otherwise we will both die. I am heavy, you are not strong enough."

"It's all right, God will help." He said and kept dragging—he had to drag me for about 200 yards. The Germans detected the movement and started shelling even harder than before. Splinters flew all around like peas, and the firing of the automatic rifles forced the lieutenant to lie still for a while, as blasts of dirt flew with each bullet, I lost consciousness. When I came to, I heard as in a fog the sounds of explosions and I could feel that I was being dragged along the ground. Where was I being taken? To our lines? To the enemy? My friends later marveled that it was possible that the tiny lieutenant had been able to pull me, such a heavy man. There was quite a bit of talk about it. The lieutenant and I received medals for this. When I got better, they were ready to send me on another mission. I looked at the lieutenant with love and wanted to thank him. He answered me with a smile, "You see, Platon, God did help us!" I thought he was joking.

We were sent behind the lines again. The Germans had become even more cautious, so that anyone who was sent got killed. We knew we were going to our deaths—but an order is an order, so we had to go. There were six of us—and I will tell you ahead of time, all six returned safely, which amazed everybody in our division. We brought back some very important information, as well as a German prisoner who gave the authorities some other critical information. For me this mission grew to be extremely important, because it was, in a way, the beginning of a new life. It was the time which showed me that I was not living as I should. We reached a place about 30 kilometers behind the lines, near some village. On its outskirts stood a little church near a forest.

Four soldiers went to reconnoiter, while the lieutenant and I went toward the church. It was quiet all around us, the moon was new, and the cross on the cupola shone with a bluish silver light. I suddenly thought that there was no war, and that there shouldn't be war in which people kill one another. But my automatic rifle was slung around my neck, I had a knife strapped on my side, bandoleers of bullets for my rifle on my back, and death was watching us from all sides. The lieutenant went toward the church, moving from tree to tree; I went to walk around the graveyard, but didn't make it and returned to the place I had left. And what do I see? The lieutenant is standing by a tree, looking at the church and making the sign of the cross. Looking up, he crosses himself slowly and whispers something. I was amazed. The lieutenant, an educated man, who is fearless and a good soldier is suddenly displaying this primitive belief, this lack of awareness. I cracked a branch then walked over to him and said, "So, Comrade Lieutenant, it turns out you believe in gods."

He turned around, frightened, but he controlled himself and answered me, "No, I do not believe in gods; I believe in God." From that day on, there was a distrust between us and we began to watch each other carefully.

It's a long story, but we all returned safely. As I said before; we went through a lot! Everyone thought that we were just lucky. I think now that it all was part of God's plan. We returned, and the thought would not leave me. How can a Soviet person believe in God? He is obviously educated, so he must have read the books of Yaroslavski and of Stepanov in which it is clearly proven that God does not exist. If you still believe, you have a bourgeois mind and are therefore an enemy of the people.

"He is a wolf in sheep's clothing," I thought. "He's only making believe that he is a real soldier. It's true that he is courageous and that he saved my life and also that his findings behind the lines were important. Perhaps his camouflage, his masking all had a purpose. The enemy is smart and shrewd." I could find no peace of mind. I went to talk to the authorities. I was received by a young lieutenant and told him about my doubts. He got excited and pleased, and took me to see his superior. The superior was a major from Latvia who was always sad and always tired-looking. He listened to the young lieutenant telling him that Lieutenant Kamenev was an enemy hidden in our ranks and that he should be eliminated. I was asked how he behaved during our missions, what was his relationship with the soldiers during times of inactivity. The major thought for a moment, called someone on the phone, asked a question, and said, "Comrade, Sub-lieutenant, you are going today on a reconnaissance mission behind German lines to gather information about Lieutenant Kamenev. You may leave now! As for you Skorino, please remain!" The young lieutenant turned pale and tried to say something, but the major only hushed him.

When the door had closed behind him the major told me, "Listen, Skorino! I know a great deal about reconnaissance, and I also know a lot about the lieutenant and about yourself. But would you please tell me: is that a head on your shoulders or an empty vessel?" Here he tapped my forehead with a finger. "You are a fool! So what if he is a believer, so what if he made the sign of the cross? You saw him in action. You worked with him. He saved your life; he brought back priceless pieces of information. And now you tell me that he is the enemy. In 1941 I walked home from the border: I saw the retreat. I saw people surrounded by the enemy. I saw panic, fear, courage, true fearlessness, true love for our country. This is when you really see people as they are. I wish all of you could fight like Kamenev does. Did you know that at the beginning of the war he led a whole train of the wounded from behind enemy lines? He carried a wounded general off the battlefield. You know nothing about people if you judge them on little things. Today you will be sent on a mission with the young lieutenant and with your Kamenev—and just you watch them both in action. Throw out of your mind your silly thoughts and do not speak of it to anyone! Just go now, and learn to read people better. When I was young I too was over-zealous, and I splintered many a log, and now I am sorry for it. Go!"

I was amazed at this conversation. But that night we went on a mission to catch a prisoner who would talk. The young lieutenant turned out to be a coward, hiding behind us, never raising himself far from the ground. He refused to go forward, always hanging back. We took a prisoner and started to drag him home. The young lieutenant got excited and started to run, and that is when a bullet took off half his head.

A week later we were sent on a mission one more time. Everything went well until we ran into a group of Germans in the forest. We were almost goners, but we made it. When we came to the meeting place we had agreed on, we divided into two groups. The lieutenant took me with him. We walked for two days or, rather, for two nights. We met a number of tanks, and we tried to work our way around them in order to measure the strength of the enemy at this point. We barely made it back. It took us a while, but we did make it.

In the forest we found a sort of a hole filled with leaves. Because we were tired, we lay down in these leaves, and decided to take turns sleeping, but neither of us was able to fall asleep. At this point I decided, "Whatever may be, I just have to admit to the lieutenant that I went to report on him." I also wanted to tell him what I feel about religion.

When I finished talking, the lieutenant was silent. Then suddenly said, "Do you know what faith is?"

He did not wait for my answer but kept talking. As he talked something totally new opened up before me. In the beginning it felt like an interesting and sweet fairy tale—he was talking about the life of Jesus Christ. Then when he started talking about the meaning of Christianity, I got all shaken up. He spoke about the goal of people to become better human beings. He explained to me what prayer was. He spoke about the lack of faith and about anti-religious propaganda. I began to see religion from a different perspective—it was not just primitiveness, manipulation, lies. We spoke for about three hours, until the sun began to rise. I was able to ask only one thing: "But they say that priests are fakers, who are looking for their own advantage. How is this compatible with religion?"

The lieutenant answered, "A lot that is being said about our priests is a lie—few of them are bad. Any good thing will attract evil people who will take advantage of it to get richer or whatever."

"Are you the son of a priest, Comrade Lieutenant?"

"No, I'm not. My father is a doctor and my mother is a teacher. They are both believers. I myself live only for my faith. The fact that you tried to report me to the authorities was also the will of God. You heard what the major told you about people. Even up there, there are good people."

I will never forget this conversation. We got back to our meeting place. Two others had gotten there before us. They sent their messages and turned to go back again. We walked for two more days trying to cross the German lines. The Germans dispersed our group. Only the lieutenant and myself remained, while the others died. To this day, I still do not know how we made it back.

I became very fond of the lieutenant, but he was soon transferred with a promotion. My contact with the Lieutenant Kamenev left a permanent mark on me. It made me think about many things and probably it prepared me for receiving my faith. He was a good man.

I was sent away to a hospital near Viatka, in Kirov. I stayed there for five months, then I was transferred to a nursing home for two months. My wound became infected and septicemia set in. No medication helped. Looking at the faces of the doctors I could see that they had lost all hope. They transferred me to a single room, which alone was proof that I was going to die. They were just waiting for me to die. Of course I wanted to live, but I was tired of suffering, of pain and treatments, and the expectation of frightful things unknown and oppressive. I was afraid not of death, but of other unknown things.

There was a nurse in our hospital; her name was Marina. She was thin and tiny and had brown eyes. She was cheerful, kind, and especially attentive to each patient. We all loved her for her sensitivity and her never-faltering readiness to help us. It so happened that every soldier who was on the mend would fall in love with her. Although she was kind to every one, she kept her suitors at a distance.

When they transferred me to the "hopeless" room I was unconscious almost all the time. But every time I regained consciousness, Marina was there. Sometimes she would be giving me an injection, other times she would be wiping my forehead, or changing my sweaty clothing. Once, as I lay there with my eyes closed, the head doctor entered with a group of younger doctors. He was making rounds. The doctor responsible for me reported to him on my progress and ended by saying, "He is lost, he has septicemia—an infection of the blood."

The chief looked me over and also pronounced, "It's hopeless."

Although I was lying there half asleep, I heard and understood everything. I didn't know if it was day or night, I regained consciousness and could feel that Marina was standing next to me. She was saying something in a half whisper while sponging my forehead with water. I understood that she was praying for my health. I opened my eyes and she said to me, "It's all right, Platon, it's all right. You will be well," and she gave me some water to drink.

I later found out that it was holy water. Marina kept on praying. This went on for about two weeks. She would bring a little bottle with holy water, or a little piece of blessed bread (prosphora), and gave them to me every day. As soon as she came near my bed she was constantly praying. She came to my bedside even on her days off. It was she who cured me, it was she who obtained my recovery from God.

When I got better, she spoke to me about faith, and taught me a few prayers. I left the hospital a true believer. She together with Lieutenant Kamenev turned my life around.

I loved Marina as a mother, in spite of the fact that she was my own age. The chief doctor said to me when he sent me to the nursing home, "We pulled you out of the 'other world,' but without nurse Marina we could not have done anything. You must bow deeply to her."

I already knew that, but I knew Who along with Marina had helped me. I swore to myself then and there that if I live, as soon as the war was over, I would become a priest. I told this to Marina.

The war was finally over, I was demobilized in Berlin. I returned to my dear Leningrad and immediately went to the seminary. I went to them, they looked at my papers and then returned them to me. They did not want to accept me in spite of everything I could say. I was called to appear before the War Committee. They mocked me, and tried to dissuade me: "Listen, Skorino! Are you crazy? You have won all the medals possible, you are a full lieutenant and you want to become a priest, a preacher? You are shaming the army!"

But I persisted and was admitted to the seminary. It was very hard for me to study as I was totally uneducated. I had only finished the lower grades of school, and that was of course very long ago. Yes, it was very difficult. I felt that sometimes people got in my way on purpose. I finished the seminary and wanted to become a monk. Now it was the seminary's turn to make fun of me: "What, you, such a healthy man, so inexperienced, and you want to become a monk! You'd better get married; you'll still be a priest." To be honest, they were right, I wasn't right for monastic life – and besides, where could I prepare myself for it?

So I had to get married before becoming a priest,[3] and there I was, studying in the seminary. I never went anywhere and didn't know any girls. They were ready to assign me to Irkutsk, and I was not even a priest yet. I had to find a bride fast! Before the war I used to have many friends, but in the course of those years in the seminary I had lost them. I wasn't interested in women then and hadn't thought about marriage. And now I had to find a wife, which is indispensable for a priest. I went to church and started praying, asking God to help me. I prayed for a long time.

I came out into the street and I saw a one-legged man hopping along on crutches. As I passed him I recognized the former captain of our regiment. I forgot to mention that I had finished the war with the rank of full lieutenant—I had started as a simple soldier. I ran up to the captain; we were both happy to see each other. He invited me to his apartment. We started remembering our times together, and then talked about today's problems. The captain was a good person, cheerful, hospitable. I told him I had finished the seminary, that I wanted to become a priest and that I now had to find a wife. He thought I was joking. "I have the woman for you!" he shouted. "My first cousin Nina."

I met her two days later, I liked her and I thought she liked me. I decided to marry her, so a few days later I asked her to marry me, and told her everything about myself. At first she didn't want to believe that I was going to be a

3 In the Orthodox Church, priests may be married if they wed before ordination.

priest, but after she had thought about it she accepted my proposal, saying, "But, Platon, I am not a believer."

Well, I thought, I had been an unbeliever myself! I spoke about this in the seminary. They listened to me carefully and gave me their blessing. In two weeks I had gotten married, and they ordained me a deacon and later a priest. We had to leave. Nina told me, "You go, Platon, I still have to stay for a year and a half to finish my studies in nutrition!"

I can't understand how I could have forgotten that she was still studying. She had told me, but I forgot. But I had to go. We decided that she would join me after she finished her studies. I will be honest, it was hard to leave her behind. I loved her and had no doubt that she would join me.

Yes, now I want to speak about my Nina. She is not very tall; she comes just above my shoulder. She is slim, but well built. She has big gray eyes. She is very beautiful. She has a sharp tongue; she knows how to talk.

I was sent to Siberia, to a village beyond Irkutsk. The village was large, but the church was closed because the priest had died. No one was taking care of the church building, and it was partially in ruins. I tried to put it back in some kind of order. Two old women helped me. I started holding services at the church, but only three people came, so I got worried. Where were the parishioners? I decided to serve every day. I served for a week, a month, three months. Still nobody came. I fell into despair. I went to talk to the bishop, telling him that I was serving daily and nobody was coming. What should I do? The bishop listened carefully to me and said, "God is merciful! Everything will happen in due time."

After I left the Bishop I stopped by the local city church. I waited for the end of the service and went up to the old priest, and told him my sad story. He invited me to his home and was kind to me, saying, "God called you to be a priest. He will not leave you. Everything will be all right—parishioners will start coming and your wife will join you. Pray more!"

I became friends with Father Peter and visited him often. He gave me a lot of support. He was a very spiritual man.

Half a year went by and I still had only eight parishioners, but I kept on serving. I honestly had no money to live on. In my free time I started to work. I would fix a roof for somebody, I would help store timber, I would fix locks. While I was working I would talk to the owners of the homes I was working in. It was of course interesting for them to have a chat with a priest. Some of them started asking about the faith. I was glad to answer; they listened to me and some of them began to stop by our church. At first they just wanted to look around, but then they came to pray.

Of course I worked honestly, conscientiously. I suppose I had learned something in that factory in Leningrad. I had as many orders as I could handle. By the end of the year 80 to 90 people were coming to church, mostly middle-aged people. During the second year young people started coming.

At first, when I had only just arrived people did not receive me well. I would walk in the street, and boys would shout, "Look, there goes the pop with a bald top." and often they would use swear words. These guys would mock and laughed at me. They would walk into the church and start laughing, not wanting to let me serve. When I would ask them politely to leave, they left swearing hard. They thought I would never defend myself. Once a group of young men beat me up seriously. I was taking a walk in the evening when they attacked. While they hit me I only begged them, "Don't do it, please stop." They had fun beating up a "pop."

It was very difficult. I missed Nina badly. When she finally came, I was very happy, but in the beginning she had a hard time. She had never imagined herself in a rural life with a country priest. She now had a diploma, and found a job in the big milk factory in our village. They hired her easily, but started giving her trouble when they found out that she was the wife of a priest. She was very knowledgeable, she worked well, and was an example for all.

Once in the evening when Nina and I were walking home, four half-drunk guys attacked us. Three started beating me but one was interested in Nina. I begged them to leave us alone, to let us go. Nina is screaming, "Help! Save us!"

The guys keep beating me up and I see that one of them is throwing my wife to the ground, the two others looking on. "Hey, Father Platon!" I thought. "You were trained to fight, you have tricks up your sleeve and you are very strong." I let myself go! I let them have it. I threw one over my shoulder, hit another in the stomach, hit a third with the side of my hand on his neck, and ran to the one who was attacking my Nina. I was as angry as I could be and so I hit the guy hard and threw him into the bushes. Nina was standing amazed. The two who had been watching tried to help their friends, but while I beat the one up they both ran away. I picked up the guys I had been fighting and let them have it again. It was all such a surprise for them all. They thought a "pop" was a weakling and that he would be easy game. I decided to teach them a lesson: I forced them to crawl for 50 yards—I am ashamed of this now. They crawled, and when they tried to resist I let them have it again. Ninka was laughing: "I didn't know you were like that, Father Platon!" I was very angry then.

After this encounter people started to respect me. The guys I had beaten up came up to me and said, "Father Platon, we thought you were just an uncultured 'pop,' and it turns out you are a sportsman!" I served the marriage ceremony for one of those guys in church a year later, and I baptized the daughter of another.

I know! You probably blame me for this fight, because a priest should not fight. But I had no choice. Had I been alone, it would have been another thing, but my wife was with me. I later told all of this to my bishop; he laughed sincerely and said, "In this particular case, you were right to act as you did; in any other case I would ask you not to use your physical strength. God will forgive you!"

⁜

We lived in this village for several years. On May 9, 1965, we celebrated the anniversary of the end of the war and our victory over the Germans. Both the leader of our collective farm (*kolkhoz*) and the head of the village were veterans. They declared there would be a big celebration in the club. They invited all those who had been in the war, and they asked that each wear all the medals he had received.

"Platon! You must go for sure!" said Nina.

I wore my civilian clothes and pinned on all my medals. I had many of them: three Medals of Glory, four Medals of the Red Star, the Medal of the order of Lenin, the Fighters of the Red Flag, three special medals for bravery and plenty of others as well.

When I go in the club, the leader of the kolhoz almost doesn't recognize me, and then he says, "Where did you get all these medals?"

I answer, "What do you mean where? I received them during the war."

He was faced with a problem. Where was he supposed to seat me? All those who have medals were supposed to sit on the dais, and I have more medals that any one of them, but... I am a priest. He asked someone's advice and said, "Comrade Platonov, I would like you to come and sit on the dais," and sat me in the second row. I should mention that many called me Platonov as a last name, although Platon was my first name. The veterans who had been involved in combat each recounted a particular memory of their experiences. I thought it over for a minute and decided that I would also recount my memories. Of course I knew perfectly well that this might mean trouble for me from the church authorities, but I decided to show people that believers and priests were not just uneducated or stupid people, but that they really believe in God, walking toward Him, despite all odds, seeking no personal advantage. I even became friends with the leader of the kolhoz. After this event he began to appreciate me. He told me that his superiors had blamed him for letting a priest speak at the celebration.

We stayed in the same village for twelve years. God was merciful to us, He did not leave either of us. The church was full of people, they liked me, and even the authorities did not create too much trouble. My Nina did not take to religion right away, but now I think she is stronger in faith even than I am. She is now a sincere believer, she knows the church services well and is my support and advisor in all church affairs.

They have now transferred me to a big city. It is difficult for me to get used to it, but I am trying.

I think that this is all I can say about my life and the path that led me to God.

Wait, I apologize! I just remembered how I heard about God for the first time from a believer. I was very impressed by this encounter, and it started me thinking. It left a mark on my soul, a mark that I would think about every so often—but I was only fourteen then and living in the orphanage.

We had a teacher of sociology. His name was Nathan Aronovich—I don't remember his last name. He organized evening get-togethers, discussion groups, conferences. He took us to museums and led an anti-religious propaganda club. He was constantly with us.

A boy also aged fourteen came into our orphanage. His name was Vovka Balachov. He came from an educated family. He was a good student, but he didn't like to talk—he was an introvert. He had stayed with us for six months when one of the boys noticed that he was blessing himself with the sign of the cross. He denounced Vovka to the teacher in charge. I don't know what was said between them, but this was a time when debates were in fashion in our school. We would pronounce judgment on such literary heroes as Chatsky, Onegin, Tatiana Larin, Bazarov,[4] and others. One of us would be the prosecutor, another the defender, and of course one was the accused, the literary hero. There was always a teacher present, but he would try to let us proceed without helping.

4 These are all heroes of famous novels by authors such as Griboyedov, Pushkin, and Turgeniev. All Russian teenagers are familiar with these characters.

Nathan Aronovich decided to arrange a judgment on Jesus Christ and on Christianity. We decided that Vovka Balachov would play the role of Jesus Christ, and dressed him in a sheet so that he would look like Jesus. Nathan Aronovich prepared us well as to what to accuse Jesus of. The prosecutor was Iura Shkurin, the defender Zina Fomina and the presider Kolia Ostrovski. There were seven witnesses, and two classes formed the public.

We all got very involved. We worked for ten days on making a case, without Vovka knowing what we were doing. We started calling him "Little Christ." Only one day before the case was to be tried did we inform Vovka that he was to be Christ. Vovka tried to refuse, but nobody listened to him. We later heard that many teachers were against the whole thing, but Nathan Aronovich insisted. We noticed that in the course of this one day Vovka seemed to have lost weight and became very nervous.

We gathered for the "court session." The presider opened the session. Balachov refused to wear the sheet. He stood pale, without a hint of blood in his face. The girls started to pity him and we, the public, also felt uneasy. The presider asked Vovka, "Do you plead guilty?"

He only had to answer, "No, I am not guilty!" and then we would have started the discussion, arguing. It would have been interesting. It always was: we brought up arguments and quotes from literature; we all always learned a lot from the experience and understood the hero better than before. The important thing was the discussion. Vovka surprised us all with his answer, "I am a believer! I do not accept such a judgment. Every person has a free conscience." Then he sat down.

They started to interrogate him. He was silent. We didn't know what to do next. Nathan Aronovich signaled to the presider to make a plea. Iurka stood up and started to say, "Vestiges of capitalism, the rich farmers, the priests, the relics..." and ended by saying once again that this was vestiges of capitalism. He spoke well and we all applauded. The defender also brought up for consideration the dregs of capitalism, a lack of culture, the influence of the society, etc., etc. Her speech was as much an accusation as that of the prosecutor. We all applauded again.

Witnesses were called to the stand. They each quoted books of anti-religious propaganda. Somebody showed a caricature of Christ from a comic book. Everybody had fun and got involved. The presider suddenly realized that the speeches of the prosecutor and the defense should have followed the appearances of the witnesses, but since he could do nothing about this any more, and pleased with how the case had proceeded, he offered the accused Vovka Balachov to make the final statement.

Nathan Aronovich was pleased. As always when he was in a good mood he rubbed his hands.

We all thought that Vovka would remain silent. But he got up, stood tall and straight, and started speaking as if some weight had been lifted from his shoulders. We listened to him, stunned. He spoke about good and evil, about the teachings of Jesus Christ. He explained why he himself believed in God. He said that we were poor and to be pitied because we had no faith. Our souls and minds were empty. He was never alone, because God was always with him. God was his hope and his strength! As he spoke, we thought he would cry.

Nathan Aronovich signaled the presider to stop Vovka, but the presider did not want to interrupt. Vovka finished his presentation saying, "Yes, I believe in God and it is my business. Nobody has the right to judge me for this. Each person has a conscience which is free and nobody should impose their ideas on others. I believe in God and I'm happy I do!" And he remained standing.

He spoke so well that he caught all of our attention, we were impressed. We gave him an ovation. None of us had ever thought that Vovka could speak in such a way. Where had he found the words?

Neither the prosecutor, nor the defender, nor any of the court knew what to do. Kids are basically honest. They understood what Vovka was saying and they understood that we have no right to accuse people for their convictions. On top of it, Vovka's speech sounded so sincere and unforced.

Nathan Aronovich jumped to his feet and shouted to the presider, "Read the verdict!" Kolia Ostrovski only answered, "But he is not guilty."

The question nobody dared ask was, "Who is not guilty? Jesus Christ or Vovka Balachov?"—and so it seemed that neither was guilty.

Nathan Aronovich was so angry that his face was covered with red blotches, his voice trembled, and he said, almost hissing, "Enough of this farce! There is no Christ. Christianity is only an unsuccessful imitation of Judaism. This is all lies! There is no God—Balachov spoke dangerous lies. Read the verdict!"

The presider, Kolia Ostrovski, after conferring with his assistants announced, "The court cannot pronounce a verdict because of circumstances beyond our control."

We left the room with a heavy heart. It had been no fun. Many conversations followed this event, because we each had been touched in some way.

About two weeks later Balachov was transferred to an orphanage for "difficult" youngsters. Nathan Aronovich lost our affection and we didn't want to be around him any longer.

Looking back I can see the different ways God led me to Himself. Lieutenant Kamenev, the nurse Marina, Vovka Balachov, my studies in the seminary, my marriage to Nina, the difficult life I had in the beginning of my priesthood, the fact that I did reconnaissance work, and much, much more than I have told you about. All these were steps by which God led me to Himself.

✥

I asked Father Platon, "And how did you meet Father Arseny?"

"In the church where I serve now I have a spiritual son who is a good friend of Father Arseny. He asked Father Arseny permission to bring me here to him. So I came. I thank God for this. I put my whole life into his hands, and I leave a renewed man. And as soon as I get home I will convince Nina to come here as well. Father Arseny said she should come!"

Mother Maria

THE LONG YEARS of life—with all their joys, worries, difficulties and griefs—in the end become the memories that a person carries within himself. The bright and joyous ones light up your life as it proceeds; they cultivate your soul. The dark and loathsome years—those you try to forget. But memory will not allow you to forget, and these recollections haunt and oppress you; they make you suffer. The life you have lived inevitably turns into a series of memories.

I want to tell about some people whose life is not in the distant past but is still real today, in spite of the fact that it arises out of my personal memories. True love enriches a person, brings him happiness, and gets reborn again and again in others. But if there is a power stronger than love it is self-denial for others' sake. It is kindness, limitless faith in God, prayer and the help of others.

Both Father Arseny and Mother Maria were people of that quality. I want to tell about them, because you just have to be told about those who helped the people around them, alleviating their suffering, teaching them, and leading them to God. I am sure that many of those who will read about Father Arseny and Mother Maria, about their good deeds and their way of being, will find new life in their example and will find the proper path. This is why the stories of Father Arseny and Mother Maria are not memoirs but are life itself; they are the living source that gives you the strength to believe and to renew your ability to live as you should.

To write this account I have relied on the notes I made almost daily at that time. Of course some things may be subjective and were written under the influence of the mood of those days. As I was writing from these notes, I tried to delete my personal remarks, but I am not sure I always succeeded.

✥

I came to see Father Arseny for my holiday. I loved the little town where he lived, I used to walk its beloved old streets every day, visiting its monasteries and churches which were half in ruin. On such walks you would find yourself in the fourth century, then you would be thrown into the ornate eighteenth, and then to the more pompous nineteenth. I became friends with the curators of museums, and I was given the chance to see such beautiful mysteries of antiquities that not many tourists or inhabitants of this town had ever had a chance to visit.

205

I was 27 years old then and I could walk miles in the environs of the town. In the evening, when Father Arseny was free, I would pray with him, talk with him or just listen in on his conversations with others. Every time I was able to do this I learned things about the spiritual life and the faith. When I left Father Arseny I always felt spiritually enriched.

One morning I visited a monastery built in the sixteenth century. Much of it was still standing, but everything was old and decrepit. Especially beautiful was the main church building, where you could still see a seventeenth-century iconostasis. I came home tired, and rested for two hours. In the evening, at about eight o'clock, Father Arseny received a visit from a young woman he did not know. She brought a note. Father Arseny read the note and told me, "Tomorrow morning we will go to Moscow. Evdokia Ivanovna writes that Mother Maria, a nun she knows well, is very sick. We'll have to leave on the first train, at five in the morning. Please buy three tickets and come with me. We shall stay in Moscow for perhaps four days." Then he started to talk with the young woman who had brought the note.

I didn't have time even to look at the young woman, but went to gather a few things for Father Arseny and for myself. Nadezhda Petrovna, in whose house Father Arseny lived, helped me put all the necessary things into my briefcase. When I returned to Father Arseny's room he was not there.

The young woman was walking all around his room, looking at the books on the table and the shelves, looking at the paintings and icons that were hanging in the corner. She looked over all his belongings in a rather cavalier way. When I walked into the room, she paid me no attention but kept looking around at everything. When she had finished, she sat back in an armchair and said, "I never thought that a priest nowadays would be interested in art, medicine, philosophy, or Marxism. I thought that priests only knew about services, the Gospel and the Bible. I am surprised at your Piotr Andreyevich." Then, having looked me over very carefully, she said with a trace of mockery, "Tell me, are you also one of 'those', like Piotr Andreyevich?"

The tone of her conversation and her impudence were unexpectedly hurtful to me. I was hurt for Father Arseny, and I said angrily, "Yes, I am one of 'those!' But before you say anything more about Father Arseny in such a tone, why don't you take a look at some of the books he has written."

"Books?" she said, all surprised.

I opened a cabinet and showed her a few of the books he had written. She took one of them in her hands and leafed through it stopping every so often and reading a few pages. She then said, "He is a learned man and a priest! What an unexpected combination. Life goes forward, materialism is recognized in almost half the world and has entered the minds of all people. Many books have been written that prove that religion is absurd, but religion is still alive...

"Scholars believe, writers believe, famous painters believe, doctors, professors and teachers believe. Millions of highly educated people in the West believe. Our churches are full of people, and not just old ladies. (When I was a little girl, the old ladies used to irritate me awfully by the way they tried to teach me how to behave.)"

And as if she was answering herself she said, "Yes, much is written, but nobody has yet been able to prove that God does not exist."

Addressing me, she continued. "You know, I've read many atheistic books, but I have the distinct impression that they are unable to prove anything. They either try to discredit religion or they argue with God, trying to prove to Him that He does not exist... My grandmother Katia believes unconditionally. If only you knew what a human being she is! She is better than anyone else. She is even better than my mother and father. If only everyone could be such a believer." And unexpectedly she asked me, "How about you, what do you think about God?"

I was going to answer, but then I saw Father Arseny standing at the door, looking at the young woman with such a welcoming warm and gentle smile that I decided not to answer.

"So, are you ready?" he asked me.

"Yes, I will be at the station tomorrow at four in the morning, and I would ask the two of you to be there at five, for the arrival of the train."

On the train the next morning we were silent. Father Arseny looked fixedly out the window. We passed forests and fields, stations, crossings; various buildings flew by. We saw people walking on paths. Praying, he was unaware of all this.

The young woman in our company, whose name was Tatiana, read a medical textbook. I tried to concentrate on the short story I was reading. We traveled for a few hours. Two or three times Father Arseny addressed Tatiana and asked her something.

Moscow was noisy and you could see that Father Arseny, who was now used to life in a small town, felt somehow lost and unsure of himself here. When he sat in a taxi he found it difficult to shut the door, and he looked bemusedly at the buses, trolleys, cars, and people rushing by. A tall modern building greeted us with the sounds of shrieking children, and the sounds of a radio playing music. We heard the noise of slamming elevator doors and the clicking of thin heels against the asphalt of the sidewalks. We saw rushing pedestrians looking suspiciously at the old people who sat on benches near building entrances.

All was quiet inside the apartment. The sun was shining through the windows. We went to wash our hands after the trip. Tania went to see her grandmother, said something to her and offered us some tea. I refused, and Father Arseny kept silent. Tatiana, full of energy, was setting the table with cups; she started slicing bread, cheese, and some kind of fish. In about five minutes probably everything they had in the kitchen was on the table, and we started to drink some strong tea.

Then we walked into the bedroom. On the bed was an old woman whose hands were lying on top of the blanket. Her face was serious and sad. Her big eyes were gray and looked at us with curiosity and gentleness.

"Babushka, I brought you the friends of Evdokia Ivanovna!"

"Yes, I heard you talking for a while," the babushka answered.

"Sit down, Father!" she said to Father Arseny. "You too, 'smartie,' do sit down, and listen. Tania will go and take care of something she has to do."

"Why did she call me 'smartie'?" I wondered.

We sat down. For a few seconds we were silent. Father Arseny, it seemed, was observing something; he was thinking with great concentration.

"You, dear Father, sit closer to me. First I will tell you about myself, so that you know my life, and then please hear my confession. My voice is now very quiet."

Father Arseny took his chair over to her bed and again I noticed that he was observing the face of the old woman with concentration. You could see that he had summoned up all his spiritual strength and from the gentle movement of his lips I guessed that he was praying.

There was silence in the room. It was strangely quiet. Father Arseny did not talk, and Maria did not talk. The sun was bright through the window on which there were white sheer curtains. On the walls you could see copies of paintings by Nesterov. In the corner above the bed there was an icon of the Mother of God of Vladimir. It was surrounded by an embroidered towel. You could see that it was arranged in such a way that the icon could be covered if needed.[5]

I was impressed by the face of Mother Maria. You could tell that she had been very beautiful. She still was beautiful through the web of wrinkles that covered her face, but she looked extremely tired and sad. Her large gray eyes looked at Father Arseny in request and hope.

Her long hands, covered by a net of visible veins, didn't move, but they were tense. It seemed as though she might all of a sudden use them to help her sit up. Her simultaneous immobility and tension made her hands look like those of a statue. Looking at the hands of Mother Maria, I tried to imagine her personality and I remembered Nesterov's portrait of the academician Pavlov, where his hands on the edge of the table also spoke so clearly of his character.

"Bless me, Father, bless the nun Maria. My baptismal name was Ekaterina. I want to tell you about myself so that you know whose confession you are going to hear. Perhaps it will seem strange to you, but my spiritual Father Ioann told me once, "When it is time for you to die, you must tell about yourself to your confessor. Do not forget this!" I want to do what he ordered me to do. Please, Father Arseny, do not be cross with me for my story."

Father Arseny came close to her, bowed low and blessed her in an especially touching and loving way. Mother Maria received his blessing with reverence and a sense of unworthiness.

"Father, I was orphaned at age six. I was taken in by my grandmother, a poor peasant. We had to beg for bread in villages, and beg for money near churches. This was what we lived on. The local landowner, Elena Petrovna (God rest her soul) took me into her service. When they got used to me, I started to play with her daughter, Natalia Sergeyevna. We became friends, we loved each other. Elena Petrovna was kind and fair. She was responsible for the whole household. She loved me like a daughter, she acted like a parent to me and gave me warmth. I studied together with her daughter. This was a good time, Father! Yes it was good.

"I grew up. I was seventeen years old by then. God gave me a good figure and a pretty face. It sometimes happened that some guests would mistake me for the daughter of the lady of the house. Elena Petrovna and Natasha didn't mind this. They were true saints, yes they were!

5 As it was dangerous to keep icons on display, they needed to be easily covered.

"Sergei Petrovich, the husband of Elena Petrovna, loved women. He gave much grief to his wife with his numerous escapades. Otherwise he was a good man, God rest his soul.

"I was growing up. Sergei Petrovich loved me, treated me like his daughter, kissed me and hugged me, but then he started to try to see me alone in the garden or in a room. I understood what was going on and tried to avoid him. I was scared and so ashamed in front of Elena Petrovna and in front of Natasha. They had accepted me as one of their own, and this horrible thing was happening!

"Ever since my childhood I had believed in God and I wanted to become a nun. Even Elena Petrovna jokingly called me 'my little nun.' I used to pray for long periods of time.

"Sergei Petrovich used to stop me and I would beg him not to touch me. His answer was, 'you little fool, you don't know where your happiness lies!'

"Once, Elena Petrovna and her daughter went away to visit somebody. Sergei Ivanovich also went off. I had a headache and stayed home. I was sitting in my room, when Sergei Petrovich suddenly rushed into my room and said in an emotional voice, "I love you, Katia! Let us leave this house. I will take you with me to St. Petersburg...to Paris!" and he started embracing me. He pushed me down, started tearing my dress off, and kept saying things. I kept pushing him away, praying all the while, 'O Lord, save me; O Mother of God protect me! Help me!' He was going crazy and tore my underwear. I fought, tearing myself away from him, begging him and crying, 'Sergei Petrovich! I don't want anything. Have pity on me! Don't shame your family. This is a sin, a terrible sin. Do not destroy me! I want to go to the monastery.'

"He became as angry as a beast. I started crying aloud saying, 'O Mother of God, help me!' At that minute Elena Petrovna opened the door and screamed, 'Out of my house! I never want to see you here again!'

"I leaped up. With my hair all over the place and my clothing torn, I wanted to run away. But she halted me screaming, 'Stop, Katia! I'm not chasing you away, it is him I want out of the house.' And she did throw him out. For a whole year he didn't come back.

"She took me in her arms and crying, she said, 'Forgive me, Katia! I doubted you. I was watching you and just now I was standing behind the door when all this happened, and I heard you. I understood everything.' She kissed me many times. I was sobbing, I couldn't stop. This woman was a real saint.

"I didn't stay long in that house after what had happened. I wanted to go into a monastery, but Elena Petrovna tried to prevent me."

"A young engineer, the son of one of Elena Petrovna's friends, wanted to marry me. She tried to convince me to accept his proposal. She offered to give me a nice dowry. I insisted that I only wanted to be in a monastery. So Elena Petrovna went with me to a monastery where the abbess was one of her relatives. She paid for my stay there and I became a novice.

"Elena Petrovna and Natasha cried when we parted. I couldn't stop crying either. O Lord, what good people you sent me. Your glory is in them.

"I was happy in the monastery. I learned a lot and understood much. I met many good people who taught me how to go toward God. I sang in the choir, I learned the services, I learned how to sew. All of this helped me later in my life. But I didn't stay long in this monastery—I came in 1914, and in 1919 the authorities chased the young novices out of monasteries. I stayed another year in a private apartment where other nuns lived nearby. I would visit them. But then I had to leave, as the president of the kolkhoz started courting me and refused to leave me in peace.

"I moved near Riazan, where I started working as a cleaning woman in a church. The priest was a good man. His name was Father Ioann. He let me lead a monastic life. He had a great soul and was a prayerful man, but I didn't stay there long either. The church got closed down and Father Ioann was sent to Siberia. We corresponded. He was old and was unable to survive in exile for very long. He taught me a lot. Perhaps it is a sin to admit it, but he gave me more than my life in the monastery had.

"I moved near Kostroma because I knew somebody there. I started living near the church. In the beginning all was well, but all of a sudden Father Gerasim started to love me. One evening while I was cleaning the church after vigil, he attacked me, threw me to the floor and wanted to rape me. I begged him to leave me alone and I pushed him away. He insisted and swore in a dirty way. I hit him on the face. He beat me to a pulp; he tore my dress to shreds. I was able to escape. Two weeks later the police came and arrested me, saying that he had reported to them that I was agitating against the government. I stayed in prison for three months. Then some people stood up for me and I was set free.

"I left. It was only with great difficulty that I found a job in a sewing factory. I knew how to sew. Later I started to study to become a medical nurse.

When I finished, I started working in a hospital as a surgical nurse. I moved to Moscow, where a nun I knew helped me. She was working in a hospital herself, and she helped me to get hired. I worked there from 1924 on. I am now retired from there.

"All this time I corresponded with Elena Petrovna and Natasha. Life had pulled them apart. Sergei Petrovich died in 1919; we accompanied Elena Petrovna to the cemetery in 1927. She had come to have an operation in our hospital and only lived one year after this. Natasha used to come to visit me in Moscow quite often. I used to visit her too. She had a difficult life; she suffered much. She was killed along with her husband in 1937.

"In the hospital I became friends with a doctor. Her name was Vera Andreyevna. She was middle-aged and her husband had left her. She was left with two children: Alexei and Valentina, who is the mother of the Tatiana who brought you here.

"We started raising the children together. It was not easy, but God helped us. We raised them well. In 1943 Alexei was called to the front. He was killed almost immediately.

"Vera Andreyevna worked in the army hospital whereas I was a nurse in the local hospital. Valentina wanted to become a soldier, but instead later became a doctor and got married. First they had a daughter, Xenia, and then another, Tatiana. I became their second grandmother.

"That is my whole life, Father. It was spent in a hospital or at home taking care of children. Is this a monastic life? You can see for yourself. It was just day-to-day life. May God forgive me! Oh yes, I forgot the most important thing. In 1935, I did become a nun. I was tonsured under the name of Maria. I was tonsured secretly. My family heard about it only a few years afterwards. And so I lived in the world. I was a nun only in name. I know this is a great sin. I really never became a true nun, no, I never did. I loved to pray when I could and I loved going to church.

"You could be on duty at night in the hospital. You would just get started praying but when the bell rings, you have to run. Or else you would have to sit all night next to a critically ill person, or another who had just been operated on. When you are in the operating room, your attention is focused on the instrument you have to give the surgeon. At home you have to take care of the children, you have to cook, you have to talk to them.

"I never even came close to real prayer. Only sometimes I could pray while I was on my way somewhere. Sometimes in the course of a whole day I would be able to say "Lord, Jesus Christ, Son of God, be merciful to me a sinner" only a dozen times. At night, when I would start to pray, I would have no strength and I would fall asleep. I couldn't even perform any good deeds, as I was too busy with day-to-day things. When I retired, I was able to pray more, but became unable to help others. I am now old and weak. So you see, although I had been so anxious to become a nun, I was unable to fulfill my promise to God. I am a sinner.

"A long time ago, when I was still living in the monastery, a staretz (my spiritual adviser) told me once, 'Do good to people and pray more—this is the salvation of monastics. Ekaterina, your path to monasticism will be long. You will have many difficulties to overcome, but God will not leave you. Go!' Father Ioann of Riazan told me the same thing. I did not fulfill their advice. I sinned much, and I almost got married. This was in 1930, but God stopped me.

"Since early childhood, I had wanted to be a nun. I continued to have this desire when I became a novice. It took me twenty years to become a nun, and then I was a bad one. This is my whole life, Father! I told you everything because I was told to do so by my father confessor, so that you know whose confession you are going to hear.

"I summoned you with great difficulty, but I didn't dare hope that you would come. The day before yesterday I was in church and I felt strong, but when I got home my strength gave out and I knew my hour was near. I told Valentina and her husband that I would die on Tuesday. They made fun of me: 'What are you saying, Babushka?'

"But the doctor who listened to my heart said that my heart had suddenly gone very weak. I know it, and I know that nothing can help. I am so grateful to Evdokia Ivanovna that she agreed to send Tania to you with a letter. I am not imagining things, I know that I'm going to die. I raised Valentina and Tania as believers. But they believe in an intellectual way only. It is my sin that I didn't know how to transmit to them what I knew. I will have to answer to God for this.

"Andrei Ivanovich, Valentina's husband is a very good-hearted man. He does a lot of good for other people. He never speaks against any one, but I have been living with him for 30 years and I am still unable to figure out whether he believes or not. Perhaps he does, but is an introvert. Please, Father, hear my confession. As for you, 'smartie,' go out to the other room. Go join Tania."

Throughout her story, Father Arseny was unusually serious and he looked as if he was concentrating on some thought. At the same time his eyes were full of light. When I got up to leave, Father Arseny said to Mother Maria, "The mercy of God is always with us, and His will is over us."

I left the room and sat down in the larger room, near the window. I will be honest and tell you that Mother Maria's story had not impressed me much. Her life did not appear to be exceptional. Many people had much more complicated lives, more painful and more ascetical. I couldn't explain to myself the seriousness I saw in Father Arseny. It seemed to me that this life was like any other.

I could hear sounds Tania was making in the kitchen. I sat alone for half an hour and then went to join her. She was wearing an apron and peeling potatoes over the sink. On the refrigerator I saw a medical textbook at which she glanced every once in a while.

"So you talked with them and now you've come to get in my way. I am cooking and studying." I turned around to leave. "Don't get sore, you get hurt too easily. I saw that yesterday when I said that you were also one of 'those.' Just take a peeler and help with the potatoes. After all, aren't you going to be eating with us?" she said, laughing. I picked up a peeler. Tatiana let me have her apron and asked in a worried tone of voice, "How is Babushka?" I only shrugged my shoulders. What did I know?

Tatiana turned to me and said, "If you only knew what kind of a woman she is! She did so much for my other grandmother, for my father, for Xenia and for myself. She raised us, and we all depended on her for years. She helped so many people! Yes, so many!

"She spent nights with sick people without being asked, and took no money for her help. She helped people she knew and people she did not know, she helped, and helped everyone. She'd never ask "Do you want me to help?" She simply did it. Not for one moment did she live for herself. My father is a reserved man, but he loves Babushka more than he does my mother, more than Xenia, more than me, and more than his own mother. And this is not because she took care of him when he had a heart attack. No, not because of that. He loves and respects her for her actions and for her never-ending help to other people. No one could count how many people received her love and help. She paid for it all with her time, her strength, her health, her sleeptime. My friends, when they came to visit me, would talk with her for a while, and then came back to talk to her again, asking her advice as they would from their own beloved mother. She would give gifts, and always the right gift for the person's need or enjoyment. We, her family, had gotten used to her and did not always pay close attention to what she was doing.

"But from the outside people marveled at her goodness. Life with us has not been easy for her. She doesn't dare to hang her icons. She doesn't want to. Papa has told her many times, 'Please, go ahead and hang them on the wall, and we won't let anybody into your room.' No, she doesn't hang them, because she doesn't want to embarrass us, and so she answers my father, 'It's all right, I'll go to church and pray; there are many icons there.'

"We know it hurts her that we are not believers. It is not really so. Of course we believe, but not in the same way that Babushka does. We believe in our own way." As she was talking, Tania was crying, but she did not seem to mind my being there. When she had finished talking, she went to the other room and waited impatiently for Father Arseny to come out. She kept talking to me and told me more about Mother Maria.

About three hours later Father Arseny came out of Mother Maria's room and told Tania that her grandmother wanted to see her. He took off his priest's stole, sat in an armchair and sank deep into thought, not noticing anything around him. Tania came out, went back in and called the doctor. The doctor came. All the while Father Arseny sat seriously, and focused inwardly. Not to be in his way, I went in the kitchen, because I thought he was praying. After the doctor left, Tania came into the kitchen.

"What did Father Arseny say?" she asked me, whispering.

"I don't know. I didn't ask," I answered, also whispering.

"The doctor said that her heart is seriously worse. I also listened to Babushka's heart and I called my parents at work." And then she started to cry softly, putting her head on the table.

Three hours ago Mother Maria's story had looked almost uninteresting to me, common, like that of many other people. But what Tatiana had been saying revealed Mother Maria in a totally new light. The life I had encountered here became somehow part of my own life and I felt I had to get involved somehow.

Father Arseny touched the lives of so many people, taking upon himself their sufferings, their martyrdom. He reconciled them to their life or to their imminent death. Father Arseny always remembered these people, he suffered their pains and anguish; he tried to help those who lived and prayed for those who had died. I knew that Father Arseny had seen and borne so much while in camp, and that he had been in contact with exceptional people. The events and the encounters of those times had left a permanent mark on him; it seemed that now nothing could surprise him. What was it then that amazed him now?

Valentina Ivanovna, Tatiana's mother, came home.She spoke with Tania, greeted Father Arseny, and went to Mother Maria's room. Andrei Fyodorovich also came home, greeted us, and also went to join his family. From the room where Mother Maria was we clearly heard his voice, "We do live, Babushka Katia!" and after that everything was quiet. In about ten minutes Valentina Ivanovna came out of the room and, addressing Father Arseny, said, "Babushka asks you to go in."

"I want, Father Arseny, to bid my final good-byes to everybody," said Mother Maria. Calm and joyous, radiant, she was lying on her bed wearing a black dress. The good-byes were painful for all the relatives. Blessing each one, Mother Maria loudly said to him or her words that were probably especially meaningful to him or her alone.

Andrei Fyodorovich cried like a child, sobbing, and he could not leave Mother Maria's side. I was standing right next to Father Arseny. All of a sudden Mother Maria addressed me.

"Come near, my dear! You should also say good-bye to me, so that you would not have come for no reason. Come close!"

As she was blessing me she said loudly, "Do not forget my Tania; do not hurt her in any way!" These words were incomprehensible to me and sounded very strange.

Father Arseny, who stood in a corner of the room during these good-byes, came over to Mother Maria after I did. He blessed her three times with his chest cross, bowed down in front of her three times, bowing so deeply that his head almost touched the floor. Then he straightened up, and remained standing—straight and serious with eyes alit and joyous. It seemed he had seen something unique and mysterious, and was afraid to lose that something, which was so greatly important.

☩

The funeral is over. An ache of sadness stays with me. My memory is full of the words I had heard from Mother Maria, her conversations with us, her good-byes. The faces of her family are lost and downhearted, and the face of Father Arseny is concentrated. The painful separation from Mother Maria moves me and disturbs me. I would like so much to help, to give something of myself so that things could be easier for them all. But I am unable to do that.

It is sad, heavy and painful. It is time to say good-bye. In the apartment are only the family and Evdokia Ivanovna.

Valentina Ivanovna asks Father Arseny for his blessing; Xenia does the same but she feels shy about it. Tatiana, with her eyes wide open, goes to Father Arseny, takes him by the hand, then hugs him several times and kisses him impetuously but shyly. Father Arseny's face lights up with a kind smile, the kind of smile that goes with serious thoughts and suffering. Andrei Fyodorovich doesn't know what he is expected to do saying good-bye to a priest, a priest he likes and who did much good in his house, and to whom he is grateful, but he has no idea how to express himself. He shakes Father Arseny's hand for a long time, asks him to come back some time, and finally tries to give him some money, as you might to a doctor when he has made a house call. His hand hangs in space, Father Arseny hugs him and, smiling broadly and openly, gives him a kiss.

They all say goodbye to me as if they had known me for a long time, and they ask me to come see them again. Tatiana also asks me to come back. Having said good-bye to every one, Father Arseny bows and says to them all, "Thank you for having called me. You gave me the opportunity to see a remarkable person, a true ascetic, a Christian who brought only goodness and joy to people. I learned a great deal about perfection from Mother Maria. Thank you! She was a rare and exceptional person!"

After he had once again bowed low, Father Arseny, calm and serious, left the apartment. There were three of us: Father Arseny, Evdokia Ivanovna and myself. Father Arseny was silent and concentrated. "Let's take a walk in Moscow," he said to me. I gave the briefcase with our things to Evdokia Ivanovna who went back home, and we started walking along the streets. We walked along the Garden Ring Road, the crooked little back roads, and narrow streets, past dark old houses with peeling paint and new ones that were tall and surrounded with little gardens, trees, shrubs.

"I want to see Moscow," says Father Arseny.

I hail a taxi and we ride toward the Kremlin. The weather is sunny but a little windy, the air light and easy to breathe. We walk slowly in through the Borovitsky Gate, go up the hill, walk along the wall, circle the cathedrals and approach the bell tower of Ivan the Great. I hang back a little, feeling that Father Arseny wants to be alone for a while. He walks slowly, looking at each ledge and each curve in the stone, carved many hundred years ago.

In the Cathedral of the Dormition there aren't many people today. You can see so well the frescoes, the icons, the fine ironwork of the gates, the tombs, the inscriptions, saints' relics. In this cathedral you encounter the whole past of the Russian people, its faith, greatness, hopes, and dashed dreams.

The icons and frescoes: Father Arseny stands in front of them for a long time, lost in his thoughts; he is serious and stern. Here is the wall along which are buried all the hierarchs of Moscow, including Metropolitans Alexei and Peter.

Father Arseny walks slowly up to these tombs, he bows three times to the ground, crosses himself, and stands for a long time without moving. As he is bowing, we hear a voice from about six meters away: "Citizen! This is a museum, you are not allowed to pray in it!" Father Arseny does not turn around but continues to stand as before near the place where the saints of Moscow were buried a few centuries ago.

He walks slowly around the cathedral, stays looking at the iconostasis a long time, concentrating on the faces of saints in the icons. Every so often he freezes in one spot, or returns again and again to the same icon.

We move on to the Cathedral of the Archangel, then we cross the Red Square and walk to St. Basil's Cathedral, where we catch a taxi and leave. While we ride along, Father Arseny names some of the streets we pass, stops the taxi, and gets out to look around at some churches. He looks at them for a long time with great attention. There are many churches, of which some are closed and some open:[6] the small church of Trifon the Martyr, the Andronikov Monastery, and the Donskoi.

The driver asks me, "Is the old man a tourist or a scholar?"

"A scholar," I answer.

We visit three cemeteries. Father Arseny walks for about half an hour in each, first in Vagankov cemetery, then Vvedenski Hills, and then the Piatnitskoy cemetery.

The taxi driver, a young man, is starting to get nervous. I calm him down, saying, "Don't worry! We will pay what we owe you."

We return to the center of town, circling the familiar little streets and squares of the oldest parts of Moscow. We stop near ancient homes, tiny wooden houses built deep in a courtyard and ready to fall apart.

6 In Stalinist Russia, most churches were closed. Some of these were maintained as museums; most were used as factories or warehouses, or simply left abandoned.

Sometimes we see a new house built two or three years ago and replacing another which had been familiar to Father Arseny. We pass the Sivtzev Vrazhek, Molchanovka; we go to the Taganka, then up a hill to the church of the Martyr Nikita, and from there Father Arseny walks to an old and decrepit house and stands near it for a long time, looking at the windows, the courtyard, the surrounding houses. It seemed to me at that point that he discreetly wiped a tear from his cheeks.

After all this, we traveled to the other side of the river, the Zamoskvorechie, to Evdokia Ivanovna's apartment. She started to fix us something to eat and put plates on the table, but Father Arseny suddenly got up and said, "I'll be back soon!"

I tried to go with him, but he didn't want me to, and so he left. We were left upset and worried about him and I started remembering all the events of these past days: the unexpected trip to Moscow, the death of Mother Maria, my meeting with Tatiana, Mother Maria's funeral, Father Arseny's deeply serious mood, his obvious concern, his "tour" through Moscow.

Moscow was the town of his childhood, his youth, the establishment of his character and his convictions. It is here that, when he was still in high school, he wrote his first articles, and then his books. He became a famous scholar. Here in Moscow he was tonsured a monk and then was ordained a priest. He served here for a long time, then moved into the smaller town near Moscow where he created a community which he loved and supported constantly. Still in Moscow he had set the cornerstone of faith in many people and on this stone he was later able to build his strong community of faithful.

In the new town where he lived, he received visits from many Muscovites, and it was clear that his community was made up mostly of people from Moscow.

He loved his new town, there his spirit had grown; but it was here in Moscow, the city of his childhood and his coming of age, that he had built the basis of his faith. It was here in Moscow that he had learned to love people. This is why Moscow was so precious to him. This is why he was so moved today when he visited the fragments of his life, remembering his beloved past. But why was he so unusually serious? Why?

Though his sternness was so unusual for him, you could detect a secret sadness. He probably was remembering people he loved who had died long before. But there were still many people in Moscow now, people he loved and knew. Why did he not ask anyone to visit him at Evdokia Ivanovna's, why did he not go visit his spiritual children as he always did when he came to Moscow? And again I asked myself: why? But was this for me to know?

At about nine o'clock Father Arseny returned, joyous, and started to tell us how he had gone to his church, how he had met many of his friends and acquaintances there (he never called them his spiritual children, but simply his friends).

"When they saw me they were amazed, and asked me how it is that I am in Moscow, and especially in church. You will have to forgive me, Evdokia Ivanovna, but I told them that I am staying in your apartment, so they will probably come to see me." In fact very soon we heard the door bell ring many times and sixteen people came in. I knew many of them. The remaining hours of the evening and well into the night Father Arseny heard confessions or simply talked with them. We left Moscow at eleven o'clock the next morning. Before that a few more people came; Father Arseny himself called three or four others on the telephone—they were "camp friends," as we called among ourselves his spiritual children, friends and acquaintances who had spent time in the same camps as Father Arseny.

Father Arseny left Moscow tired and without enough sleep, but he was especially joyous. Many people, I think all of those who knew he was here, came to see him off. Tatiana was also at the station, somebody having told her the hour of his departure.

After he returned home, Father Arseny had to rest for two days. Only Nadezhda Petrovna was admitted to his room; she told us later that he spent all his time reading the daily offices or praying.

✤

Six or seven days later Father Arseny invited me to come for a walk. We walked out of the small town and came out to the banks of the river, and then to the fields. The narrow country road meandered and ended in a field full of ripening wheat. Birds were flying out of it, a mild wind bent the stalks of heavy wheat, blew lightly through our clothing, and ruffled our hair. We walked in silence; the road changed and we continued walking on a narrow path. The sun was beginning to set with the shadows getting longer; we breathed lightly and easily.

Self-contained, separated from everything that was around him, his glance slid over the wheat, the long shadows of grasses, the orange disc of the sun, the meandering path. He was deeply involved in his thoughts, known only to him, or perhaps was he praying? He walked along having forgotten about me, the fields, the grasses, the wheat, and the sun. At times he would slow down and seem to be looking carefully at something or other. The wheat was as high as our shoulders and hid the horizon. When we walked up a hill we could see the whole field again; we could see where it ended at the beginning of a dark pine forest. The wind stopped.

Father Arseny stopped and said to me, "You remember Mother Maria's death?" and without waiting for my answer he continued. "I have seen a great deal in the course of my life, I have met many people and have been able to get something unique from each of these meetings, something new, something greatly needed and deeply instructive. I always perceived the will of God, His great wisdom and His Providence.

"There were no big or small encounters. A human person will always be a human person and, whoever he is, he is made in the image of God and this always stays with him. Only in one case did sins make this image pale; in other cases, the great power of a man's efforts in the name of God can make this man shine so that he is as bright as an angel of God. I have encountered such great servants of God three times in my life. My meetings with them were a spiritual joy, an enrichment and a revelation of God himself.

"From each and every person I met I carried away something good, I have taken the best, I was able to learn something from each one. But the confession of the Monk Mihail in the camp, my meeting in the far north with the simple country priest Father Ioann, and now my meeting with Mother Maria were revelations for me, they were a spiritual turning point for me, which made me understand and evaluate in a totally new way all of life, people, and my own whole life's journey.

"You heard Mother Maria telling her own story, but I could see that you didn't appreciate it and did not understand it at first. Her life looked banal to you, common. You weren't the only one: her own family saw it the same way. When you are close to a mountain you see the stones that make it up, not the mountain as a whole—it is the same way with the life of a person.

"Think about her life, look seriously at it. It was absolute self-denial; she didn't exist for herself, but only for God and the people who were around her. As a little girl, a young orphan, she always wanted to belong to God. She was a young girl in the rich house of a landowner and she still yearned for a life in God. A novice in a monastery, a cleaning woman in a church where the priest wanted to rape her, a worker, a nurse. Wherever she was, her thoughts always turned towards God and she completely dissolved her own 'I' in the lives of other people; she abandoned it for them. This is what you didn't catch in her story, what you didn't feel.

"As I listened to her story I was very moved. I was amazed at the power of her spirit and her constant yearning towards God, which vanquished all obstacles and all possible difficulties. Her last confession opened for me even more the perfection of her soul, her great humility and her love for other people. All this was lived in an everyday life, among the plain people that surround us and the modern destructive vanity of vanities. The fact that her deeds went unnoticed, the humility and personal sense of the nothingness of her deeds, vividly underlines the greatness of the effort sustained by Mother Maria.

"Mother Maria knew how to be patient. This is the most important thing in the life of a Christian: knowing how to be patient and not thinking that what you are accomplishing is something difficult. While doing good to other people you just have to remember that the one who is suffering and who needs your help is your brother. You bring help to him not from yourself but from God and in His name. Mother Maria knew how to do this, forgetting herself. Listening to her confession, I was overjoyed and my spirit was uplifted. Even her sins, and there were some, were a proof of the value of the person, when her behavior as she fought the good fight to correct these sins evidenced the victory of the spirit over the flesh, of faith over sin. Do not forget this family. Mother Maria gave them so much. Don't you forget them!"

(I did not forget them. Tatiana and I were married in a year's time. Each of us helps the other nowadays.)

Father Arseny stopped and, tearing himself away from his thoughts, he looked at the field. It seemed he only realized now that we were standing amid wheat and that the sun was setting towards the forest, that we could smell mint and wormwood and that we were walking on a meandering path into the warm summer evening. He touched ears of wheat, bent over to a pick a flower, smiled a little and said, "I do not have long to live, and this is why my meeting with Mother Maria was indispensable to me. God sent this meeting to me to show me a righteous woman of our time and again and again to humble me."

We were walking back. Father Arseny came alive and looked with interest at the silhouette of the town, its churches, the church domes and bell towers. He told me a great deal about people whom he had known and whom he loved. He was joyous and transparent and his eyes became deeply thoughtful and sad.

When we were already close to the town, he turned towards me and said, "It's true! What a person can achieve with the help of God. Mother Maria. Mother Maria!" he said this several times, and then as if he was pursuing a thought known only to him, he said:

To see everything, to understand everything,
To know everything, take everything in,
To take into your eyes all shapes, all flowers,
To walk the whole earth with burning steps,
To perceive everything and to give form to everything anew.

"That poem was written by a very good man and a remarkable poet called Maximilian Voloshin. He loved people, did much good, walked his path to the Light in a way known only to him. God was an abstraction for him, a convention, and this is why his path was tortuous. He constantly turned back on his steps. Did he ever arrive where he was going? Only God knows, but his soul and his life were good.

"I knew him, but the year was 1925 and in those days there were for him many difficulties and much wavering.

"Mother Maria was a simple Russian woman, he was a famous poet, and they both were going toward the same goal, but how different were their paths!

"Lord, forgive us!"

We found ourselves right next to the house where he lived.

K.S.

O Mother of God, Help Me!

On The Second day after the war started, on June 23, my husband was mobilized to go to the front, and I was left alone with Katia.

The alarms during the night, the volleys of anti-aircraft fire, the rays of searchlights in the sky, the moaning of sirens, the cigar-like barrage balloons—zeppelins hanging over the city—and all the alarming news we heard about our retreat from large cities and even whole regions, accounted for the sad and concerned faces of people. The words "war" and "front" drove all other feelings and emotions out of our minds.

This is what Moscow felt like in 1941.

Each time there was a bombing I had to run with my little Katia to the shelter under our house and stay there until the end of the alarm. I lived through this thousands of times. I was constantly frightened and I had the feeling that something tragic and irreparable inevitably was going to happen. I very seldom received letters from my husband; he never got mine. The division of the army in which he was serving was constantly thrown from one place to another and his address changed every time, so my letters never reached him. My husband kept asking why I didn't write, but I couldn't answer because he didn't get my letters!

Many children were evacuated from Moscow. They evacuated the kindergarten which my Katia attended, but as she was sick, she couldn't go and had to stay with me. I had to work and used to leave her with kind-hearted friends during the day. In September they evacuated the company where I worked, but Katia was still sick, so I could not go with them. In September Katia got better, but by then there was no way to leave with any company at all.

The Germans had broken through the front and were marching toward Moscow. Every human being felt the weight of something fearsome and tragic. The city was emptying out; people were leaving by train, by car, on foot. Overcoming a whole series of difficulties, we also left. The trip was a nightmare. Everyone was trying to get rid of everyone else. People pushed, swore, made you change trains, or simply threw you off. The train was bombed three times, and near Riazan somebody stole all my belongings. The trains were so full that people had no space to breathe; they hated and suspected one another. The saying that "man is man's own wolf" proved true. I do not know why, but I didn't meet any nice people in those days. During our travels Katia caught a cold, had a headache, and was in a terrible mood.

We had crossed the Ural mountains and were now in Siberia. We passed snowy steppes, and only very rarely a station flew by. The wind was fierce, the blizzard strong. Finally the train arrived at the place we were going to. We gathered up what we had and left the train. Beyond the platform we could see an old Siberian town. It was cold, unknown and unfamiliar.

Where should I go? Where should I stay? How could I live? I understood only then how foolish I had been to agree to evacuate from Moscow where I had friends, an apartment, work, and a salary. It was morning. The wind from the steppe was fierce. There I stood afraid and lost, deafened by the noise and the bustle of the station. I had no money, no clothes, and no food coupons. I went to the war committee, but there was an enormous line there. I tried to go this way and that, but nobody cared about me. I got to a major with great difficulty, I told him my husband was in the army, that he was an officer, that I had come from Moscow. I showed him my papers and I pulled Katia along by the hand.

He responded, "There are many people who have come. The town is full. Manage by yourself as you can!" But at least he gave me two coupons so that we could have dinner. What could I do? We went to eat and then went to the market to sell my good sweater, the one I was wearing. We offered it to many people, but nobody wanted it. Many people were standing there trying to sell their clothing, but there were no buyers.

It was getting dark. Katia was crying; she was cold and tired and she wanted to sleep. I decided to go to the railroad station, and then see what would happen next. We took a tram. It moved slowly through unfamiliar streets. The windows of the tram were iced up so you couldn't see through, but I knew that the station was the last stop. I breathed onto the window, melted a bit of ice and looked outside. I was angry at everything and everybody. The tram stopped and did not move for a long time. I looked through the window and saw a church at the end of the street. People were flocking to its doors and going in. I don't know why, but I got up, left the tram, and walked up to that church. I was holding Katia by the hand and walked in.

Some kind of a service was going on. The church was filling up and I pushed my way to the front and stood in front of a large icon. The church was warm. I untied Katia's kerchief and unbuttoned her coat. I could not stop thinking, "What can I do? Where can I go? Katia is here with me, she is hungry and cold. We are alone." Had I been alone I wouldn't have been so afraid, but

I had with me my little four-year-old daughter. I wanted to scream, demand, ask, cry—but whom to address? Whom to ask? Why had we come here?

I cannot say how long we stood there, but Katia pulled me by the sleeve and said loudly, "Mama, I'm tired of standing!"

People started whispering. An old woman said to me, "Why did you bring a child here at nightfall? You sure found a place to stand!" Then she tried to push me away from the icon.

The church was filling up with people and there was nowhere for me to move. "Even here they chase me away," I thought. "I expected that here they would speak of love..." I lifted my eyes to the icon in front of which I stood.

The eyes of the Mother of God looked at me from the icon. Her face was bent toward her child, who pressed His cheek tightly against hers. In this embrace you could see the unbelievable love and desire of the Mother to protect her child, to warm him with her love, the love only a mother can give. The eyes of the Mother of God were so full of light-giving warmth that, looking at them, each person could find calm and consolation. The Mother of God looked at us with sad eyes, full of pity and warmth. It filled you with hope and you felt consoled. My faith was always weak and insignificant. When I was a child, my mother had taught me how to pray "for mama and for papa" and had wanted me to learn the "Our Father" and the prayer to the Mother of God. Later, I forgot everything and it became a long-forgotten memory, a little funny, a little sad.

If people laughed about the rites of the church, I laughed with them, but somewhere, deep inside, I had a little feeling that perhaps God did exist. But only possibly.

The face of the Mother of God which was looking at me now from this icon suddenly turned my soul around and, in spite of the desperate situation I found myself in, I understood that hope could only exist in her. And I started to pray. Not knowing any words I prayed. I simply asked the Mother of God, I begged her to help us. And I believed she would help us. How could I, an unbeliever, believe such a thing at this time? To this day I do not know. I think that the unusual, divine warmth of her gaze made me believe that she would help.

Katia was sitting on the floor, the old woman was whispering things and trying to push me out of the way, but I was praying. I remember now that my prayer was only asking. My whole being was begging for Katia, "O, Mother of God, help us, help us!" I repeated this hundreds of times. Tears were running down my face. I was looking at the icon in prayer and I was shivering.

The service ended and people were leaving. I was still standing there and praying in front of the icon. The church was almost empty and Katia was asleep on the floor. The priest was walking towards the door. I approached him and asked him to help me. He listened to me, sadly spread his hands in a gesture of helplessness and, quickly buttoning his overcoat, left.

After the priest had left, the old woman who had tried a number of times to push me away from the icon, now grabbed the sleeping Katia by the collar and shouted loudly that this was a church, not a rooming house, and that I was rude and worthless. And she dragged Katia to the door. Katia woke up and started crying. I went back to the icon of the Mother of God and, venerating it, could only beg her again and again to help us. I was absolutely sure that she would, and I went to the door. Out of the darkness of the church a woman suddenly appeared, took me by the sleeve, and said, "Let's go." We left the church. I only had time to think, "Here is another person trying to chase me away!"

The woman was holding on to me tightly and was leading us somewhere. It was very cold and I was frozen to the bone. The snow crunched underfoot. The streets were almost completely deserted. The only things that passed us were occasional cars in a rush. We walked in silence past small houses and fences. At times I wanted to ask, "Where are we going?" but I did not ask, hoping that something good might happen. The thought that the Mother of God would not leave us did not leave my head, and as I was walking into the unknown, I never stopped praying. I remember that thousands of thoughts, worrisome, troubled, frightening thoughts came to me, but as soon as I closed my eyes, I could see the icon of the Mother of God and everything that was troubling me stepped back and disappeared.

We stopped at a high picket fence. The gate squeaked sadly and we entered a small front yard covered with snow. We walked up to a small one-storey house. The woman searched for her keys while muttering angrily.

She opened the door and said, "Come in quickly and take your coats off. Hang them in the hallway and sit on this bench, so as not to contaminate the house in case you have lice. My name is Nina Sergeyevna. Now, please wait. I will call you!"

I heard her talking in an adjacent room. I heard an irritated voice say, "Nina, whom did you bring?"

"The people I brought are the ones that God sent."

Nina Sergeyevna left to go somewhere. I heard the sound of pails; I could smell some smoke and the aroma of cooking potatoes. I was shaking with emotion and exhaustion. Pressed against me Katia was soft because she was warm and was half asleep. What was going to happen?

They will let me spend the night, and then what? I shivered more and more. The door opened and Nina Sergeyevna said, "So, my dear, here you sit. Why don't you come help?"

I got up and went to the kitchen. The stove was hot and water was being heated in big pans. Not far from the stove I could see an enamel tub used for bathing. "Pour some hot water in and some cold too. I am going to wash your daughter myself. Tell me your name. I already know that of your daughter."

I told her my name. "Your name is Nina, like mine. Do you know the date of your namesday?"

I did not know it. "You have to know it, my dear, if you visit churches. Nina is commemorated only once a year—on January 27, Old Style."

Why she was telling me all this, I did not understand. The kitchen was warm, the smell of smoke and of cooking food was pleasant, and I was filling the bathtub with water. I was embarrassed to be in a strange house, and creating so much trouble for people I didn't know. I said this to Nina Sergeyevna. She stopped me and said, "Don't be so sentimental. Bring me your daughter and I will wash her. You are both dirty from your journey, and you might have lice."

I undressed sleepy little Katia. She squealed with joy and played in the water, she grabbed the neck of Nina Sergeyevna with her wet little hands and was telling her something. I stood next to the stove almost unconscious; all this looked as unreal to me as though I was dreaming. "Now it's your turn," I heard Nina Sergeyevna say.

She carried Katia out of the room. I undressed and stood in the tub. I was shivering so much that the washcloth fell several times from my hands and I could barely stand on my feet. Nina Sergeyevna came back into the kitchen. I was shy. "Stop being embarrassed. I am a doctor. Listen, my dear, you are shivering seriously. Wash quickly. You are sick!" Nina Sergeyevna, the kitchen, and the stove swam in front of my eyes and I could tell vaguely that somebody was washing me, drying me, and dressing me in a nightshirt. Every so often I could hear a voice saying, "Wait, stand up, don't interfere with me."

I was led somewhere, I was lifted onto something, something hot was put on my chest, and they gave me some water to drink.

I was told that four days later I regained consciousness for a short while. I can only remember that while I was unconscious I had before my eyes the icon of the Mother of God of Vladimir and I was praying, I was praying for Katia, for myself and for Nina Sergeyevna who had taken us in to her house. In my dream somebody was trying to tear me away from the icon, but I fought back and shouted, "Mother of God, do not forsake us!" Every time that I lost my strength I could only stretch my hands toward the icon, while again and again I was pushed away, but I walked towards it and then the face of the Mother of God would light up and I would feel calm, and I could breathe easier, but then the fight would start all over again. If you only knew how afraid I was and how painful this fight was. A frightening horror possessed me whenever I thought I might be pushed away from the icon. I only wanted to be near the Mother of God.

I understood that only she could help Katia and me. If she showed mercy and gave us her hand, we would live. If I could only explain now how I was able to pray while unconscious! When finally I regained consciousness, I could hear the regular sound of the pendulum of the clock, the squeaking of a board in the floor, and somebody was whispering. I was so weak that I couldn't even move a finger, and I could scarcely open my eyes. I see an unfamiliar room, and a window covered with a curtain. I move my eyes very slowly and suddenly I am overcome with enormous joy: in a corner hangs an icon with a little green oil lamp burning in front of it. It is the same icon I saw in the church, the icon before which I was praying and crying (I later found out that it was the icon of the Mother of God of Vladimir).

I look at the icon and I can only repeat what I was saying when I was unconscious, "O, Mother of God, do not forsake us!" and I begin to cry. I can feel somebody's hand wiping away my tears and I fall asleep for the first time without dreams, without fear, without fearful thoughts.

I woke up the next day. While I still had my eyes closed I could hear the same sound of the pendulum as yesterday, and a rustle. From the other room I could hear Katia's voice and somebody else's low voice reading a fairy tale. I tried to cry out, to call Katia. I opened my eyes and again I could see the icon looking at me. I felt at peace and tried to call Katia and Nina Sergeyevna again. The floor squeaked and I saw bent over me a face wearing glasses, a nice, soft and welcoming face. "Katia is here, Nina Sergeyevna is at the hospital, working, and she will be back late. It is good that you have woken up. Now everything will be alright. The Mother of God helped you; you kept calling on her while you were unconscious," and the woman's hand gently stroked my head. "You had pneumonia, the flu, and a nervous shock, all at the same time." And in the same breath she continued, "Nina Sergeyevna is a good friend of mine. We are both from Moscow. We came to live here in 1935. My name is Alexandra Fyodorovna. I am also a doctor, an internist. Katia and I have become good friends. Nina and I have decided that you are going to live with us."

I stayed in bed for another five days; Nina Sergeyevna allowed me to get up only then.

People totally unknown to us had taken us in, had cared for me while I was sick, had fed me, had given me water to drink, and had taken care of Katia. Why had I gone into that church? Why did I stand in front of the icon of the Mother of God, praying and trusting she would help us? Why was her face constantly before me during my whole illness, and why was it that the first thing I saw was her icon again? Why? While I was still lying in bed I came to the conclusion that all this was truly, a great and real miracle which God and the Mother of God had sent me, a sinner, as a great mercy. When I realized all this, I felt even more overcome with gratitude and love for her and for the people who had saved Katia and myself.

I told all this to Nina Sergeyevna and to Alexandra Fyodorovna after my illness, while I was still bedridden. They both enabled me to become a true believer. They baptized Katia and taught us everything that would help us to truly believe. We lived together for three years, while I worked in a factory. Then I had to return to Moscow not to lose my apartment. They kept Katia with them. She finished school there, graduated from the Institute in 1960, and only then did she return to Moscow along with them, her "Babushka Nina" and "Babushka Sasha."

There's no need to describe what kind of people these two women were. In recounting this important period of my life I think I have already told all I could about these two true Christians. I will add that they were spiritual children of Father Arseny; they'd had to leave Moscow in 1936 to avoid the epidemic of arrests that was occurring then.

In 1958 they introduced me to Father Arseny, who had been freed from the camp the year before. This is how we both became his spiritual children. In 1960 both of the old ladies came to Moscow and bought a little house, but in actual fact they nearly always lived with Katia and her family.

I thank you, O Lord, for the enormous mercy you showed me. I also thank Our Lady, the Mother of God, for the miracle that brought me to the faith, to the Church and to the source of life. I thank you, O Lady, for having shown me two of your daughters and for sending me such a spiritual father and teacher, the priest Arseny.

Glory to Thee, O God!

On the Roof

LIFE WAS CONTINUOUSLY difficult, full of the most unexpected dangers and fears which constantly threatened our physical and spiritual life. But the Lord and the Mother of God were merciful to us in times of imminent danger and never abandoned us. Whenever I would get estranged from the ways of God, He would send me someone to help me find my way back onto the true path and would help me avoid mistakes and errors. If at times of physical danger I would call on the Lord, He would always help me. So many times in my life I was shown that prayer, sincere prayer, is true salvation. Prayer to the Mother of God was always the most saving and unfailing protection from all physical and spiritual dangers.

I want to tell you here about our spiritual father's power of prayer and about how the event I am going to recount influenced us all.

People were hungry in Moscow. We had coupons for an eighth of a loaf of bread a day, and the bread was full of chaff. You could find nothing, no potatoes, no cereal, no cabbage, and we couldn't even remember the last time we had had butter or oil. The currency had no value; the peasants would accept only goods in exchange for what food they were ready to sell, and of course they demanded exorbitant prices. "City people" were treated like enemies and we had to literally beg to obtain bread or potatoes in exchange for a fur coat or a gold chain. We were hungry, we were cold, and we were constantly afraid.

Sasha, Katia and I went to our spiritual father, Mihail, to ask him to allow us, three young women, to go to the country to get some food. So many people went with their goods and brought back food. Father Mihail listened to us attentively, shook his head disapprovingly, went to the icon of the Mother of God, prayed for a long time and then, turning to us, he said, "I entrust you to our defender, the Mother of God. You must each take a little icon with you and pray to her the whole trip. She and St. George will protect you. It will be very difficult for you. I will pray for you from here!" And he said to himself, "O Mother of God! O blessed St. George! Help them, save them, and protect them from all danger and all fright and blasphemy." He blessed us, and fell silent.

He turned back to the icon of the Virgin of Vladimir and started to pray as though he had forgotten us.

So we went. During the trip we tried to guess why he had said that St. George would protect us. We were just young women, life appeared to be simple, and we were not afraid of anything. But of course we didn't know much about life. We had always lived in the city, our families were well educated and we didn't know country people at all. We were studying in different departments at the University, and what united us was the Church. Our families didn't want to let us go, but finally we went. We traveled from Moscow standing between railroad cars. The end of September was nearing.

We obtained about thirty pounds of flour and thirty pounds of wheat. We carried all this ourselves although it was heavy. It was difficult, but we were extremely happy. We had gotten some food! Our families would be so glad. But we were stopped somewhere far from Moscow. There were "anti-profiteering detachments" everywhere, who would take your grain and bread from you. They wouldn't let you onto the trains, where only military echelons were allowed.

We were surrounded by people sick with typhoid, people who were hungry. It was a disaster. We were stuck at this station for three days: we ate green onions and chewed uncooked wheat. I can still feel that taste in my mouth. One night a long train arrived. We heard it was an army train going to Moscow. Early in the morning the doors opened and soldiers jumped out of the cars to exchange what they had for apples, pickles, cooked beets, and onion. We were afraid to ask if we could get into one of the carriages. The women say that it's dangerous to get into a car with soldiers. They tell awful stories. There are rumors that the white army has penetrated the lines and is advancing, and that bands of deserters are roaming the region, stealing from and raping anyone they find. Somewhere there was an epidemic of cholera. It was all scary and seemed hopeless. We remembered then the words of Father Mihail. The cars were full of soldiers, horses, field weapons, and wagons. Soldiers were sitting on the floor, smoking on bunks, laughing and chewing sunflower seeds, and shouting to women who were sitting on the platform: "Hey! ladies, we will give you a ride! We are leaving soon!" We are afraid. A few women decide to go. Soldiers help them in with jokes, taking in their bags and their bundles. There are rumors that for several days there will not be another train. We are worried and try to decide what to do. Meanwhile people are climbing onto the roofs of the carriages; there are many people on them by now. You can hear laughter from inside the carriages, and people playing harmonicas. They say that the train is going to Serpukhov.

A group of women—us included—decide to climb onto the roof, because we can not see any other way to go. We climb up with difficulty, pulling up our bags and helping each other. The sun is hot. We lie down on the middle of the corrugated roof and press ourselves onto the warm metal.

I am praying, asking the Mother of God to help us; I try to make the sign of the cross without being noticed. Sasha and Katia do the same. The roof is covered with people, mostly with women. The smoke from the locomotive is acrid because they are burning wood. After a while the train begins to shake; it seems to hesitate whether to go backwards or forwards but then slowly begins to move. Moving forward, it gathers speed.

We pass a station full of people who try to jump onto the train, some miss and try again; not many are successful. The train is now crossing the steppe, which is quiet and unpopulated. A single track cuts through the dried grasses and the dying steppes.

Black smoke with bright sparks periodically envelops us on the roof. The sparks burn our hands and faces, and burn holes in our bags. We try to brush the burning sparks off like flies. We brush them off each other, and shake them off ourselves. I am at peace, even forgetting to pray for a while, and watch with interest the passing steppes, the roofs of the other cars which are also covered with people. Sasha keeps praying, you can tell by the serious look on her face and her barely moving lips. Watching her, Katia and I start to pray again as well. Praying to the Mother of God calms us and gives us assurance. Sasha whispers that we should all lie with our heads together, so we carefully move together and she starts to recite the Akathist to the Virgin of Vladimir. She says it several times. Our neighbors do not hear her: the train is noisy, each car makes its own sound. Sasha continues to pray, selecting such prayers as, "O Mother of God, we come under your protection, we put our trust in you and we glorify you. Protect and save us by your mercy. We entrust ourselves into your hands, you are our hope and our salvation."

And every time she says the Akathist I feel that we three are not alone, but that the Mother of God is with us and will protect us.

It is sweltering hot, and it's difficult to put out the sparks and to hold on to the ridges of the roof at the same time. The bags are slipping and have to be gripped at all times. The train stops at small stations and the soldiers load up wood. The locomotive fills up with water and we move on. We pass little shacks and small villages but mostly we cross the big steppe, dry and hot. We travel for a while, but suddenly the train stops. People jump off it and discuss something. The train is stationary but we stay lying down. The sun has set, so it is a little cooler. We are thirsty. The car doors slide open and soldiers jump out onto the embankment, and laughing they walk to the sparse bushes, laughing and swearing for fun. We watch them from on top. Suddenly one of them says, "Why don't we go visit the women? Look how many there are on top of the cars..."

And the mood changes. The cars empty out, and many soldiers start climbing onto the roof.

"O, my Lord!" I thought. "What can we do?" Soldiers start appearing on the roofs, at first only a few and then there are more and more of them. We hear screams, sobs, begging. "You good-for-nothing, what do you think you are doing? I could be your mother."

"Soldiers, please do not touch the bags, my children are expecting the food, they are hungry."

"We are not interested in your bread. The administration feeds us well."

Boots tramp noisily on the roofs; it is very frightening. One woman sobs hysterically and begs, others jump off the roof, hurting themselves. Our roof is still empty of soldiers, but suddenly several appear on it. I keep praying to the Mother of God. Katia is right next to me crying and praying. Sasha glares angrily at the approaching soldiers. I know our Sasha; she will never give in, she will not stop resisting. Her face is full of assurance; I know she is praying hard. I remember the words of Father Mihail, I know that the prayers of a spiritual father can help, and I also remember that he said to ask St. George to help us. I start praying to him. Sasha! I trust her prayer and put my hope in her. She is serious and calm and remains lying down while the rest of us are sitting up. One soldier walks around the other women and walks directly to us. He has high cheek bones and a bald head, and his slanted eyes show no evidence of thought. He grabs me by the hand and says, "You lie down and I won't hurt you!"

I push him away and, still looking him in the face, I make the sign of the cross several times. He is in a good mood, so he smiles to make fun of me. I step back. On the roof some are still fighting, some are giving in and there is a lot of noise. There are many soldiers and they are having a very good time, thinking all this is very funny. Their regiment has been fighting hard, they are now being taken back for a rest. They have seen death and danger and they feel entitled to everything. The fact that the women resist excites them even more. When they were going through villages they got used to taking any woman they saw, women who resisted and were scared. (All these thoughts came to me only when we were back in Moscow, of course.)

The man walks up to me and I step back again. Katia shouts, "You are at the edge of the roof!"

I turn and see that I cannot take even one more step back. A sailor climbs up onto the roof. He has a tee-shirt on his big wide chest. He looks very angry. His eyes sparkle—yes, exactly, they sparkle. The sailor frightens me so much with his decisiveness, his anger and his energy that his face is etched in my memory forever. I cannot step back any more, one man coming up in front of me, the sailor behind me.

The sailor grabs me by the shoulders, pushes me away and says, "Stay calm, there will always be time to jump off the roof. I will take care of your problems."

He walks over to the soldier, punches him in the chest, and says to him, "You, worthless thing, get out of here," at which point the soldier immediately jumps into the space between the cars. We are left alone. The sailor walks across the roof to another soldier who is lying down and shouts to him, "What are you doing, you dirty rat, putting our army to shame?"

The soldier swears mightily, tries to hit the sailor, but the sailor punches him in the face. The soldier starts fighting, and the sailor grabs his revolver and shoots him. The body falls to the ground below.

"Comrades," shouts the sailor. "We are soldiers of the Revolution, we are here to build up and protect the Soviet government. We are for the people and we ourselves come from among the people. What are you doing? For shame! The Red Army protects the working class and here we are putting ourselves to shame. Each rapist deserves to be shot on the spot! You should be ashamed! Our own sisters or wives may be sitting on some other train, on some other roof. All of you who are true Communists, come with me!"

The soldiers are noisy and some of them try to fight, but they climb down from the roofs. They gather into a Communist meeting to discuss what has happened. The sailor speaks passionately, simply, eloquently. At first some of the soldiers were making noise, grabbing for their weapons, but the sailor was joined by other soldiers and commanding officers. After a while the soldiers calm down.

Only the women stayed on the roofs. The soldiers quickly buried the soldier who had been shot and went back into the car. The sailor came back to us and said, "Well, girls, do come down into the cars, so you can be more comfortable." Sasha got up and said, "Let's go."

The train moved slowly for 48 hours. The soldiers were good to us. They fed us barley soup and let us drink some smoky tasting tea which they had saved from a burning car. The sailor's name was Yuri[7] Nikolaevich Tulikov. He was the Communist supervisor of the regiment. He sat with us, and Sasha, who was usually so silent, couldn't stop talking. I thought she was wrong to tell this man so much about us, about the Church, about the university, about our friendship. She also told him how we had been praying to the Mother of God and to Saint George. The sailor listened without ever making fun of us or blaming us.

We slept in the corner of the car; we also talked a great deal. In the evening we prayed together—especially Sasha.

Two or three times we encountered blockades that tried to take us off the train. But the soldiers fought them off. The train took us up to Podolsk. This was its last stop. Yuri and some others helped us onto a local train which took us to Moscow.

As we were saying good-bye, Yuri said, "Maybe we shall meet again! Life is full of unexpected encounters!"

Sasha, our reserved Sasha, always so moderate in her words and actions, came up to Yuri, put her hands on his shoulders, and said, "May God protect you and keep you for other good deeds. Remember always to be as warm-hearted as you have been today! Good-bye!" And, taking her hands from his shoulders, she bowed low to him. This all was very unusual for our Sasha.

Our families were very happy to see us come safely home. As soon as we had washed, we ran to see Father Mihail.

Father Pavel met us at the door and said, "Father is waiting for you. He knew you were coming and sent me to meet you. All through these days he was praying for you!"

We went into the house. Father Mihail jumped to his feet, hugged us, gave us his blessing and, turning to the icon of the Mother of God of Vladimir and to that of Saint George, he began to pray aloud, thanking them for our salvation. When he had finished, we told him what had happened to us. As we were talking, we saw his lips moving in prayer. When we finished, he said, "I thank Thee, O Lord, for Thy great mercy." He then told us, "Don't dare forget the sailor Yuri, who has a spark of God in him. Pray that the difficulties of this world do not extinguish that spark. Pray for him. One of you will meet

7 Yuri is a version of the name "George."

him again, and then you will be the one who will have to help him. You will just have to help him!"

✢

More than twenty years went by. It was now 1943—a war year. Father Mihail had died in a camp, and our beloved and prayerful Sasha had also died in exile. Being separated from Father Mihail was very painful and difficult for all of us. Occasionally he was able to send us a short letter which we received through friends. Father Mihail had been arrested in 1928 for his religious activities. I visited him several times and lived near the place where he was, sometimes staying a month at a time. Sasha, leaving everything behind, moved permanently to the place to which he was later exiled.

So many things happened in those years, and so many people died. Life without Father Mihail was difficult, but he had left us to the care of Father Arseny, who was his spiritual son and who lived in a little town not far from Moscow.

Sasha had died, and Katia had gotten married a long time before. We were in close contact. In 1943 I was working as a surgeon in an army hospital, sometimes eighteen or twenty hours a day. I couldn't get home for weeks at a time. I could go to church only every so often. I prayed when I could, always to the Mother of God.

During those awful war days memories from the past became dulled. Our awful journey on the roof of the train was almost completely erased from my memory. The hospital where I worked was for officers. I was so busy that often I didn't even have time to look at the face of the wounded man—I would only see and tend to the wound.

One night they brought in a colonel. His wound was infected, and I had to operate during the night. The intervention lasted four hours, and we had to give him blood several times. When the operation was finished the whole team was exhausted. We could barely stand on our feet. I fell asleep without undressing—the nurses helped me. I slept for something like four hours. As soon as I awoke I rushed to check on the colonel.

Very gradually, life began returning to him, in a slow trickle. We had many setbacks and difficulties trying to bring him back, but we all really wanted him to live.

I came to his bedside on the twentieth day after the operation. He was lying very weak, pale and transparent—only his eyes were bright. He looked at me and suddenly said very slowly, "Mashenka, you visit me so often and you still do not recognize me?"

I got angry and answered harshly, "I am not Mashenka to you—I am a military surgeon."

It upset me because I had come with many other doctors, on rounds. He only smiled and answered, "Oh, Mashenka, as for me, I have remembered you and Katia and Sasha all my life!"

That was when the past came back to me. "Yuri!" I cried out, and before I knew it I was hugging him.

The doctors and nurses stepped discreetly out of the room. As for me, I was hugging him around the head and crying like a little girl. I looked at the tag with his name, where it said, "Yuri Nikolaievich Tulikov." How could I not have noticed it before?

Yuri's eyes were shining and he said, "Go on your rounds, but stop in later."

For two months I would visit him after my work was done. We talked a great deal, and very well. We covered many subjects, but his first question was whether I was still a believer. I told him about Father Mihail, the dead Sasha, the married Katia, and about myself. I also told him about Father Arseny who was by now in a prison camp.

He told me a lot about himself. He'd lived a hard life, but he had a pure soul, clean and open. What Sasha had told him then in the train had remained embedded in his memory and had left a mark that had never been erased. It brought him to see faith, religion and people with care, attentiveness and good will.

He said, "In 1939 I was already a colonel, but I was sent to a camp. I saw good people and evil people there, but out of all those I met I remember one especially. I will remember him as long as I live. He carried so much goodness and warmth to people that everybody loved him, even the criminals. He was the one who introduced me to God—yes, exactly—he introduced me to God. In early 1941, Gleb had died in camp; I was liberated in August and sent back to fight on the front lines. I worked up to the rank of colonel again. I commanded a division until I was wounded. When I am better I want to return to fight. I have taken part in many wars—the Spanish war, the Finnish war and now the Patriotic War."

Yuri and I parted as dear friends, and we wrote to each other through the rest of the war. In 1948 he moved with his family to Moscow, and we got together often. He is now retired. He lives outside Moscow, in a country house, and is raising his grandchildren. We see each other just as often, but now we meet mostly in the cathedral at Trinity-St. Sergius Monastery in Zagorsk. How inscrutable are Thy ways, O Lord. Father Mihail had been so right when he said in 1920 that I would meet Yuri again. The power of human prayer is great, but even greater is the prayer of a spiritual father for his spiritual children. Great is the mercy of the Mother of God and her care for us sinners. By his prayer to the Mother of God, Father Mihail saved us from death and from sin and through our salvation he brought Yuri to the faith. Most Holy Mother of God, save us!

Excerpt from the memoirs of M. N. Ar.

An Admission

WRITING ABOUT FATHER Arseny always means telling about yourself, your life and actions, your doings that are connected in one way or another with him as your spiritual father. His unusually clear mind, his understanding of people and of life in general, his deep knowledge of people's souls—which you could also simply call intuitive knowledge—his constant prayerfulness, and his complete selflessness for the benefit of many many other people, all these traits put him in a unique place among the many priests I have known in the course of my life. To hide anything from him, to omit anything during confession was impossible; you could not avoid telling him the whole truth about yourself. You stand in front of him and you feel that he sees you in your entirety and that he knows ahead of time what you are going to tell him.

Before the war, both when he was in exile but still free to see people, my mother and I visited him often and I became his spiritual daughter. I was eighteen years old then. Later Father Arseny was in prison camps for many years and only very rarely did we receive little notes from him, with his spiritual direction to us. Starting in 1949 we, his spiritual children, completely lost contact with him and we didn't even know whether he was alive or where he was. I am providing here some memories which I wrote down, but I don't want to mention my name. These notes are much too personal.

In the forties I got married to a man who was a believer; he was calm and good-hearted, an introvert. He didn't talk much, not even with me. He was ten years older than I.

The Patriotic War was finished, and the years of repression between 1946 and 1952 did not touch us personally. We had two daughters, and my mother lived with us. My husband loved me in a consistent, calm way. He spent a great deal of time with the children, and he raised them in the faith. We lived comfortably, prayed often at home, on Saturday and Sunday we went to our church where we had a very good priest, Father George. It seemed that there was complete unity and peace in our family.

But the spring of 1952 came and what happened to me left an imprint on my soul for the rest of my life. The imprint had two sides to it: I committed a grave sin which I was perfectly aware of and which I confessed with all sincerity, but at the same time I felt I had grasped an enormous happiness, and the kind of total joy which can occur only as the result of real love. This second layer lies in the depth of my soul, covered by my repentance, but it is still alive and I am aware of it. I confessed my sin to Father George, and I thought that my confession had cleansed me in a way from my sinful past.

In 1958 Father Arseny was freed from camp and it is impossible to convey the joy which we, his spiritual children, felt when we saw him again. It felt to me that we were all closer to God, in a new way. Everything was told and confessed to Father Arseny, but I was unable to tell him about what had happened in 1952. I was too ashamed, and I was at times afraid he would reject me if he heard what had happened.

What was it that happened? As I said, as a family we lived in harmony. But suddenly, in 1952, an enormous love seized me and engulfed me. I fell in love with a man who was totally foreign to my way of thinking; he did not believe in God. But he was good-hearted, responsive, very intelligent, and strong willed. This love struck suddenly. It was he who was drawn to me first, with a gentleness and a winning tenderness, with an attentiveness and a caring which all people, and perhaps women especially, appreciate and need. I am sorry to say that my husband was never attentive or tender to me. He was a man of duty and moderation.

In the beginning the attention and tenderness of Fyodor (this is not his real name) surprised me and even scared me a little, but at the same time I was drawn to him: I wanted to look into his soul and understand the secret of his being, and also I wanted to help, yes, exactly, to help! In what way? I did not know myself what I could do for Fyodor. O my God! A kind of attentiveness and a gentle, caring word can mean so very much to a person, especially a woman. Our life was moderate and habitual. Each one of us knew what he or she would say when getting home. I knew what my husband would ask, what my mother and my children would say. The interests you establish in your family become immutable, and they do not exceed the expectations you develop during years of life together.

Fyodor was broad-minded, his knowledge was extensive, he was energetic and tall, his face was attractive. People liked Fyodor, but he remained humble, not talkative, reserved and, as far as I knew, had never been interested in other women. He loved only one woman, his wife, who had been a good friend of mine for years. In 1943 Aniuta was 43 years old and Fyodor was 46. Fyodor and Aniuta lived a moderate life like ours. Aniuta reminded me of my husband, in the sense that she too was silent, an introvert, pedantically organized, not tender, and very thrifty.

Fyodor lived for his work. Our lines of work were similar and, in spite of the fact that we worked in different departments, we used to cross paths at some meetings and even sometimes had to collaborate on various projects. Fyodor and Anna often came to visit us and we used to go see them. Fyodor and I would start talking about our work, and Anna would then say, "Is it really necessary to talk about work even at home?" But since she saw that this made no difference, she would talk with my husband or other guests. Our friendship would probably have continued the same way, without complication, for many years to come—if only something terrible had not happened.

Yes, exactly—if only. In the spring of 1952 my husband and I were supposed to go and spend some time in a sanatorium where we loved to go.[8] We loved the countryside around it and went there many times. But, all of a sudden my husband was unable to go. He was sent by his job on a lengthy assignment, far away. His authorization to stay at the sanatorium was going to be lost. We decided to offer it to Fyodor because he had a month's vacation left. "This way you won't be lonely, you will have somebody you know with you," my husband said to me.

It was the beginning of the month of May, the weather was sunny and warm, the greenery was still pale and transparent. There were hills in the distance, the forest was sparse, and wildflowers had started to appear. All this unwittingly created an atmosphere of happiness and excitement. The sun was reflected in small lakes that were connected by streams; there weren't many people around the sanatorium, everything was peaceful and reminded one of the paintings of Levitan or Nesterov. That spring everything seemed perfect to me. During the first five days of our stay Fyodor and I enthusiastically walked around the surrounding countryside and talked about everything. The usually silent and withdrawn Fyodor disappeared. Our conversations were very interesting. We discussed various topics: religion, faith, the beauty of nature—and we seemed to love the same sights. I was happy and enjoyed everything. I suddenly saw Fyodor in a new light, as intellectual, gifted, tender. After the fifth day came the sixth day, and on that day my whole previous life fell to pieces and this was the beginning of a totally new life filled with the joy of our meetings, with the light of another person, with an enormous all-consuming love.

My family, my husband, my faith, the words of my spiritual father, my own womanly modesty—all this disappeared, swept away by the tornado of a love such as I had never experienced before. This was a human, earthy love

8 The Russian sanatorium is a quiet and restful place where people go to take healthful walks and breathe the good air while receiving medical attention.

which made me believe that it was a kind of love you encounter only once in your lifetime. I was unable to push it away and, even worse, I didn't want to push it away. Each day I lived with Fyodor was happiness, a discovery of new feelings and new joys. The world around me became beautiful and everything that had seemed dull and gray before started to shine, acquire colors, become beautiful and full of light.

The things I discovered in those days carried me along like a torrent which washed away everything that I had loved before and that I had thought to be precious to me. I awaited each new meeting, and new conversation, every new closeness impatiently. I had never experienced such feelings toward my husband in spite of his love and our spiritual closeness—in spite of the fact that we were both strong believers. Nothing could be compared to my relationship with Fyodor. My feelings for him were burning me; I forgot everybody and everything, and I saw that the same thing was happening to Fyodor, but perhaps in a bigger way. He became another man before my very eyes.

Perhaps you will find it hard to believe that during the seven months of our relationship not once did I feel repentance or regret that all this was happening to me. I loved him as more than just a man; in my attraction to him I discovered a whole new world that had been totally unknown to me before. I lost the ability to see what was happening to me critically, from a spiritual perspective. I write now about how I felt then, and I am trying to tell only the truth. Fyodor changed; his energy was amazing, and the enormous knowledge which had sat like a clot in his brain suddenly became attainable to others. At work he made discovery after discovery. He became much more outgoing, and the people around him were surprised to see that they had never known him to be this way.

He discovered that I was a believer because he saw the cross and the little icon which were pinned to my undershirt. He looked at them with surprise. Yes, this is how it was! Even his question, "So, you are a believer?" didn't call to my mind even for a second my entire past; it didn't make me stop and think.

The time we had at the sanatorium went by in a whirlwind. We returned home, but we were changed people. We did not stop meeting. On the contrary, our relationship became even stronger. At first we met wherever we could in secret, then we were able to find a room where we could meet. We were afraid of everything, we were afraid to be seen by people we knew, by our colleagues, or by members of our families. We would leave work as if to go to libraries or on assignment and would meet in our room. We stole love from our families, from our conscience; we stole it in the face of humanity and I stole it before the face of God.

I sometimes felt that I was like a thief in somebody else's house. I was snatching precious things and I was afraid all the time that I would be caught. Every sound, every squeaking door frightened me. Most of all I was afraid of being caught by my mother or by my husband. Even in my dreams I had the same thoughts. I was afraid to start thinking about what was happening to me. If I did, my past would enter into my present life, and the courage that was based on my stolen happiness would desert me—and then my fall into the abyss of doubt and suffering would be unavoidable. I had enormous fears, both of the pain I would feel if my love were to be broken, and of my suffering in connection with my broken family if our subterfuge was to be discovered. I could love only in secret, and only if I did not try to think about what was happening, I tried not to analyze. I lied to my husband, I lied to my mother, I abandoned my children, I evaded all my duties, but I met Fyodor, and I couldn't stop myself from doing it. I thought that my husband didn't notice anything, and to this day I am not sure he did. He was always so silent. He never reacted when I told him I was delayed at work, or when I was nervous; he just began to be even more caring with the children, spending a lot of time with them and praying a great deal.

I don't know how long such an affair could have lasted, but in the beginning of the seventh month my oldest daughter became seriously ill. First we tried to take care of her at home: the sleepless nights, the calling of doctors, the care for her fell on the shoulders of my mother and my husband. Her state of health became worse and she had to be hospitalized. Here again my husband carried the brunt of the care. Even during these dangerous days I managed to find snatches of time to spend with Fyodor. I felt then that I had the right to forget all the difficulties of my life when I was with him.

One day my mother telephoned me at work and told me that my daughter had taken another turn for the worse. At that time I was supposed to meet Fyodor, and regardless of everything I still went. At about three o'clock I stopped at home to pick up what my mother had cooked for my daughter to take to the hospital, and found my husband praying on his knees before our icons.

"O Lord! Do not forsake us sinners, heal and save us, visit your servants (he named our daughter and me) and visit them with your grace!"

I walked carefully out of the room, grabbed the package my mother had prepared and ran to the hospital. The thought of my daughter's illness, my fear for her life, and the clear vision of my spiritual degradation turned my soul around in that moment. It was as if a curtain had fallen from my eyes. I, a believer, a spiritual daughter of the Father Arseny who was now suffering in a camp and who was leading me on the path of faith—I had become much worse than the unbelievers to whom I used to compare myself, thinking I was better than they because I had faith!

I ran into the hospital and I found my husband bent over our daughter. I thought she had died. I ran up to her, but my husband stopped me and said, "Don't wake her—she is sleeping after an injection," and he took me aside, over to a window.

"I have been waiting for you here since morning," he said. "Now the crisis is over, and you have both come back!"

This sentence puzzled me: what did he mean by "You have both come back!"?

I thought that perhaps my daughter had died and my husband didn't know what he was saying. I looked at him and started sobbing. He gently hugged me, touched my shoulders and repeated, "It's all right, now it is all over, all of it!"

I understood that my daughter was alive, but his words meant something which probably had to do with me. What struck me was that he had been in the hospital since morning, but in the meantime, I had seen him praying at home. What was this? We sat together at our daughter's bedside all night long. We were both silent, but we both had a lot to think about. . . . My whole life passed before my eyes and I saw myself as I truly was. I was afraid to look at my husband: his humility and his patience did more for me than any amount of accusation could ever have done.

From this day on, my relationship with Fyodor ceased. I knew I had been a weak toy in the hands of sin and I was ashamed that I had stepped away from God, that I had forgotten everything Father Arseny had ever told me, and that I had chosen the path of infidelity and vice.

Many years have passed since 1952 and although I repented very sincerely for what I had done, and although I realize and am aware of the sinfulness of what I had done and I ask God to forgive me, in spite of all this, I cannot regret that all this happened. Our love for each other was too sincere, too real and beautiful. Yes I was wrong, I went astray—but I truly loved, and even then I begged God for His forgiveness, as I continue to do now.

People have told me, "If you say this, it means you have not repented, that you have not realized the depth of your fall." This is not true, I did realize everything but I am unable to curse my past, and I do not want to do so. I can be judged in many different ways.

✠

My life with my husband went on as it had before, but I was now different. An invisible line of secrecy separated me from him, but it seemed to me that he did not feel it. As always, he was quiet, a man of few words. I know he loved me, but too rationally and calmly. I sometimes had the impression that I was one of the objects in our apartment, I was the mother of our children but I was not a "wife," I was not a "woman."

Fyodor, for all intents and purposes, was completely out of my life. We never even hinted at our previous relationship. We met when he came with his wife to visit us, or when we visited them. We couldn't stop being friends because my husband and Fyodor's wife would never have understood. Our break seriously affected Fyodor; he lost all his newly acquired energy, he became sluggish, his work suffered. It was only some eight years later that he became himself again. The most unpleasant part was that Aniuta confided in me that she had had a feeling in 1952 that Fyodor was infatuated with another woman. It was a hard and shameful thing for me to hear.

This is what happened to me then.

Five years went by after Father Arseny had returned from camp in 1958. I visited him every month, went to confession, asked for his advice and left calm, peaceful, and renewed, but my past still weighed heavily on me.

In 1963 I went to see him in October. Father Arseny was especially cheerful and energetic. I prayed with him during vespers, in his room. I made my confession sincerely and deeply. During this confession Father Arseny was unusually silent. I spoke about myself in detail. When I finished he asked, "Is this all?"

"Yes, this is all." I responded.

He sighed deeply and asked again, "Is this all?" and when he heard no answer he covered my head with his epitrachilion and read the prayers of forgiveness.

Next morning I received communion along with a few others who had come to see Father Arseny. The weather was bright, but windy. I went outside and sat on a bench in the garden together with Anya. Because of yesterday's confession, today's communion, and the sunny day I was cheerful and at peace.

After a while Nadezhda Petrovna gave us tea with some cake and fried potatoes (only she knew how to cook those so perfectly). While we were eating we talked, we reminisced, told stories. Father Arseny went for a rest after the meal, and after that he expressed the desire to go for a walk in the forest, which was about a kilometer away. Irina the doctor was opposed to him going out because of the wind and the dark clouds gathering, but Father Arseny put his coat and hat on. Nadezhda Petrovna insisted he dress warmly. Irina and Anya wanted to go with Father Arseny. Of course we all wanted to go with him, but since those two had expressed their desire first, the others refrained from speaking. Anya and Irina went to fetch their coats, and Father Arseny was still in his room. When he came out of his room and saw them dressed, he looked at me and said, "I will go with L., she needs to take a walk with me!"

We went out and walked through the streets, past vegetable gardens, old barns where people were drying bricks, and found ourselves in the field. The wind was tearing the grass out, dark gray clouds gave the impression they were holding onto the ground, branches of trees were bent in battle with the strong wind. The wind was lifting the fallen leaves, pushing them forward and tossing them at our feet. The wind was whistling, the dead leaves were rustling, and it felt as if we were walking on something alive, moaning and begging.

I felt uncomfortable. I glanced at Father Arseny. He was walking along calmly, concentrating on his thoughts. Sometimes a faint smile would illumine his face.

A narrow path went into the forest. In the forest you could feel the wind even more. The trees bent under the wind's pressure moaning mournfully. The leaves which covered the ground would suddenly lift and move slowly in the direction of the wind, bumping into the roots of the trees, falling onto each other, only to be dispersed once again by the next gust. All of this depressed me, spoiled my mood, worried, and troubled me. "Why is it that Father Arseny wanted to take me for a walk?" I thought. "Why?" He never did anything without a reason. He always thought about ways to be helpful, ways he could direct us—his spiritual children—toward God. Probably he hadn't called me out without a good reason. Yesterday I went to confession, today I received communion and...suddenly the memory of 1952 pierced me.

"Father Arseny!" I cried out, and stopped him. "I must tell you..." And I started talking, barely breathing because I was so moved.

Father Arseny stood right next to me and looked at me attentively and gently. After he had heard the first words of my confession, he bowed his head, crossed himself and told me, "Don't tell me! It isn't necessary! Your sin is great, but God has already forgiven it, you confessed it to Father George. Do not repeat your story!"

I cried, tears were running down my face, I tried to continue talking, I was shivering because of my inner fear, embarrassment and shame.

"Don't. I have understood everything. The fact that you didn't tell your husband is both bad and good. He loves you; if you had told him you could have wounded him deeply and it could have created serious problems for your family. He knows anyway. We are all sinners—remember your sin before God and before your family. You must pray and pray, and ask for forgiveness. I will pray with you. What is most important is that you were able to talk about it with your spiritual father. Truth cleans a person, especially truth admitted in confession. Let us go." And he blessed me.

We had not gone very deep into the forest. We turned back to go home. The wind was still strong and cold, branches still swept the ground, leaves still rustled on the ground, dark clouds rushed about in the sky—but I had regained the peace and calm I had not known since 1952. Now this awful sad weather did not scare me, it didn't tear my soul apart. On our way home Father Arseny was lively and joyous. As we were walking he told me in detail the life of St. Mary of Egypt. Each and every word he said carried a special and deep meaning for me.[9]

At home Father Arseny was joyous and prayerful throughout the day. He told us a lot about the different people he had met during his life in the camps, and quoted from the Gospel and from the fourth-century Fathers of the Church. He spoke about unconfessed sins, about prayer. He talked at particular length about prayer. He spoke mainly about the power of prayer when two or more people agree to pray about one thing and he remembered how several times he had prayed in camp asking for the salvation of his friends. Alyosha (the student, now Father Alexei), who was sitting around the table with us said, "Yes, Father Arseny. Do you remember how we were saved in the prison cell? Our common prayer performed a miracle."

I will always remember Father Arseny saying that when two or three agree to pray for the same thing, if their prayer is sincere and comes from a true

9 St. Mary of Egypt had been a prostitute, but suddenly realizing her sin, she fled to the desert, living there in solitude and repentance for 37 years. She was discovered by a monk, Zosima (her eventual biographer) who found her to be a holy person.

faith and a pure heart, this prayer is always very powerful before God and the Mother of God.

"Sin," said Father Arseny, "is unavoidable for the great majority of people, because we live on earth. But the main thing in life is the person's relationship with God. We have to turn toward Him in prayer, a sincere and informal prayer—repentance, confession, the awareness of our sinfulness, the doing of good deeds, love for others, for animals, for nature!"

"We must constantly remember," said Father Arseny, "the words in the Scriptures: 'Vengeance is mine, I will repay, says the Lord' (Romans 12:19). The feeling of vengeance must never visit us; if it comes, we have to fight it with prayer, in remembrance of the lives the Fathers and of how they fought this passion and conquered it."

When the thirst for revenge visits us, Father Arseny advised us to put ourselves in the place of the one you want to take vengeance on, to see the irrationality of your wishes.

In the course of the same evening he spoke of the attention we have to pay to others, how we must listen when a person tells us about his sorrow; even if we do not agree with what he did with it, we have to see his life through his eyes, deeply and without accusation. Life is so complicated that most of the time a person does not even know ahead of time what he is going to do.

As he was speaking Father Arseny often looked at me at length. I felt then that when he was looking at me, he could see my whole soul.

The sin I had committed did not disappear; it remained. By confessing and repenting of it I did not erase it. I know that I will have to answer for it at the Last Judgment, but confession and repentance have given me the opportunity to realize my actions fully. When I admitted it all to my spiritual father I felt nailed to a "shaming post," but in this way I became less torn apart by what had occurred, and understood my own insignificance.

When he was saying good-bye to me, Father Arseny said, "Always remember and pray and ask forgiveness again and again. Do not forget your sin against your husband, and forgive him much."

I left calmer. During the trip home I kept thinking, I tried to understand how it was that Father Arseny knew about my confession to Father George; I had never told anyone about it. Father Arseny really was a reader of the human soul. His spiritual eyes saw and read what was most secret in us.

✢

Father Arseny died, leaving us orphaned. My husband, before whom I was so guilty, also died, and the children left. I now have plenty of time to remember, to ponder—and I decided to tell here about that enormous help and spiritual strength which Father Arseny gave to us all.

A Note

I was given a note to pass to Father Arseny, and on my way, I lost it. When? Where? I couldn't understand. I discovered the loss only when I arrived.

I was distraught, I was miserable and immediately upon my arrival, I told Father Arseny about it. I knew that the note was very important; the person who had written awaited an answer as soon as possible. But I didn't know what the note was about, I didn't even have an approximate idea of what was in the note!

After he heard what had happened, Father Arseny said, "This is also the will of God!"

The next day, as I was leaving he blessed me, gave me a note and said, smiling, "Please do not lose this one!"

I left, and as soon as I arrived I ran to M. and even before I gave her the note I told her that I had lost hers. M. was terribly upset and even began to cry. But after she read Father Arseny's letter she was overjoyed, crying this time from happiness, and repeated again and again, "Lord! What a joy! Father Arseny wrote me a full answer to my note. You understand, he wrote everything. So you were joking that you lost my note? How could he have found out about my problems?"

I also thought... *How?*

A Panikhida

———

THE MORNING OF March 21, Father Arseny served a liturgy. On Saturday three people had come, and four more came with the night train.

He gave communion to all of us who had gone to confession, finished the liturgy and said that if we wanted we could leave and have tea in Nadezhda Petrovna's room. He explained that he would come in about an hour; he wanted to serve a *panikhida*.[10]

We did not leave. Father Arseny started serving a *panikhida* for the newly-departed servant of God Kyril. He cried as he served. The whole *panikhida* was a "groaning of the spirit," a true lament from the heart for a dear, departed friend. He did not notice any of us, it was as if he was completely alone in the room. There was only the limitless prayer for mercy, for forgiveness, for the soul of the departed servant of God Kyril. None of us there knew who this Kyril was, but we understood that he was a friend, a very beloved friend of Father Arseny.

Father Arseny finished serving, took off his vestments and, very sad, joined us all for tea. Nobody felt like talking; we all sipped tea quietly. Father Arseny was also silent. Then he left to go to his room, and we stayed at the table.

At about three o'clock a telegram was delivered, addressed to Father Arseny: "On March 21, at seven o'clock in the morning, Kyril died of a heart attack. Signed—son Igor."

The telegram had come from Yaroslavl.

When we heard the telegram many of us remembered dear Kyril Sergeyevich, a kind and good man who had done time in a camp with Father Arseny.

We looked at each other, and we all thought what a seer you must be to know about the death of your spiritual son before the news comes.

Great is Your power, O Lord, in Your chosen children!

10 A *panikhida* is a memorial service for the dead.

I Deliver Letters

AFTER SHE SPENT two weeks at Father Arseny's, Natasha brought back a whole pile of letters which had to be delivered as soon as possible.

I was asked to deliver half of them.

The times were troubled. Many of us had been arrested, and the rest of us sensed that we were being followed—so delivering letters was a dangerous task.

Natasha told us that when she had been staying at Father Arseny's it was obvious that the house was under surveillance. In addition, Nadezhda Petrovna and some neighbors had been called in for interrogation; they were asked who comes to see him, who writes him, who stays there, and whether Father Arseny holds services in the house.

"As I was traveling home in the train, I constantly had the feeling that somebody was behind me. I was traveling in a crowded train, and several people got onto the train with me at my station, but my attention was definitely drawn to a woman who 'happened' to be near me wherever I was sitting or standing.

"All the way home I was thinking—what should I do with the letters if they arrest me? But I couldn't think of a solution and remembered the words of Father Arseny when he blessed me saying good bye: 'He will protect you, He will be with you. Do not be afraid of anything. All will be well!'

"I got off the train in Moscow and felt that nobody was following me. I felt calm and went peacefully home. The stress was off, and I even thought that I might have imagined everything."

This is what Natasha said as she was giving me the letters. We put the letters on the table and sorted them according to the people each one of us knew. I spent the night at Natasha's. Half the night we talked about Father Arseny, about his teachings, about his way of life.

At seven in the morning, I put on my coat, put a kerchief on my head, and left the house carrying the letters. It was Sunday, and there were few people in the streets. I walked joyously, excitedly. The letter I had received myself from Father Arseny had done me much good; it had reassured me and my unsettled state had been alleviated.

I had walked for some fifty yards when I felt that somebody was walking behind me. I turned around and saw a woman. A thought came to me: "they are watching me." I decided to test this impression. I walked faster and turned into the next little street. The steps were still right behind me, I turned again, the woman was still behind me. My heart skipped a beat, my legs did not obey me any more—I didn't know what to do. I was carrying the letters, and if they were confiscated they would cause serious trouble for many people. I walked a little further and crossed the street; the woman did the same, keeping some 50 to 70 yards' distance behind me. It was now undeniable that I was being followed. A thought crossed my mind: perhaps I should throw away the letters and start running, but obviously they would be retrieved, and they know who I am—I was walking from Natasha's.

After I had controlled my feelings and gotten hold of myself I started praying. At first prayer did not flow easily; then I concentrated on it. I walked slowly.

Perhaps I was daring, but I prayed to the Mother of God with these words: "O Mother of God! I put my trust in you and I count only on your help. Take me under your protection, I put myself in your hands! Help me!"

So I walked and I prayed, counting on the protection of the Mother of God. My fear left me, also my worries left me—I was sure of the fact that I was not alone. The Mother of God protects me; if something is to happen that means that it is the will of God—whatever happens. "Everything depends on you, O Mother of God. Whatever you will, so it will be!" I walked calmly, I was not afraid of anything and I kept hearing the clicking on the asphalt of the heels of the woman behind me. I wasn't rushing any more—I started walking more slowly because I understood how inescapable my situation was. My hope was fully in the Mother of God, so I was serene and calm. I kept walking and praying and I didn't even notice where I was going. Only one thing was on my mind—the Mother of God. I heard footsteps get nearer and nearer to me. I came to a crossroads, I turned the corner and I saw a woman dressed exactly like me, my age, with the same kerchief on her head, the same coat, the same purse on her shoulder. She began to walk next to me, turned slightly toward me. Her face looked familiar to me; it was bright and seemed lit up with an extraordinary light.

I looked at her once more, and could not look any more—her face was so light and so perfect. So we walked together and I rejoiced that I was not alone any more. I kept walking and I kept praying. I didn't understand who my companion was, but I kept hearing the heels of the other woman behind my back. We walked up to a street corner, my companion turned to me and said, "Stop here and stand. I will keep walking." She said this sternly, but her face was full of goodness and of light. I stopped, and she—my companion—kept walking ahead. She was identical to me in the way she looked and the way she was dressed. This felt strange to me, but I stopped. The woman who had been following me stopped next to me, looked me over from head to toe. She looked surprised, walked around me and ran to catch up with my companion who was walking very fast.

The woman who was following me had such an angry face, she looked as if she hated everything alive.

So I kept standing. I did not have the strength to walk. I only watched the other woman who looked like me walking on, followed by the agent who had been following me all this time. They came to another intersection, turned a corner and disappeared from my sight. I came to and went the other way. By two o'clock I had delivered all the letters.

I often wonderd whom the Mother of God had sent to me. I knew it had been her gracious and great help.

A year after this I was arrested. My interrogator kept asking me who the woman was who had walked with me, and where did we both disappear to? They even confronted me with the woman who was following me. She said, "There I am walking, comrade Lieutenant, following her, she turns corners to lose me. But I follow her... When I came to the corner of Kazakov Street, somebody was standing, and another woman looking exactly like the first one walked away. They were identical, dressed the same way, same kerchiefs, same boots, same coat, same purse, same gait, same turn of the head. I followed them, but I couldn't figure out which one I had been following from the beginning and which one appeared on that street corner. I followed the one who was walking away, I walked behind her for some ten minutes when she suddenly simply disappeared into thin air. I swear I am telling you the truth—she simply disappeared. Ask this woman, let her tell you what she did. It was just like a disappearing act in the circus."

What could I answer? The interrogator was shouting, he even hit me, and I remained silent. I only answered, "Well, I do not know!" and I kept praying, and suddenly I could not resist any more and simply said, "I did not hide anywhere, I did not disappear. The Mother of God saved me. I had been walking and praying to her all the time." The interrogator started laughing, but didn't hit me any more.

The punishments were fierce at this time, but again the Mother of God helped: I was exiled for three years to live not nearer than 100 kilometers from Moscow. This was the smallest possible punishment.

Whom did the Mother of God send? Or did she come herself? Did she send a saint or my guardian angel to lead away the woman who had been following me? But I did see her, I heard her voice: all this is written up in my interrogation report.

After this, I only got to see Father Arseny again in 1958. I told him all about what had happened, asking him what he thought had happened.

He said, "In answer to your prayers the Mother of God, our Protector, sent you a great grace and protected you. The grace was important both for you and for me. If they had intercepted my letters many people could have been arrested and sent to camps.

"Glory to Thee O God, glory to Thee! Most holy Mother of God, save us. Always keep the icon of the Holy Virgin of Kazan with you. Pray before it often."

From the memoirs of A. V. R.

Lena

———

I CAME TO see Father Arseny to tell him about myself, to go to confession and to receive advice concerning many questions which had come up in my life, and which worried me. He was ill, however, so I had to stay for a few days as a guest with the hospitable Nadezhda Petrovna, waiting for Father Arseny to get better and be able to see me.

On the day after I came two other people arrived, a husband and a wife. Yuri Alexandrovich was about forty years old, and his wife Elena Sergeyevna must have been thirty-five. They were both tall, handsome, a little noisy and excited but very united in everything having to do with faith, life, and their relationship to people. I liked them.

The next day I went with them to see some ancient churches, monasteries, and museums in the area. We talked a great deal and by evening, without even noticing it, I told them about how I had come to the Church, to faith. When I finished talking I asked them, thoughtlessly and somewhat tactlessly, "And what about you: how did you come to the Church?" Yuri looked at his wife and said, "Well, through her." And for some reason they both laughed.

"Perhaps you could tell me about it?" I asked again, but Yuri and Lena looked at each other and changed the topic of conversation.

The third day we were together brought us even closer. Father Arseny felt better at last and could talk to us. We stayed on another two days, after which Nadezhda Petrovna, as usual, organized what she called a "farewell tea."

Father Arseny even got up from bed, came out of his room and joined us at the table.

Irina, his spiritual child and also his doctor, had come from Moscow especially to take care of his health, and was closely watching his every step. Father Arseny asked us about news from Moscow, and told us many interesting and useful things. He looked at Yuri very warmly, talked with him, and all of a sudden he said, "You shouldn't have hesitated to tell Alexander Alexandrovich (this is my name) how you came to the Church. Be sure to tell him about it, or write about it and give him your notes. Be sure you do this!" repeated Father Arseny.

We were all surprised that Father Arseny knew that I had asked and that they had not answered.

Back in Moscow Yuri and Lena became frequent guests in our home. My collection of old books was of great interest and delight to them. It was about two months after we had met at Father Arseny's, and with some embarrassment, that Yuri passed his notes on to me. With his and Lena's permission I will let you read them. Father Arseny wanted this.

✦

I finished high school, applied to university, and became a student. Sports, books, theater, and hiking were my passions. I enjoyed life, I was carefree, but I was a good student and went right on to graduate studies. Once I had my master's degree I was feeling very important and went to do research far away. I was very involved with my work. Just as I had as a student, I spent my vacations and my days off on hikes and excursions. I gathered a large collection of books. And yet I was not satisfied; something was always missing. I was looking for something new, something wonderful.

During my hikes in the mountains I would see the unlimited world of mountains, air, clouds, alpine meadows, and forests bright with their fall colors and chaotic rock formations. A light mist would cover all with its mysterious and magnificent beauty. It almost hurt to see all this beauty, this boundless perfection. I felt like bowing before nature, thanking it for its beauty freely given as a gift to mankind. Our thick northern forests reminded me of the world of Russian fairy tales. I often felt like a pygmy lost in a land of giants.

When we rested we sang Russian songs of those days. We had good times, and life was interesting, but whenever I got home I felt an inner emptiness, I was unsatisfied and nostalgic for something.

I fell in love several times. Each time I thought that it was the real thing, but time would go by and it cooled off, and love was replaced by indifference. I brought sadness to many, and I myself was also sometimes in despair, but I only thought of myself; I never gave any thought to the suffering of others. At times love would come to me like the onset of a severe illness—I would shake, I would be deaf and blind to everything; at other times it would creep in as a colorless, boring love which only served to pass the time.

This is how my life was going. It looked great from the outside, I was successful and had interesting work, but inside it was empty, and I realized this at times.

In our construction department there worked a young woman aged 25. She was gifted, willful and stubborn. Her colleagues referred to her formally, as Elena Sergeyevna. I was told that when she had first started working there people used the more familiar form of her name, "Lenka," or "Lena." She said very seriously, "Why do you make it so complicated—why not just call me

Elena Sergeyevna," and that is what everybody did. I often worked with her, but was never interested in her as a woman. I didn't think she presented any interest, but because she was very serious and knowledgeable, I thought of her as a "blue-stocking." I worked with her for about a year without noticing her.

We went on an excursion to northern Rostov; I had been there several times, but I went again because at home my usual friends were celebrating somebody's birthday and I didn't want to be there.

At seven o'clock in the morning, we all boarded a bus. It was full of older people; only four people were young, one of them was Lena. We arrived; as usual we first visited the churches and the museums. A guide told us about everything, but Elena Sergeyevna went off by herself, looking carefully at icons, frescoes, churches. I didn't listen to the guide either.

I joined Elena and asked, "Why don't you listen? What he says is very interesting."

"It doesn't interest me, I interpret ancient Russian art in my own way."

So we walked through the museum together. She spoke almost like a guide, but her tone was different. When she spoke about historical events, about the lives of saints, her stories were warmer, more sincere—you saw the relationship of the believer to faith and to God, and how everything was reflected through the soul of a believer. When we entered a church, she was lively and her explanation of the Rostov frescoes made me see them in a new light.

She saw the frescoes, the icons, and the architecture on a higher plain, one of spirituality and majesty, tying everything into the faith and the life of our people and their past.

I became interested in Elena Sergeyevna. At work I came to her desk often to talk with her. We went to Suzdal together, then to Uglich. Each of these trips opened up something special for me. I asked her how she knew so much about ancient Russian art. She answered, "I got interested and I read up on it." So it went. I started courting her, but without great interest. I thought that I would soon win her.

Once as I was accompanying her home in the evening, I took her in my arms, rudely, strongly, and kissed her. She pushed me away, tore herself away from me and left. This got to me. At work I tried to approach her again and talk to her. But she avoided me and wouldn't talk to me. After work I caught up with her and tried to talk again – again she was silent. She stopped walking alone. She only told me, "I didn't expect you to be so rude. Art doesn't truly interest you—it was just for show!"

At work my colleagues, especially some women who always noticed everything, began making fun of me, seeing how I was trying to pursue my relationship with Lena. They told me, "Well, unrequited love has finally caught up with you too!"

Summer came, and I went south for the holidays. I met a friend there, and what with the mountains, tents and hikes, I developed a crush on her and forgot Lena. But on returning to Moscow I found that I just could not live without Elena Sergeyevna—I needed her like I needed air. I tried again to talk to her, to get closer to her—but to no avail. She was silent, she didn't answer my questions. When I talked with her about work, her answers were monosyllabic.

Once, I decided to try to make some conversation with her out on the street. I followed her out. She took the subway, we rode for one stop, she left the metro and took a few little streets up to a church. She went in and made her way among the praying people, toward the front, and stood before an icon, which I later found out was the icon of St. Nicholas the Wonderworker. She blessed herself several times with the sign of the cross and began to sing with the choir. I stood off to the side and watched her. Her face became transfigured, bright and focused. I had never seen such a Lena.

From that day on I went to this church, secretly, every Saturday. I would stand among the praying parishioners and watch her. But in about six weeks she noticed me. I wanted to talk to her, to say I was sorry, but nothing helped and soon she left her job at the institute, because of me. Our colleagues understood even this!

But still I went to that church. I wanted to find out what could make a contemporary person believe, and especially a young woman like Lena. So I would go, and listen. I tried to catch the words, I tried to understand them, I wanted to understand the services. I understood how one could be interested in architecture, in art, in history; you could love antiquity, but how could you believe in God? What for? And pray? How could one stand next to all those simple old people, how could one listen to the readings of the priests—it all sounded so difficult to understand and so unconvincing. Of course they sing well, but to hear good singing you could go to a concert hall and hear a beautiful concert sung by professionals—and there you didn't have to stand; you could sit among civilized people.

And here?

I decided to look deeper into the nature of contemporary faith. I wanted to find out what attracted and compelled man to believe. After Lena had seen me she stopped going to that church. But I continued to go, trying to get a good look at things, to study it all. I noticed that not only old people came, there were some young people too. Healthy guys dressed a modern way, girls, women with children, even intelligent-looking men. What was it that brought all these people, and Lena, here? What? I wanted to ask, I wanted to talk to somebody here about it.

At first I came to church only on Saturdays, then I started coming on other days. I listened carefully, I tried to understand, but I could catch only a few words or phrases here and there. But I would think about what I had heard. It was so hard to make sense of it all. The thought came to me that for two thousand years people believed in God, in Jesus Christ and in the Mother of God, they prayed, bowed to the ground, suffered martyrdom, died for their faith. All this couldn't have been just because somebody had forced them to do so. Probably there is a need in the human soul for faith, a necessity. Or maybe this was one of those psychological or psychic phenomena which have not yet been studied.

I would hear prayers: "Lord, now lettest Thou Thy servant depart in peace...," "O Gladsome Light of the Holy Glory..., " Bless the Lord, O my soul..." I would remember the words, write them down as soon as I got home, and think about them. Gradually, like an ancient inscription, I began to decipher these words and phrases. Much became clearer, but I was still completely in the dark. When people sang in church I sang with them: it lifted my spirits and appealed to me. I tried to find out as much as I could about Christianity. I realized that I had very little to work on from modern books about iconography and architecture. I looked further. I managed to obtain a Gospel, a Bible, books about the Church published before the Revolution, and I talked to certain relatives and friends.

Some things became clearer, but then reading the Bible confused me. The thoughts in the Gospel were understandable and kind, but a little naive for modern life. I went to the library, and found some essays on religion, but there everything was disparaged, made fun of, and criticized. I felt that approach to the problems of faith was superficial and full of lies. I didn't know anybody in this church, I didn't know who to ask. By luck I found in the home of some relatives an old book—a catechism. I devoured it, and much became more clear to me, but the book was dry and heavy, stiff and official.

Still there were explanations of some prayers and some services. I was familiar mostly with vespers and matins because those are the services I attended.

To study, to understand almost became my hobby, my passion. I entered a world I had never known. This world is not separate from modern life, but to my surprise includes it.

I still love nature, I love my trips but now there is something new in my life which makes everything more meaningful, more inspired, more full; but still there are things I find strange, antiquated, intellectualized. I have not seen Lena for a long time now. I have visited other churches, but did not find her there either.

It took me more that a year and a half to understand the services and to absorb the main tenets of faith, but I still knew so little then.

Much of my past had left me, and new interests entered into my life. I now spend my holidays in Trinity-St. Sergius Monastery. I rent a room and go to the Monastery every day. I was standing at the relics of St. Sergius once and there I met a seminary student. He explained many things I hadn't understood and answered my questions. This was such a happy meeting.

Finally the day came when I understood why people believe in God. I used to come to church just to see Lena; now I came because I just couldn't not come. Do I believe? Or have I simply gotten used to church services? It is now difficult for me to answer this question. Now I don't just listen to the prayers, I let their meaning enter into me, and sometimes I catch myself praying. After church, the words of the prayers and hymns and readings stay in my soul for a long time.

Two years have now gone by since I first came to church. First I went to catch up with Lena, then I went out of curiosity, and now I go as a believer.

It is Pascha;[11] Great Lent has ended. The Matins are sung, all those attending are joyous. People are singing "Christ is risen from the dead, trampling down death by death..." Of course I sing with them. I am full of an unexplainable joy, I am enraptured by this joy, my soul is uplifted, I want to embrace everybody and everything. There is neither tiredness, nor hurt feelings, nor concerns.

The Paschal Matins have ended, and I stay for the Liturgy. When it ends and people are ready to leave, so many people crowd the door that I decide to leave through the side door. On the steps I see Lena. I am not even surprised

11 The Orthodox commonly refer to Easter as "Pascha," the Greek and Hebrew word meaning "Passover."

to see her, I simply say, "Christ is Risen!" Lena lifts her head towards me and looks at me with joy. Her eyebrows fly up with delight, her eyes shine from an inner joy, her face is moved and happy. I look at her and I repeat, "Christ is Risen, Lena!" "Indeed He is Risen!" she answers and unexpectedly approaches me. We kiss each other three times on the cheek, as is the tradition. We run down the steps together and walk together. Where are we going? What for?

The sun is just rising, the city is quiet, the air is fresh and transparent. I take Lena by the arm and I say, "Lena, I came to this church two years ago because of you, at first because of curiosity and now I come because I believe!" And I tell her about myself, I cannot stop talking. My soul is full of the Paschal service and my heart sings: "Christ is Risen!"

Lena walks next to me and listens to me, I look at her and I keep talking. We walk down little streets, big streets, boulevards, quite aimlessly; there must be passers-by, but I don't see them. Right now I am full of the paschal joy and I must admit that I am also full of joy that I am walking with Lena. Everything today is wonderfully good: Pascha, life, my mood, and the fact that I am with Lena. I feel like I have been reborn. I am speaking with Lena about Pascha, about faith, about my life and about her. She walks along, her arm in mine, listening but saying nothing, only glancing at me every once in a while. I become concerned, even fearful about her silence. Squeezing her arm I babble on, losing my breath: "Lena, you know, Lena? You know what I want to tell you." I keep repeating the same thing, and I just cannot finish the sentence.

She doesn't push me away, she only looks at me with her big dark eyes, then she looks down shyly and says, "I know."

If there were passersby, they were probably surprised to see some big guy giving a hug and a kiss to a young girl right in the street... perhaps nobody was there, I do not know.

"Yuri," says Lena, "I knew that you kept on going to church. Now it is going to be our church—both of ours."

I do not answer, I just hug Lena and we keep walking; we find ourselves in front of the church we had left after the service—now another service was being held.

We go inside, we walk up to the icon of the Mother of God, we venerate it, we pray and leave.

Lena says, "Let's go to my mother's, she is expecting me after the service."

And this is how I came to the Church, all the rest you can well imagine without my telling it.

We met Father Arseny through Lena's mother, two years ago. Now I visit him very often, and each time I carry home a joy which can't be compared to anything—the joy of knowing God, and the guidance of Father Arseny about how we have to live as Christians in today's world.

I wrote all this story in one long evening, making myself remember my past. It is a past that is actually not so far away. Lena and I have been married for only four years."

Liuda

IN MY FAMILY, religion and the church were respected, even honored, but only superficially, without reflection. Yes, the church did exist, but why? what for? We didn't care.

My father was a skeptic, he made light fun of the church and its rites, and he looked down on the clergy, calling them "long maned."

My mother visited the church, but only visited, on Christmas and Pascha, as well as when something bad happened, or for funerals of relatives and friends. She took me to church rarely (that was how it was done, it was proper), but I was taught to say the "Our Father," "Rejoice, O Virgin Mother of God," and to pray for Mama and Papa. That was all I knew up to age fifteen.

I studied in a school where the children came from very different backgrounds—there were children of educated people as well as those of workers. As always everyone was drawn to things new and contemporary, and made fun of everything from the olden days. The kids made fun of priests, of nuns, and I was no exception. In school I became friends with a very nice girl—Sonia. We became inseparable.

Once, during a holiday from school, we had nothing to do and decided to go into a church to see what was going on there. It was August 19, the feast of the Transfiguration (Old Style). We had no idea what this meant. We made our way to the front and looked and listened. We didn't understand what was going on but we liked it. It drew us in, and elevated us somehow into something lighter and brighter. We stayed till the end.

As we left the church, Sonia said to me, "Liuda, I feel so good, and joyous." After that time, we visited this church regularly. Sonia got to know a number of parishioners, talked with them. She went to confession, and then convinced me to do the same.

I prepared myself to tell the priest about my ideas and my moods. I was met by a skinny, tall priest. I knelt down, looked at him and saw that he was young. For some reason I suddenly felt embarrassed and forgot everything I was going to say. He waited. The silence lasted a few minutes; then he said in a gentle and attentive voice, "What did you come for?" I started talking about myself, then I talked about Sonia. After that I told him what I like and what I dislike in church. I finally said that the church services felt complicated and unclear to me.

266

The priest listened to me never interrupting me—I was thankful to him for that. When I had finished, he started asking me questions—he asked me about the meaning of faith and the purpose of life, and if I remained silent, he answered his own questions for me. He spoke about prayer, about sin, about the meaning of mercy toward others, and simply about everything that was good. He asked what worried me or made me suffer. I shrugged my shoulders and said that nothing worried me or made me suffer.

"I am going to introduce you to a person who knows Orthodoxy and who is a kind and good person. Spend some time with her. She will help you sort things out and understand a lot. Then you will come to confession as to a great Christian sacrament, which cleanses the human soul from all evil and sin. You must learn a great deal." He blessed me but did not give me absolution, explaining that I had not been ready for this confession.

During the service that followed I wondered who that person would be whom the priest wanted to introduce me to. I was afraid it would be a boring old lady. I was tempted to leave, not to have to deal with moralizing lectures.

The priest, Father Arseny, introduced me to Natalia Petrovna. How grateful I am to her. She gave me so much of her time and energy, and I can truly say that she turned me into sincere believer, revealing to me what I did not know. I called her by her formal name, Natalia Petrovna, in spite of the fact that she was only 24 years old. It was only ten years ago that I dared to call her Natasha.

Six months after I had met Natalia Petrovna I went to confession to Father Arseny, understanding its meaning, knowing that it was indispensable for a believer.

I listened to his sermons, I came to talks, participated in discussion groups; I read spiritual literature under the supervision of Natalia Petrovna. Years were passing and I understood services, I developed a way of thinking and a moral code of behavior, and became, as it seemed to me, a true Christian.

All through the first years, my mother and father made fun of me. They felt that going to church was a useless but harmless childish passion. Papa was disparaging as always, telling jokes about clergy, about monasteries, and quoting the ideas of Voltaire on religion.

Later, things got worse. They didn't want to let me observe the fasts, they tried to distract me when I was praying. Without telling me, my mother went to talk to Father Arseny. She waited through the whole service, but was able to see him only after the service on the next day.

Having seen my mother in church, I was worried, expecting the worst, but Natalia Petrovna said, "Don't worry, rely on the mercy of God!" In fact there were no more derogatory talks at home, the only difference was that after her visit with Father Arseny, my mother started going to church.

And that is how my mother and I became the spiritual children of Father Arseny. Papa didn't make fun of us any more, probably Mama and he had talked. He calmed down about it all and accepted it as a given. Papa was an exceptionally good-hearted man, he was very educated and intelligent, but he had no opinion of his own, so he relied on that of my mother, whom he loved unconditionally. Papa even came to our church several times and talked to Father Arseny. The Church and faith gave meaning to my life. It is only thanks to this that I have been able to lead a pure and happy life, in spite of the great trials which befell me.

I was neither a favorite nor a less favored spiritual daughter of Father Arseny. He loved us all equally. But some of us were able to give more to the Church than others. I was a receiver, I came to be consoled, led, directed and fed from this Tree of Life. The Church gave me much, I learned and understood a lot, but I was always looking for advice, support, leaning on a person stronger than myself, more spiritually experienced. God always provided such people for me.

It was toward the end of the twenties, that blessing me, Father Arseny said, "Liuda! God has given you much, you are successful in life in many ways, but in questions of faith you are to be a follower, you need to be led." This is when Father Arseny gave me a guide. Her influence on me lasted my whole life long.

A Few Sad Thoughts

DURING THE TWENTIES, the thirties and the forties, we were young, energetic, and outspoken; we were burning with the desire to help each other. In the beginning Father Arseny was with us, he led us, and even when he was in exile, he instructed us all. Our church had been closed down, and we had to serve in people's homes, our community now functioning in secret.

Many of us were arrested, some were sent to camps or exiled; others, scared, left our community.

The war separated many of us: wartime hunger, evacuation, and mobilization spread us out across the country. We had no news about Father Arseny; people said he had been shot, or had died of hunger in a camp. Even during those grim times, we, his spiritual children, continued to hold together.

The war ended, almost all of us gathered in Moscow. We met, prayed together and tried to care for each other as we had done before; we tried to read and study, we tried to take care of those of us who were sick, but somehow it didn't work.

Those of Father Arseny's spiritual children who had after the war become priests left Moscow, and visiting them often became impossible.

By the end of the forties we suddenly realized that we had aged, we had lost our spiritual energy. We had become unfeeling, callous, impatient with each other. We still spoke about loving and helping each other, but in reality we wanted others to help us. We had changed.

We each had a family, our own problems, illnesses, work, and children—and our faith and our good intentions had been diluted by all these concerns. There was no one who could lead us and set us straight.

A small group of us gathered around several of Father Arseny's most steadfast spiritual children, but others left, choosing rather to go to open, "safe" churches. We met only rarely, by chance, more at funerals and major church feasts.

Conversations were about health, who got married, who had died, who had had children or grandchildren, had obtained an apartment, or had finished his or her studies. The usual arguments and interesting conversations on serious religious topics or religious literature were a thing of the past.

The light had become dull, our spiritual life almost gone. "I shall strike the shepherd and the sheep will disperse ..." (Zechariah 13:7).

And suddenly, in 1957, we learned that Father Arseny was alive and free. Our first meetings, conversations, confessions, were an enormous joy for all of us, an incomparable joy. All of us were drawn to his little house, under his protection—or almost all of us were. There were those whom we lost to fear or indifference. We were embittered by people's lack of gratitude, hard-heartedness and forgetfulness, and Father Arseny suffered for us all.

A year went by, and the number of people appearing in that little house in that small town far from Moscow grew: it included not just us, but many of those whom Father Arseny had met during his time in camps. The return of Father Arseny and our meetings with him led many of us to live a new life, to shake off dust of worldly life and to draw closer to the Church. As before, we all attended services in different churches in Moscow, but we carried our souls to Father Arseny and left with him our bitterness, our pains, our burdens, our doubts. We brought him our sins and received in exchange his spiritual direction, instruction and consolation. All this gave us the possibility to live in the faith.

I will never forget the words of Father Arseny: "In this world, you must walk the paths of God's commandments, be merciful to one another; in your behavior and actions try to be like monks—even though you live in this stormy sea of life. Then God's mercy will not leave you." He also said, "Prayer to the Holy Mother of God is one of the most important and strongest prayers for the believer. Every day, look at all your actions and answer to them before yourself and before God."

In spite of the fact that Father Arseny was among us and gave many of us a new life, we had changed. We were no longer young, life had worn us out and broken us down. I felt that in our prayers we now asked for help more, and glorified God less. It didn't used to be that way.

I asked Father Arseny once, why is this so? He answered me somewhat sadly, "In a way this is natural. People have lived through too much, through too much difficulty. Everything was done to eradicate faith from the souls of the people. Conditions were such that it became necessary to think only about how to survive, to overcome the obstacles which had been created. Just look at the life which has now been created: radio, magazines, television, newspapers, cinemas and theater create a standardized way of thinking, the same for everyone. This leads to a person being unable to be alone with his own thoughts, to feel the presence of God.

"The pace of today's life, so quick, and so constantly pressured, makes people think only according to how somebody wants them to. A person is never alone; even when he is sent to a sanatorium or rest home for a rest, there is always a definite rhythm and program to follow, everything is decided for you. People are fed, informed, and taught what someone else has decided they need. Huge numbers of people are gathered together, but they are separated by the daily battle for life.

"All this has affected even believers, brought them closer to the 'norm,' made them indifferent. A prescribed way of thinking makes it difficult for a person to become a believer and makes it difficult for the believer to preserve his faith. But do remember, Christ's Church will live eternally even under these circumstances. Preserve your faith, fight for individuality of thought, pray more, read the Scriptures, and God will preserve you, He will not let you lose the clarity of your thoughts, He will not let you think like the faceless mass of indifferent and cold people."

Pavel Semionovich

GOD PROTECTED US in His mercy. In 1957 Father Arseny decided to move to my house for good. At first he did not see anybody, then he wrote several letters and people began coming, just a few on weekdays, and on Saturdays and Sundays up to ten people!

I used to remind Father Arseny that this was dangerous, but he left it all in God's hands. I was worried and tried to arrange it so that people would take turns in coming, especially on Sundays and on feast days, not to attract the authorities' attention. Some good people lived on our street, but also some not-so-good people. I am sorry to say that these were more numerous than the others.

Of course times had changed a little for the better since the death of Stalin, but still, both Father Arseny and I had both been arrested and spent time in camps. Father Arseny is a priest, and he doesn't serve in any officially open church. Anything could happen.

About a year after Father Arseny moved in the local police inspector paid me a visit. His name was Pavel Semionovich, but people called him "the grabber." He must have been 35 years of age. He was not too tall, red-haired, blue eyed, he had an open face with a wide smile. I must admit that it was because of this smile that we were all afraid of him. He would fine you, or give you a warning, and never stop smiling.

He came into the house, said hello, asked me about my health, asked if everything was in order and then he started asking me about my lodger. Who is he? Where is he from? Laughing, I answered, "Pavel Semionovich, my lodger is officially declared to the police; they know everything about him. Tell me, what do you really want?"

"Actually, I don't need anything. Your neighbors are talking. They say many people visit you. We know your tenant is a priest, perhaps he holds services in the house? You do know that this is strictly forbidden by law. There are some churches which are open for such activities."

While we were talking Father Arseny came out of his room, greeted the visitor and sat down.

"Are you asking about me?"

Pavel Semionovich was taken aback, but he answered, "Yes, about you, Mr. Streltzov. I was asking whether you conduct church services at home. I hear you came here from a camp?"

They started talking. Pavel Semionovich said something sympathetic, and then mentioned something about a foreign sect that had invaded this town. He spoke of the Jehovah's Witnesses, he said something about God. Father Arseny answered, and to my surprise seemed to enjoy the conversation. The man stayed at our house for about an hour, had a cup of tea, ate something, and then I gave him some money—about 100 rubles. He took them, as always; he never said no to money. He never touched the money, but expected you to put it directly in his pocket—he would make believe he didn't notice.

As he was leaving, he said, "Be careful about your visitors." He left, and after that he visited us regularly once a month. One time he would check the number of our house, another time he'd look to see if our fence was in good shape, or whether we had a dog. I had a feeling he simply wanted to talk with Father Arseny.

And so it was. Father Arseny met with him every time he came, coming out of his room and sitting with us so that we all talked together.

They had strange talks. For no reason, it seemed, Father Arseny would tell Pavel about his life, about Moscow, about the town we lived in, its history, and sometimes Pavel Semionovich would begin to tell about himself and his family, or would enter into a discussion about what Father Arseny had said.

I didn't like these visits. I didn't like these conversations and I said to Father Arseny, "Why do you keep on talking to him? He comes, looks around, checks everything and takes money every single time!"

Father Arseny looked at me seriously and answered, "Natalia Petrovna, you are not looking at him carefully enough; when you do you will see in him a large spark of God." But I couldn't imagine where this spark of God could be hiding in this man.

So these visits continued for two years; and every time Pavel Semionovich would manage to see Father Arseny, who would come and have tea and share a meal with us. At first our visitor took money every time, then he did not want to accept it any more. I still disliked these visits, was afraid of them; I couldn't bring myself to trust him. Father Arseny, on the other hand, seemed to be energized by these visits, and it seemed to me that he may even have enjoyed them.

In three years not only did he not accept money, but he started bringing us special foods which were completely unavailable to normal people. He did not want to be paid for it, but always said, "This is my present to you!" More time passed and Father Arseny started inviting him into his room. All his friends including myself told him that he certainly should not do this, but Father Arseny only smiled at us.

Several times Pavel Semionovich warned me about days when no visitor should come; these days I would run to the station and tell those who had come that they had to leave. It so happened that on those days I did notice that our house was being watched. Some "drunkard" would climb our tall fence "by mistake" and look around...

I don't know what Father Arseny and Pavel Semionovich were talking about, but I could tell that Pavel was growing attached to Father Arseny.

In November of 1963 Pavel came to our house very upset: his mother was dying. He sat at the table and began to cry. Father Arseny tried to comfort him.

"My mother believed in God all her life, but she couldn't go to church because of my line of work, so she prayed at home. She was upset that I was working for the authorities, but, what could I do? Please, come to visit her, hear her confession and bring her communion; come with Nadezhda Petrovna. My mother asked me to ask you. Come in the evening. I will expect you at the gate, nobody will see you."

At about eight o'clock, as agreed, we started out. Father Arseny was joyous, I did not know why. It was dark, and pouring rain. We came to the gate, Pavel was waiting there as agreed, and took us into his house. Maria Karpovna, his mother, was doing very poorly. She could barely talk, she was pale, thin and dry, only her eyes were shining.

We left the room, and Father Arseny stayed with Maria Karpovna. Pavel's wife was sobbing and kept on repeating, "You have never seen such a woman. She helped us, she raised our children, she could not go to church because of us, but never blamed us for it. She had icons hidden away and prayed at home."

In about two hours Father Arseny came out of the room and called us in. After confession Maria Karpovna seemed more alive; she asked to be helped up on her pillow and said, "Father Arseny, do not forget my children Pavel and Zina. I ask you this in the name of the Lord. They are good people. Pavel, even in his work for the police, tries to help whoever he can."

Then, looking at me, she said, "Natalia Petrovna, my dove, stay with me and read the prayer for the dying. I am going to die today, so please do what I ask."

I had never read the prayer for the departing and I looked to Father Arseny. He said, "Do stay, I brought the Psalter with me." I had learned to read

Church Slavonic and had read the Psalter many times—Father Arseny had taught me to read the services when I became a believer.

Of course I stayed in spite of the fact that obviously I was afraid. Zina went to see Father Arseny off, Pavel stayed in the room with me. We lit candles and I began to read. At first I made mistakes, I stumbled on difficult words, but then I got hold of myself.

Maria Karpovna lay peacefully, her big eyes open; she made the sign of the cross from time to time with great difficulty. Pavel stood next to me, Zina returned, put the children to bed and joined us in prayer.

It was night, it was late, I was tired, but I kept on reading. I had a sip of water every once in a while. I looked up at Maria Karpovna and saw that she wanted to say something. I came up to her.

"Please, stop reading for a minute, I want to say good bye to Pavel and Zina and then to you as well."

In this farewell there was something inevitable, and deeply sad. Maria Karpovna was serious, focused, gentle, and there was no sign of fear on her face. Pavel and Zina kissed her hands and cried quietly. But in the eyes of both there was so much deep love and an awareness, an understanding, that death was not something awful but an unavoidable reality, which we had to light up with our love and our kindness. We believed that the departing was going on a long journey and our connection with her would not end with her death.

I came up to her, and she whispered to me, "Do not leave them, pray for me, forgive me."

I kept on reading the Psalter. At about six o'clock in the morning Maria Karpovna quietly stopped breathing.

In the morning I went home, and at night Father Arseny served a *panikhida*. After the death of her mother-in-law, Zina often came and prayed with Father Arseny and anyone who happened to be there. Pavel came alone, always warning us of his coming.

In 1964 Pavel began to study law. In 1969 he left our town and began to work as a judge in another town.

Up until the death of Father Arseny in 1973, Pavel would come to visit him. After his death Pavel became the spiritual son of Father V., to whom Father Arseny had directed him.

Father Arseny told me many times that Pavel Semionovich had an exceptionally pure soul. He managed to do good things even while working for the police.

One evening, as we were talking about the strength of faith, he said, "Each person has his own strength of faith. This faith is given to him by God depending on his character, his strength and his spiritual path. To a monk or a priest who has learned under the direction of a staretz much is given, but much is going to be asked.

"Now look at Pavel and Zina, what was given to them? Almost nothing. But there was a spark of God in their souls. This spark was placed within them by Pavel's mother, and she had kept it alive in them.

"Even before they knew that they believed, they were already doing so much good around them, as we heard after they had left. Once the flame of faith had ignited in their souls, they shone more brightly perhaps than those who had 'worked from the first hour' (cf. Matthew 20:1-16). I have met such people with pure souls before in my life," finished Father Arseny.

I saw Pavel Semionovich last in Moscow, in the beginning of this year.

≈)

This story was told by Nadezhda Petrovna.

A Few Words in Conclusion

PARTS OF FATHER Arseny's far-reaching life are revealed to us through the episodes recounted in this book. We meet a kind and simple man, with an honest, open face, a man who was not influenced by the convictions nor the habits of the world that surrounded him—a world impregnated with lies, self-interest, vanity and cruelty—a world that fashioned and warped so many of us into its own image and likeness. Father Arseny was uncompromising, courageous and unswervingly committed to what he believed to be right and fair. He did not fall victim to the cruel and passionate powers that had consigned him to heavy suffering and persecution, instead he was a man who chose freely his path toward God, in the name of God. He walked this path to the end with a rare dignity, selflessness, and simplicity.

Notice with what wisdom and sadness and with what deep spiritual interest he looks into the faces of even the most fearsome and cruel people who surround him. He always tries to find a path to their hearts, ignite in their souls the spark of God, correct their ways and direct them to do good. Just see how many people he saved and supported through the most difficult periods of their lives, at times in their last hours on this earth. The young and the old, soldiers, professors, workers, peasants, doctors, engineers—all pass before our eyes as if carved in stone, their features clear and true, their being fully revealed. And at the same time we see the reality of the cruel and bleak life which surrounded Father Arseny. What we read is unforgettable.

Reading these memoirs, one can't help but remember the many people who suffered and died for the faith and for all of us.

✣

Translator's Afterword

In the tradition of this book, I want to share with the reader my own experience with it.

My first introduction to the person of Father Arseny was when I was listening to tapes of the Voice of Orthodoxy, an organization which sends religious radio broadcasts (in Russian) to Russia. Passages from this book were being read for the benefit of those who have little or no access to religious literature. I was dumbfounded by the spiritual beauty of what I heard and began to carry within me the name of Father Arseny. At that time, I was not aware that there was a whole book about him.

Just a few months later, by coincidence, a friend of ours sent a copy of the book to my sister, who was very ill. She was very moved by it, shared it with me, and managed to obtain several more copies. As these copies made their way into the homes of several friends and relatives, the burning fuse ran fast, lighting hearts and souls with gratitude to God for having let us meet His saint. Many members of my large family read the book, and each said that in some way it had changed their lives.

Since then I have met several other people who have chanced upon this book—some in a kiosk in a Moscow subway station, some in a bookstall in Saint Sergius Lavra, another had received it from a friend. Each person said that this book left on him an indelible mark. Thank God for the newly-acquired religious freedom in Russia which makes it possible for this book to now be read more broadly there.

When I decided to translate the book, to share this joy with those who don't read Russian, I asked members of my family to edit my translation. The enthusiastic response I got was very encouraging and inspiring to me. My son Alex, my daughter Tania (who edited my translation, and gave me advice and constant support), my son Peter and his wife Patricia (who went through the whole book and made the text and layout what it is now), my grandson Eugene Sokoloff, my daughter Manya Sokoloff, my niece Olga Troubetzkoy, Ruth Stankovich, my spiritual father Fr. John Breck—all undertook to help with enthusiasm and joy and were in turn enlightened and enriched from having met our dear, beloved Father Arseny.

Father Arseny, pray for us sinners!

Vera Bouteneff
Translator